CW01501568

NICE Mr

How to smuggle cocaine

by

Joseph King

Edition published May 8th 2016.

Based on a True Story

SCENE:

Colombia January 23 **1998** 10.04am

INTERIOR

A man walks down a quiet corridor in a high rise office building. He is carrying a large leather holdall. He stops at a door and knocks. "Come in!" a voice says in Spanish. He opens the door and walks into a large plush office. Sitting behind a hefty oak desk, is a man wearing a top of the range designer suit. Suspended high on the wall behind whom, the man with the holdall notices the half-smile of a decorative samurai sword.

He walks up to the desk and carefully places the holdall on it. The other man remains in his seat, and looks at the incomer questioningly, who nods, then unbuckling a large pocket on the side of the holdall, extracts a bulky manila envelope. He extends the envelope across the desk towards the seated man, who grabs it and, tearing off one end in a single strip, peers inside, before tipping the contents out onto the table. There are ten large bundles of paper money. Running his fingers through one bundle he estimates the amount. It is probably about twenty five thousand pounds. Altogether about a quarter of a million pounds sterling. He stuffs the bundles back into the envelope and pushes it to the side of his desk. Now he stands up and stretching forward, opens the holdall as wide as it will go.

Inside he can see the top of a white crash helmet. He reaches in, and gingerly lifts it up, holding it at arms' length in front of his face to inspect. It is a gruesome sight. Still inside the open face helmet is a decomposing severed head. Cloudy eyes remain half opened and congealed blood hangs from the cleanly severed neck. The man in the suit nods, and smiles. Carefully replacing the crash helmet, he closes the bag, then smiles and nods at the first man, who picks up the leather holdall again and taking it with him, walks out of the office, closing the door behind him.

*

The Guardian

Special report

26.11.99

Leaders of one of the biggest cocaine-smuggling rings ever seen in Britain face long prison sentences after seven convictions at the end of a two-month trial.

The gang is thought to have imported over $80m of Colombian cocaine in three years.

... A spokesman for Customs and Excise said: "This was a truly international, organised, criminal gang which had at its disposal vast sums of money."

*

SPIEL

I was looking for a marketable story idea. By searching on Google, I discovered that a popular written genre on Amazon, is True Crime. But where would I find a true crime of intrigue and interest, to write about? One that was a major press story but the important details of which were not reported in any media. Presumably it would not be easy to track down such a valuable gold nugget. In fact I was wrong. On this occasion, I struck a genuine gemstone almost instantly.

Pubs around the Inns of Court district in the City of London had seemed like a good place to start mining. This was the 'legal district' of central London. Perhaps I would catch the silver thread of a hushed conversational tapestry, which might lead to an overlooked seam to delve, and uncover a compelling narrative. Unveil a hidden jewel. Reveal a diamond in the rough. It was only a 20 minute bus ride from where I lived anyway, so I decided to give it a try.

Thus one afternoon when I had some spare time I travelled up to the legal district in the City of London, to hang around in a few of the pubs in the area. These were up market pubs. Some made you feel you were stepping back into the Victorian era, out of a time machine. I was sure the décor, while glistening and polished like new, had not been redesigned for 150 years. Walls were laden with enormous and ornate gilt framed mirrors. Brass hand rails and foot rails defined the dark glossy wood of the bars. Behind which cut glass mirrors reflected back bottles of the finest brands. One didn't walk in these pubs so much as hover and float; padding about on deep piled patterned carpets, all red and gold.

Some of the pubs were more like setting the dial back to Elizabethan times. Dark wooden beams dismantled from ships four centuries previously criss-crossed white plastered panels on the walls and low crooked ceilings. Wooden timbers creaked underfoot or sloped alarmingly upwards and downwards.

Others were like time traveling back a thousand years to ancient monastic orders, with oblique wooden carved reliefs full of masonic symbolism and strange archaic caricatures.

I tried to eavesdrop on conversations but even if I managed to, none of what I heard, as it turned out, was particularly enlightening. I could have listened to the same conversations in the price value pubs near where I lived, and saved myself the bus fare. In fact it was to avoid repeatedly becoming embroiled in such drunken and untethered exchanges in local pubs, that I was looking for a project in the first place.

After about seven or eight hours of applied efforts, it was beginning to seem like this had not been such a great idea after all. A little worse for wear I was seeing if I could stand up at a deeply varnished wooden bar which seemed to be moving like a viscous connoisseur brandy as the gleaming Victorian era pub started to swirl around me. I was aiming to stay vertical by leaning my elbows on the apparently moving bar while trying to keep my chin propped on my hands in a largely vain attempt to hold my head still. At the same time I was wondering if I could manage another pint without completely passing out, when my luck seemed about to change. For a moment as if by magic I was looking directly through an apparently double glazed window of opportunity. I was shown a treasure map yet it looked like there were three of them swimming in the air. Now then, if only I could see straight enough to copy it legibly.

A dapper man, perhaps in his late sixties, close shaven and with short cut grey hair, and also somewhat inebriated, took a stool beside me, held out his hand and volunteered an introduction.

He was extremely well dressed and groomed and I suspected immediately that he was involved in the legal profession. I was not overly opposed to hearing his erudite if slurred conversation. After a few minutes however I got around to laying out my own predicament as best I could, considering the state I was in.

The gentleman narrowed his eyes, and swaying like a praying mantis, stroked his chin for a few moments with immaculately manicured fingers, before suggesting that he might have just the silver thread I was looking for.

I knew I wouldn't remember much, but sensed this could indeed lead to the golden ticket I was after. So I fished the notebook and pen from my jacket pocket, and started scribbling haphazard notes even as they jingled and jangled and danced all over the page before my eyes. I remember at least that the more I listened, the more intrigued I became.

I reviewed the notes several days later, as soon as the hangover had cleared up. At first they were quite illegible, however after some minutes of painstaking labour I was able to decipher many of the hieroglyphics and even extract a small amount of crude sense from the smatterings of story ore scattered across the page. With an old razor blade I carefully scratched and scraped the mineral ore deposits into a crystal test tube, and subjected them to a bespoke, systematic process of repeated refraction and distillation. Finally, using platinum tongs to hold the test tube over a Bunsen burner flame set on maximum power, I observed the beginnings of alchemy as it took place. I could by now see that there was in all likelihood, sufficient elemental excitement to automatically trigger the chain reaction required to achieve actual atomic fusion on the page, and fully ignite the delectation of the reader.

It seemed that a friend of the legal gentleman's who was now a senior QC, at around the turn of the millennium, had acted on the defence counsel of a pertinent case. It was billed in the press at the time as the unravelling of 'The Biggest Cocaine Smuggling Ring in British History'. The story was a huge national news splash across the UK.

However the most astonishing facts were never revealed in the media. Conspiracies remained unspoken and mysteries stayed unsolved. Neither the police, nor the courts or the media were ever able to satisfactorily explain what they knew, and had no idea how much they still did not know. Not one of those convicted, whether turning Queen's evidence or not, was prepared to shed any light on the many unanswered questions. This was out of fear for their own lives.

Some people I met during the research for this book, even those who had not been party to events, but simply knew the people, immediately declined to be involved in any way once they understood the subject matter. Some were so scared of potential repercussions from the revelations made herein that they would hurriedly leave the local pubs or avoid me in the street whenever they saw me loitering with my notepad, as I pried for details. For the same reason this account has been published using a pseudonym.

Here then was an unsolved mystery, which had been eventually documented by the courts as "inexplicable". It was buried deep within a massive smuggling escapade run by chancing amateurs, which had generated many tens of millions of pounds, and resulted in hundreds of years of prison sentences. It involved conspirators, informants, spies, scallywags, liars, thieves, assassins, and smugglers: some of whom to this day continue to evade Her Majesty's justice. As I dug deeper and my scratching finger nails inched closer to the very 24 karat kernel of truth I was finally reaching for, the more terrifying it became.

The gentleman from the pub had remained friendly on a social level with one of the inside members of the ring, even after the ring member had served a lengthy prison sentence for his fringe involvement. This fellow was retired from a separate white collar career and may be interested to help as he was very bookish. Almost certainly he would know where to start an investigation with a view to my writing up the account in a book, should he agree to assist. In the pub, the legal gentleman had apparently promised to arrange a meeting for me with the retired ex ring member. He soon informed me this had been set up.

The retired gentleman was unaware of the smuggling operation at the time and was sentenced in court for handling some of the money generated. There was never any suggestion that he knew of its origins. Of medium height and slender build, he was a quietly spoken and modest gentleman, however at length he agreed to give me some introductions in return for a discreet cash payment, which I was able to arrange; and on the proviso that the names and identifying details of those members who had absconded and were still on the run, would be omitted or altered.

Over the next few weeks he was able to introduce me to other surviving ex-convict members of the inner circles of the ring. By piecing together their versions of the story, and with reference to publicly available court and police files as well as press reports, the lost truths and untold secrets of the entire riveting episode, will now be revealed.

Chapter 1

Colombia March 22, 1992: 2.52pm

Colin looked glumly out of the window at the torrential tropical rain. It made the astonishingly hot air so humid that his shirt was soaking wet, even sitting inside. He was in an empty, rather tatty classroom slowly consuming a homemade sandwich, of sliced white bread and stale cheese, no butter. The second hand ticked slowly on the big wall clock. It was nearly three in the afternoon. He had an hour to wait until the next class. An hour he wasn't getting paid for. Then five hours and forty five minutes of back to back conversation classes with no breaks until nine forty five at night. It was a daunting prospect. Still, he preferred to be earning. Where he had breaks between classes such as now, he was not paid at all. He just had to sit and stare at the clock, and wait. Even when he *was* paid, it did not amount to a lot of money. As far as Colin was concerned it was not enough to be properly motivating. It was much less than he was worth, he reflected irritably.

Following college graduation, Colin had struggled with a fledgling career in antiques but never quite managed to get it off the ground. After several years, he chose instead to complete a TEFL certificate and teach English, eventually winding up in South America. The economy in the UK in the early nineties was stagnant and many adventurous types sought job opportunities abroad teaching English for example. There was a great demand for native Anglophone teachers in many parts of the world at that time. Due to the economic climate in the UK people ventured as far as Asia and Australasia, Europe, the Middle East, and South as well as North America in their thousands in search of jobs. Nevertheless the oversupply of teachers due to the recession at home was by the early 1990's already beginning to depress the wages of such jobs.

Colin taught for a couple of years in Spain, then seeking a more exotic experience while not wishing to give up on his Spanish, had hit upon the idea of Colombia. Now in the late spring of 1992, he found himself in this old fashioned classroom which was in need of a good lick of paint, waiting to teach his next class of conversational English to a small group of local adults. The job had been supposed to provide a regular and guaranteed weekly income, however in the event he was dependent on the private college he worked at to supply a sufficient number of hours each week, which they couldn't always seem to manage. English teaching was turning out to be only marginally more secure than the antiques business which he had actually enjoyed. It was becoming a rather tedious occupation for Colin, and continued to generate only a frustratingly low income. He had sought to raise his living standard by reducing his expenditure, and thought he could achieve this by moving to a lower cost country. However while the cost of living had become much lower, his income was of course also much lower. From a financial perspective he was going in the wrong direction.

Mainly for this reason, it was increasingly evident once Colin arrived in Colombia that his foremost passion was not likely to remain the teaching of English after all. Certainly, before long his first love in Colombia appeared instead to be the rather gorgeous young woman who attended his Thursday 7pm conversation class.

Colin's mind may – questionably - have been focussed on his job in the beginning, at least in part. What is not in question is that within a few weeks he had started dating his lovely young student friend. They soon became an item, a definite couple. This helped to make the situation in a foreign land more tolerable for him. Nevertheless dissatisfaction with his low income continued to bother Colin. Perhaps even more so, now that he had a young woman to impress.

To help take his mind off his immediate money concerns, and because neither of them had much spare cash, he began to spend more and more of his free time at Ana's house; that is her parents' house. It was a very interesting insight into the local culture and lifestyle, for Colin. For Ana, it was a great opportunity to improve her English. Plus, in addition, they soon fell in love.

Ana's parents made a comfortable living running a car repair business and had a very nice home. Colin was soon making almost daily visits to see Ana, and it wasn't long before he was introduced to her two brothers. It was the second brother, Juan Pablo, who initially sewed the seed of an intriguing money making idea in Colin's head.

One afternoon, Ana, Juan Pablo and Colin were sitting together around the large oak table in the flagstone floored kitchen. It was a well to do house in a decent neighbourhood, which they had to themselves for the afternoon on this occasion, while the parents were visiting relatives. Juan Pablo, taking immediate advantage of their absence, had started to roll a joint of the local weed, on the oak table top.

"This is expensive in London, I guess huh?" he asked over to Colin, waving his half full coffee cup at the bag of weed in front of him, and almost sloshing the golden black liquid over the lot.

"Probably. How much is it in Colombia?" asked Colin.

They discussed the relative prices of cannabis in South America and Europe.

"So you could get rich very quick just by smuggling some cannabis over there, right?" Juan Pablo suggested, jokingly.

"Only if you smuggled a lot of it and you didn't get caught. And you'll have to save up for a boat." Colin laughed.

"What about cocaine?" said Juan Pablo, grinning. "That costs a lot of money over there, huh? I mean, to get properly rich it would be better to smuggle cocaine than cannabis, right?"

Colin chuckled. "I s'pose. I dunno. Perhaps you're right."

Between them in discussion they established that there would indeed be a lot of potential profit instantly available to any man who was prepared to risk his liberty by smuggling cocaine from Colombia to England. They both smiled at the ridiculousness of the conversation.

Smuggling was not something Colin had ever considered before, not even for a single moment. He was just going along with the conversation, and enjoying the social atmosphere. More for a joke really, or perhaps to make conversation, at some point he said to Juan Pablo, "So you know where to buy cocaine?"

Juan Pablo laughed at him. "C'mon, man! This is Colombia. Of course I do," he nodded.

"But could you get it in bulk, I mean? Like, maybe a couple of keys or something?" Juan Pablo nodded, and they both smiled again. They were having fun and not being serious. Colin was not remotely interested in buying cocaine, not least in bulk. He was just teasing Juan Pablo, or showing off to Ana. The intention to become a cocaine smuggler had never entered Colin's head. Sure he was aware of his environment. There had been some predictable banter with his mates at the pub the night before he flew out to take up his new teaching post.

"Next time we see you, you'll probably be an international cocaine smuggler," they had said, laughing. No one actually perceived that as an actual probability. Least of all Colin. Nevertheless at some point during the weeks following his conversation with Juan Pablo, an idea that had begun as a joke started to evolve in Colin's imagination, and to take on a life of its own.

Colin first started to wonder what might lead an ordinary civilian to become a cocaine smuggler. This interested him greatly. He decided to think himself into the smuggler's shoes, to view things from the smuggler's perspective. In trying to understand how on earth a person could assume such a role, Colin began to apply more and more of his free time to mulling over how *he* might approach smuggling cocaine back to the UK from scratch. It was just a thought experiment, but one that increasingly occupied him. It became a kind of puzzle that he enjoyed solving, a mental exercise to take his mind of the tedium of work.

As he thought it through, Colin decided that a person seriously planning such an escapade could divide the whole operation into three main elements. Firstly, the smuggler would need an identity. That is some kind of role, or persona. He could use his own passport Colin felt, but would need something to identify himself with, other than the role of illicit smuggler. Secondly, he would need a route from Colombia back to the UK which could minimise the risk of detection at the borders. Finally, should he make it safely back to London, he would need a system for distribution.

Even before considering the first two elements, a person who was actually contemplating such a plan, Colin mused, would need to know if he could sell the contraband safely. Colin was not very familiar with the cocaine distribution industry in the UK. He did know that it was hierarchical in nature. That the kind of grass-roots dealers – that is person to person retailers -

that he might be able to get introduced to, would have their own supply networks with one supplier at the top of the pyramid. It would not be sensible in Colin's opinion to attempt to infiltrate such networks at any level.

If he had not had so much time available for thinking, often isolated as he was in a new foreign country, Colin may have stopped his analysis right there, and determined that the entire notion was not practicable for an amateur. Colin had plenty of alone time however, and for want of something better to do, started to consider what other distribution methods may be available to his imaginary smuggler. Perhaps a person could set up his own distribution network, Colin wondered.

Now Colin did smoke cannabis from time to time, as did many of his friends in London, and he knew two or three small time cannabis dealers. These were generally lower-middle class people who sold small amounts of cannabis to a close group of friends and pals. Like the cocaine distribution networks, these cannabis networks were also hierarchical. The retailer would purchase perhaps 8 ounces of cannabis per week from an enigmatic wholesaler, and distribute it in sixteenth, eighth, and quarter of an ounce deals to people he knew well.

Often these people would visit the dealer on a weekly basis, and sit and chat for an hour or so. This was ostensibly a social occasion, but was really because people rushing in and out of a particular flat or house could arouse the suspicion of neighbours for example, who might alert the police. The dealer would therefore make the punters a cup of tea perhaps, and they would roll a couple of joints from the cannabis they had just purchased.

Yet while they were still hierarchical by nature, the supply pyramids in the cannabis trade were far looser. The dealers switched suppliers as and when they liked. As Colin perceived it, the illicit cannabis retail networks tended more towards the social, rather than the business side. It occurred to Colin that it might be possible to infiltrate these types of networks to facilitate distribution.

While such cannabis dealers did not habitually supply harder drugs such as cocaine, they were in general not opposed to the occasional informal handling of the 'party' drug. People even had fun names for it: 'Peruvian Marching Powder,' for example and the old chestnut 'Charlie,' of course, and they saw it as a fun occasional treat. Dealers may, not uncommonly manage to get their hands on half an ounce at Christmas say, and then sell it to many of their regular cannabis customers as a seasonal special extra. It struck Colin that he already knew three or four such cannabis dealers that he himself would be able to approach. If it were him planning to smuggle the cocaine, that is.

Chapter 2

One afternoon, as they were sunbathing on loungers in the front garden of her parents' house, Colin ran some of his thoughts past Ana. It was an attractive looking house, especially in the sunshine, with its earth red terracotta roof tiles and pristine whitewashed walls. The garden too was a lovely place to sit, in the late afternoon; the lush frequently sprinkled lawn was fringed with banana trees and papayas, mango trees and pineapples.

As Ana continued to lay back enjoying the rays, Colin, who was wearing nothing but a pair of cotton shorts, sat up in the still hot sunshine and turned round to face her. Placing his bare feet on the grass and his elbows on his knees he leaned forward conspiratorially across the space between the sun loungers, and put it to Ana that by using his cannabis network idea, a person planning to smuggle cocaine from Colombia to the UK, could certainly manage to shift a kilo or two of the stuff, over several months if need be. It would not be necessary to infiltrate any of the professional networks at all.

"Particularly, high purity cocaine," he explained, "such as Juan Pablo is talking about, would be very popular as a special extra, to many customers of small time cannabis dealers in London." Colin himself had previously been introduced to cocaine on a handful of occasions in just such a way.

Ana seemed unfazed by his comment as the concept started to run through her mind. While her parents were furiously opposed to any indulgence in recreational drugs, apart from tobacco, alcohol, coffee, and the like, she felt it was a generational thing. Many people of Ana's generation, even if they did not indulge in illicit drug taking themselves, had seen enough of their friend's and peers safely enjoying such substances, at enough parties, that prohibited recreational drugs were perceived as part of the background, the fabric of existence. Drugs were not a horror scene in some external narrative, but all around her in the hands of the people she loved. People like Ana were suddenly put outside of the law simply by association with their ordinary friends. It wasn't the people she loved that were evil, in her mind. It would shatter her psychology of course to think otherwise. So it must have been the law, or certain other segments of society that were evil, for their lack of reason and understanding. To Ana and many of her peers, the baddies were the blinkered and out of touch prohibitionists themselves indeed.

Lying on the lounger in a fleeting trace of bikini, with her eyes closed against the sun which felt so pleasant and warm on her skin, Ana's thought process continued to run. The drugs were already in demand, as far as Ana could discern, and someone was going to make money supplying them. That person wasn't necessarily intrinsically evil, they simply filled a role forged by an artificially constructed society, much in the same way that law enforcement officers did. It was nothing but a stupid game of cat and mouse from her perspective. One that probably did far more harm than good. Ana had never touched drugs in her life, but it was clear to her that if anyone was being stupid, it was the law enforcement people and the frightened and conservative prohibitionists, who so far in fact had effectively prohibited nothing at all.

The game had been going on for too many years for an intelligent person to think anything would change all the while the current policies were pursued. Someone always connected the demand to the supply. Always had. And if nothing changed, they almost certainly would still be connecting it twenty three years later, she mused randomly. Subterfuge was a vital ingredient of every human civilisation since the ancient Egyptians' nearly ten thousand years before. If it wasn't for those behaviours, why, society would be nothing more than an ants' nest, Ana thought. Human beings were contrary creatures. Not sometimes, or extraordinarily, but as part of their vital makeup. After ten thousand years those in charge were still yet to discover a way to re-engineer human nature to their peculiar liking. By 1992, it was already beginning to look doubtful that they ever would.

As she lay in the garden, bathed head to toe in lovely warm sunlight, Ana's thoughts continued to analyse Colin's comment. If a person was smart enough to outwit the 'law,' (that was not her law, but some artificial man made misconception), then good luck to him, she thought. Ana had an idea that she knew where Colin's thinking was leading him, however she didn't mind what her brother and, she hoped, future husband got up to... if they could outwit the comedians who had been erroneously put in charge. Which presumably wouldn't be too difficult for someone as intelligent as Colin, she suspected. Also, Ana was very keen on the idea of any get rich quick scheme. Ana had always wanted money.

So although she had never visited the UK, and could not have had any idea about the British based drug dealers Colin was talking about, Ana did not automatically rubbish his musings. Instead as she lay on her lounger, her eyes closed in concentration, she just nodded along, as though what Colin was saying was indisputable fact. In any case, from a money making perspective, even just as a thought exercise, she found it all very interesting.

This encouraged Colin to perceive the third element in his imaginary plan to be viable. Now he began to consider the second element. What sort of route would a person be able to take, he wondered, that would minimise the chance of discovery at border crossings?

"Obviously planes would not be my first choice, if it were me planning to do it," Colin mentioned to Juan Pablo one evening over a chilled bottle of beer in a local bar. "From Colombia, there's sure to be a surface route you could take back to Europe," he suggested. "On trains ... or lorries perhaps, you know, travelling up northwards through the States. Then over the border into Canada. From northern Canada, it's only a short trip in a local boat or light plane over to..."

"What, like a container ship all the way to Europe? Well yes, of course there is," Juan Pablo had interrupted.

*

Following these various encouragements, Colin continued to indulge his exercise in imagination. He had always been something of a daydreamer and had often been scolded as a small boy at school for gazing out of the classroom window, instead of paying attention to the teacher.

He was standing in the street near his language college outside a second hand book shop Something had caught his eye and triggered the memory of his schooldays. There was a table on the sidewalk in front of the shop, with second hand paperback books laid out for display. One of which he found himself staring at, fascinated. He walked over towards the table and picked it up to look at it. It was an old and worn English language copy of Baden-Powell's famous book 'Scouting for boys'.

He laughed quietly. He had recently entertained the idea that a scout's uniform would make an innocent looking disguise for his imaginary smuggler. But that wasn't what he was thinking about now. He was always on the lookout for antiques and collectibles. It had been his job, and remained one of his interests. "Hmm." he laughed at the book. 'You never know,' he thought to himself, 'it might be worth good money in the UK as an old edition. Perhaps I should buy it, just in case. Imagine if I let it go and it turned out to be worth thousands!'

The thought of lots of easy money appealed tremendously to Colin. He was not the sort of person that would ever risk going to prison just for easy money however. In terms of his thought experiment for example, if - and only if his imaginary smuggler managed to somehow dream up a genuinely fool proof method to smuggle at least several kilograms; and all risk of detection was totally eliminated: then and only then would he agree that it was a viable way to make money. Indeed, he chuckled to himself, a person might seem a little foolish - if they did manage to concoct such an ideal plan – and did *not* put it into some kind of trial operation. This idea amused him immensely. The more he thought about it the more he chuckled... first at the absurdity of his assumption that a fantastic infallible method might exist. Then as he recognised that he had managed to work his thinking right round; to the point where he was now chuckling at the notion of someone choosing *not* to smuggle cocaine.

And then a fully formed solution for the first and final element of his hypothesis struck him, like a bolt out of the blue. He could never remember exactly where he was or what he was doing at that moment. He may have been sitting on a park bench leafing through the second hand Baden Powell book he had just bought. It doesn't matter. What matters is that Colin experienced a genuinely creative brain wave. Suddenly he saw with full clarity. He had in that instant conceived of a hitherto unheard of method of smuggling drugs that was so ingenious it would never be detected, not in a million years. "Ha!" He laughed out loud. It was a genuine eureka moment. He had now envisioned just how an amateur could smuggle cocaine... and *never* be discovered.

Colin had always enjoyed daydreaming. His new smuggling fantasy was no exception. It had become so absorbing in fact, that during a break between classes later the same day, he found himself in the nearby library going over the local 'white pages' business directories. Locating a company that shipped freight to Europe, and seeing that it landed at Genoa, he thought, 'Now this would be a good route, for a person planning to smuggle cocaine back to London. Because from Genoa they could find a low key border crossing into France.' There were no border controls on continental Europe any more. Once inside Italy therefore, there were no borders again until Calais. At Calais it would be easy to blend into the ambulatory throngs embarking and disembarking the ferries, which foot passengers were largely waved through customs with at most a glance at the occasional passport.

Something else now intrigued Colin. That there might be cargo ships going from Colombia to Genoa was something he had never considered until Juan Pablo mentioned it. Even then he had assumed they would be for the exclusive use of large multinational companies, and not accessible to individuals. But here in front of him, in the white pages business directory was an advertisement for a carrier that not only went directly to Genoa, but also offered passage at a reasonable rate to members of the public in one of a small number of cabins made available for such a purpose. This interested Colin so much, not just from the point view of his notional smuggler but simply as a fun escapade in its own right, that before he knew what he was doing he found himself dropping a coin into the public phone on the library wall.

Of course, Colin was kidding himself by this stage. This was not just a fun escapade in its own right. The smuggler in his mind's eye was no longer notional. Even if he would not yet admit it to himself, Colin had by this time already decided that he was to become that smuggler. For in his daydreaming, he believed he had now devised a one hundred per cent sure fire method to hide several kilograms of cocaine in such a way that it simply would never be found. Having invented in his imagination such a wholly infallible masterplan, he had perhaps become bound to himself to launch it into action, and put it to the test. Somewhere deep in his mind he had already chosen the path he would follow. So now he found himself standing by a payphone in the library, and speaking to the receptionist of a freight shipping company.

She probably spoke some English, and anyway Colin spoke pretty good Spanish by this time.

"Is it true that you offer passage to Europe for individual members of the public?"

"Ola. Yes we do provide that service."

He asked a few more questions, then without really thinking it through, he heard himself booking a passage home. As he hung up the receiver he realised that he had left himself just a couple of weeks to prepare. What had started as nothing more than a thought experiment had suddenly manifested itself into reality, and was already beginning to appear on the very screen of space.

That evening when he arrived at Ana's, the instant she opened the front door, Colin said to her in a quiet voice, almost breathless with excitement, "What would you say, if I told you: I know how to smuggle cocaine, without getting caught. And that I know how to make millions. Really, I mean millions!"

Ana looked at him, nonchalantly. "And?" she said.

"And so I'm going to do it. We're going to be rich, baby!"

The latter was a phrase Ana very much enjoyed to hear. She often dreamed of having a fabulously rich husband. They would have a wonderful big house all of their own, two perhaps three, well brought up and educated children, a large lawn, an endless garden, and a life of idle luxury. A yacht might be nice, and a couple of strategically positioned holiday homes. She could swan from garden party to soirée, volunteering her presence, gracing adoring admirers with her effortless happy nature. Life would be an endless string of frivolous yet amusing engagements. She would always be well dressed in lovely clothes, radiant in perfect health, immaculately groomed and always looking her best. All her worries and concerns for the future would evaporate. All the bad bits of her life would just be filtered out leaving nothing but a golden glow of loveliness. Life would forever more be utter bliss, just like in heaven.

Returning from her reverie after a moment, Colin still gazing searchingly into her eyes, she said, "If you think you know how to do it without getting caught, then... maybe it would be foolish not to."

Colin was astonished. Ana was so perfect for him! "My thoughts exactly!" he said.

They looked at each other for a moment longer. At last Colin spoke first. "That's it then," he said, "I'm going to be a smuggler!" He looked away, lost in thought. Then he looked back at Ana with an intense gaze. Lowering his voice almost to a whisper he said, "I will be the world's 'finest cocaine' smuggler and I promise you, I *promise* you I know how to do it without ever getting caught!" He leaned forward and lowering his voice even further, whispered in her ear. "We are going to be *rich*, within a matter of weeks, you know." They stared at each other in amazement and wonder, *alive* with the chemistry. They had a quick cuddle on the step under the eaves of the porch, and then followed each other indoors.

*

Sitting at the dining room table inside were Ana's brother Juan Pablo and their father. Their mother stood serving up her famous black bean stew and jasmine rice from large cooking pots. She spooned from the pots and then from various dishes of delicious looking oven-baked vegetables onto warmed plates and passed each round the table. At the same time Juan Pablo reached round with a bottle filling glasses with red wine. Ana's father stared at his empty place mat impatiently.

As Ana and Colin sat down her mother looked at them smiling and said, "You two look excited about something!"

All eyes turned to the couple sitting on the one side of the six seater table opposite Juan Pablo. Ana's mother was standing at one end of the table and her father sat at the other. Colin and Ana stared up at her with wide unblinking eyes, as they attempted to look innocent. There was a frozen pause until Colin, seemingly almost in a trance, said, "Yes. I have a confession to make." Ana beside him tugged surreptitiously on his sleeve and shook her head slightly.

"Yes, I'd like to confess, that I've come up with a potentially very profitable business idea," Colin announced, his face aglow, unable to contain himself any longer.

While her mother looked inexplicably glum, Ana discretely but sharply kicked Colin's ankle under the seat. Juan Pablo sitting opposite frowned just perceptibly, and fixed him with an alarmed stare.

"Very good!" said Ana's father, "let's hear it."

Ana and Juan Pablo sat momentarily stunned into horrified inaction as Colin launched unstoppably into his confession, "I think I may be able to find a market in England for some antique books I can source here in Colombia." The two siblings staring at him aghast, now laughed out loud with relief. "I've already got a rare edition of a particular book that I'm going to take back with me and if I am successful, I will make enough money to buy a ring and ask your daughter to marry me."

This caught almost everyone by surprise. Not even Ana had heard of this yet. The rest of the meal was consumed amidst something like pandemonium.

*

Over the next two weeks, during breaks between lessons, on his way to and from work, having lunch, in fact any moment he was not concentrating on the day job or together with Ana, Colin spent his time absorbed in thought and research as he honed and perfected his smuggling plan. Even when he was with Ana it had become his favourite topic of conversation, although he was always careful to keep his voice low, and was wary of parental eavesdroppers. Also while he was at Ana's house, he would often spend a lot of the time these days in earnest and hushed discussions with Juan Pablo.

Ana's mother was delighted that Colin was becoming such good friends with her children. Even her husband was quietly impressed with Colin. Ana too was pleased that he was getting along so well with Juan Pablo. She was thrilled they would become brothers in law. She was confident they were both intelligent and resourceful young men.

The final few days of activities seem mundane, however Colin was now acquiring the skills that should enable him to become a multi-millionaire. Did Colin ever question the morality of what he was planning? Not for an instant. This was the early nineties and cocaine was widely used in the UK recreationally by adults. Many of Colin's peers used the drug occasionally. In Colombia some of the nice kids from good families such as Ana's used the stuff like cigarettes.

They were aware that it should be treated with respect. They knew that over indulgence could whip into a whirlwind of addiction seemingly beyond personal control, and lead to disintegration of the nose for one example. Nevertheless few people knew that cocaine can in fact also be instantly fatal even in moderate doses. However Colin wasn't planning to push it on street corners to naïve youngsters in the hope of getting them hooked as long term customers. He simply planned to sell a few ounces here and there through his existing social networks.

The final stage in his preparation was to realise his cover story. Then he would be ready to implement his new-fangled method of secreting the illegal cargo which was simply so ingenious, so cunning that the chance of detection by any customs was effectively zero and not even worth consideration. About a week before he was booked to leave port, when he had a day off, he went into town to visit the local shops. First he kitted himself out with a scout leader's uniform. The Baden-Powell book had turned out to be a fortuitous purchase after all. He studied it very carefully for several days and knew exactly what he needed. He was very particular that each item of clothing should be authentic. He purchased two long sleeved khaki shirts with patch pockets. He also bought a pair of matching khaki short length trousers and a pair of khaki full length trousers to cover him "for most weather eventualities," as he would phrase it. Next he purchased some badges to be sown onto the shirt sleeves over the shoulders. He found a small square yellow bandana and a leather toggle to hold the ends together when he placed it around his neck.

Standing in the department store he inspected his reflection in a full length mirror, very carefully. Finally he nodded slowly a few times. Yes! He was impressed with his appearance. He totally looked the part even down to the green strips of cotton fitted on the garters that held up the long khaki socks. An added touch was a green beret with a scout badge. He didn't plan to wear it but it would sit neatly on the top of his rucksack next to his Bible and his old worn out copy of Baden Powell's classic book. His wire rimmed 'John Lennon specs' completed the desired look.

Next, he returned to the second hand bookshop, and stocked himself up with a set of travel guide books and maps and the bible he needed to round off his personae. He was to be a pious travelling scout. The story would be that he had been on assignment for a few months teaching English in Colombia to help young people get ahead in the world and to develop some familiarity with the location for future scouting adventures. On his homebound journey, he was now making a preliminary expedition with a view to setting up an adventure tour of Colombia for a small group of socially disadvantaged youngsters whom he mentored in his scout group in the UK. It was a very rewarding career, he planned to say, if it ever came up. You certainly didn't want to go into a profession like this if you were interested in making money, he would laugh, if the topic arose.

He would ostensibly now be making his way homewards by boat. He had opted to travel as a passenger on the cargo ship rather than fly, he could explain if need be, simply for the fun and adventure of it. Although his scout leader pay packet was on the light side, he could mention if necessary, it was varied work and provided wonderful opportunities for travel such as this.... And so on. Since Colin had renewed his passport shortly before he left the UK for Colombia, it would not betray his cover story.

The final shop Colin visited that day was the local bicycle store.

He knew exactly what he was looking for, and was able to quickly find and purchase a sturdy framed mountain bike with fat tyres.

*

It was almost 8.30pm on the evening before his departure, and long since already dark when he wheeled his new mountain bike round to the workshop at the end of Juan Pablo's back garden. Inside the workshop were a large selection of Juan Pablo's father's tools, various battered filing cabinets, overladen shelves and a large workbench. It had been Colin's last day at work, having handed in his notice two weeks before. Now two kilos of 98% pure Colombian cocaine had been purchased by Juan Pablo and sat on the workbench, wrapped in black plastic. It would be almost impossible to find such pure product in London, but in Colombia it was standard. In London it would be in high demand and very quick and easy for Colin to shift he expected.

Turning the bicycle upside down on its seat and standing it on the wooden bench, Juan Pablo first removed the wheels and then proceeded to remove the tyres using a bicycle tyre iron. This was a fiddly job especially with new tyres, and the incandescent bulb swinging from the garage ceiling cannot have been pumping out more than about 40 watts.

Nevertheless before long Juan Pablo had removed one rim of each tyre. Extracting the inner tubes he handed these to Colin. Leaning over the wooden bench, Colin carefully ran a razor blade around the inside seam of the rubber tube. Juan Pablo had wrapped the cocaine earlier that afternoon, rolling it in black bin liner plastic, sticky taped to be water tight.

Carefully Colin inserted one kilogram of rolled bin liner containing drugs into the inner tube. It fit quite snuggly. Then using puncture repair kit glue, together they sealed the inner tube back along the seam. By the time they were done it was possible to inflate the inner tube slightly, even with the merchandise inside.

As Colin began working on the second inner tube, Juan Pablo fed the first stuffed inner tube round the wheel rim and carefully replaced the tyre using his tyre iron. Within an hour, they were finished. What appeared on the surface to be a perfectly ordinary mountain bike, now had two kilograms of finest quality cocaine concealed within its tyres. Colin paid US$1000 per kilo (about £600), and knew he would be able to sell it in quantity for at least £40 per gram to some local cannabis suppliers he knew back in London. Even after expenses, assuming all went to plan, he was looking at a profit of almost £80 000 ($120 000) for a week or two's work.

Turning the bicycle back onto its wheels and standing it on the concrete floor, Juan Pablo turned and said to Colin, "As long as you don't sit on it, you'll be ok."

The next day at a little after 6.30am, Juan Pablo and Ana tiptoed out of the house and met Colin. It was about an hour before her parents would usually arise, and they took care to avoid waking them and having to explain why Colin was wearing a scout's uniform. Quietly they collected the bike from the garage behind the back garden. With passport and maps in the rucksack, and Colin's uniform looking perfect, they walked down the garden path and out through the gate, closing it softly again behind them. Then Colin carefully wheeled the ordinary looking pushbike alongside him, as they strolled down to the bus station.

*

Weaving through bustling passengers struggling with enormous amounts of luggage, they eventually found the right bus. At 7.43am, Colin kissed goodbye to Ana, and shook Juan Pablo's hand. He wheeled the bike up to the door and looked questioningly at the driver, who indicated to put the bike on the roof rack.

Colin looked up at the large roof rack on top of the bus. A man stood up there already receiving pieces of luggage and placing them quite roughly onto the rack. This was slightly disconcerting. He could only hope the bike would not get knocked about too much.

He lifted the bike up to the man on the roof who fastened it heavy-handedly amongst the other pieces of luggage. Colin couldn't bear to watch. An image of burst tyres spraying white powder everywhere flashed before his eyes and his heart started to race. Managing to dismiss the image as highly unlikely, and regain control of his heart beat he boarded the bus, paid the driver and walked down the aisle feeling a little giddy in the rapidly rising heat of the early morning. Sidling into an empty double seat he pulled open the window. Ana and Juan Pablo were standing outside looking for him on the bus. When he opened the window and poked his head out, Ana walked over to the foot platform beside the bus, and reaching up put her arms round his neck and pulled a sad expression. "Good luck," she whispered, standing on tiptoes and stretching up to try to kiss him. "Not necessary, using loaf," Colin replied, tapping his temple, and hoping it was indeed true. She smiled, closing her eyes as tears started to well. Still holding her hands up and touching his neck she whispered. "I'm pregnant."

Just then the sound of compressed air announced the closing of the bus doors, and there was a sudden judder as the engine was thrown into gear. Colin was still kneeling with one knee on the seat and leaning out of the opened window. "*Now* you tell me! So who's the father? ... I'm joking. It's wonderful." He blew a kiss to Ana and waved as the bus pulled forward and looked back to wink and grin at Juan Pablo standing a few paces behind Ana. Colin kept waving until the bus station disappeared out of sight, then settled down in his seat.

The bus was only about three quarters full and even with the other passengers' bags and boxes, he had managed to keep a double seat to himself at the back. He had plenty to occupy him, and keep his mind off what he was doing. It was interesting to watch the other passengers as they got on and off the bus. Local people, absorbed in their local lifestyles. It was convenient for Colin to busy himself with observing what was happening around him rather than dwell on the crazy journey he had now embarked upon. He managed to continue dismissing the thoughts of despair at the lunacy of his undertaking which occasionally flashed out of nowhere across his mind.

Once they had finally got through the traffic jams and out of town, they drove through Caribbean swamps, and thick jungles and past various enormous heavy industry installations. Now and then he caught a glimpse of sparkling-blue ocean or a tropical beach. The roads were generally chaotic, and Colin wondered if there were any set traffic rules at all. Sometimes there was a bus stop at the side of the road. Mostly passengers simply told the driver where they wished to alight. Or held their hand out to flag the bus down. The bus occasionally got quite full but the locals tended to avoid him and he was able to retain his double seat for himself.

Eventually they arrived in the bus station near the port. There was a direct walkway from the bus to the docking area for the boats. He retrieved the bike from the roof rack as it was lifted down for him. A quick surreptitious inspection provided some relief from his anxiety, informing Colin that the tyres were still intact, with two kilos of cocaine still packed safely inside. Then he wheeled the bike slowly onto the walkway, taking care not to lean his weight on the handle bars. Following the other pedestrians he wheeled the bike along until after a few minutes he could see the passport control building. Glancing up ahead through the open doorway, he saw a small queue and a kiosk in which was a customs official, his head down as he inspected a passport. Colin's heart started thumping and he could feel perspiration precipitating on his brow. Coming face to face with the new reality he had constructed for himself, he suddenly was no longer certain he could handle it.

Turning the handlebars just before he reached the doorway, he walked the bike to the side and along to where there was a patch of dirt between some of the buildings, away from the thoroughfares. 'Hmm,' he thought, his heart still pumping hard. Not something he had expected. Perhaps it was the sudden news that he was to be a father. He lit up a cigarette to help him calm down, and went over his current situation again in his mind.

Chapter 3

Colin had already convinced himself he was doing nothing wrong. Certainly, up to this point, his record was technically clean. Admittedly, he had smoked weed from time to time, taken the occasional line of Charlie, or the odd 'E' at a nightclub. But that was relatively standard in that era. Sections of society across all social strata behaved like that and while it may - especially at first - have seemed slightly naughty to some, it was never considered wrong in such circles. Smuggling was a natural extension of this social behaviour and was even often seen as rather debonair, and intrinsically quite exciting. Successful drug smugglers were viewed with admiration, at least by their hedonistic peers.

The attitude of many young people even educated and middle class people towards the policy of prohibition of recreational drugs, was often one of bemusement. Drugs culture operated like a game for many. Prohibition simply enhanced a sense of camaraderie amongst users, and happened to make the supply side very lucrative. Dabbling with drugs, to people like Colin was not a moral or ethical crime. There was never a question of 'Am I doing something wrong?' To Colin this was little more than a real life game of snakes and ladders. His role was simply to avoid the snakes. Personally then, he had no moral compunction at all about what he was doing. Just the logical one embodied right now at passport control. To his surprise, approaching the starting post, he had found himself caught off balance. He hadn't realised this was going to be so hard.

Dragging intensely on his cigarette, he tried to think. Was this really something he was going to be able to deal with? Or had he already gone too far with this escapade? He still had time to reconsider. Was he being really stupid? He looked over his shoulder at the walkway. Perhaps it was best to turn back after all ... but to what? The drudgery of eking out a daily existence? No, he couldn't go back to that. He found it intolerable. He'd only end up doing something else equally as desperate. He glanced at his feet. They were pointing towards the doorway ahead. Nope, this was a sound plan. He was just suffering last minute jitters. He would keep going forward. He simply had to convince himself that he wasn't going to get caught.

He finished his cigarette and threw it on the ground, stepping on it to extinguish it. He exhaled slowly two or three times. 'Calm down,' he told himself. 'You blend in completely. Just like any other innocent passenger. They won't even notice you.' He drew a breath. 'Be calm, be calm.'

Once his pulse rate felt relatively normal at last, not wishing to allow himself too long to think, he started off towards the doorway. After a few paces, 'I can't do it,' he faltered ... but already he was too close to the entrance. If he ducked away this time it might start to look suspicious. His heart started to pound again. 'Keep going, keep going,' he said to himself. He fixed his eyes straight ahead and, confronting his fears, forced himself to continue walking. He just had to continue putting one foot in front of the other, and not miss any more steps ... but he was starting to feel light headed. The nicotine from the cigarette was kicking in.

He would not usually notice it but with his senses already heightened, he did and it seemed overwhelming. He could hear the pumping of his own pulse in his ears and feel his face getting hot as he joined the small queue to passport control. Suddenly he was aware of a single large bead of sweat trickling slowly down his temple. Should he wipe it away, or leave it? He didn't know and he was reaching a panic state. By the time he handed his passport over he was dripping with perspiration and almost visibly shaking. He tried to drag his gaze up to make eye contact. All he could think about was the two kilograms of cocaine hidden in his bicycle tyres, and that he surely had given himself away even as he showed his eyes brimming with tears of guilt and confession.

The passport inspector didn't even glance at him however. He leafed briefly through the passport and simply waved him through.

Colin stumbled forwards catching his breath when he saw he was being directed towards the side. Replacing his spectacles after wiping his eyes he looked ahead and saw a couple of tables with customs officials standing in front of them. A sign above read, 'Anything to Declare! Customs Inspection.' His heart sank. He hadn't even been checked yet. He pushed his bike solemnly forwards. To his huge relief however the first official waved him straight past, and didn't even ask him a single question.

The second official a few yards further on was paying attention elsewhere. Suddenly Colin recognised he had a chance. If only the second official would be kept busy long enough for him to walk right past. Trying not to make any jerky movements, to remain fluid and relaxed, and not lean any weight on the handlebars, Colin continued forward slowly. From the corner of his eye, he could see the second official returning a passport. Colin didn't turn his head. He continued moving forward. In the edge of his vision the official began turning towards him. Colin casually noticed a mark on the tarmac and fixed his eyes on it as he walked by, causing his head to turn slowly and naturally away from the official. The official was no longer in his peripheral vision. Colin held his breath.

"Will you come over for inspection please, sir!" a voice rang out. Colin's heart jolted. Feeling dizzy he slowly turned his head and exhaled. The official was looking behind Colin, to another passenger. Bolstered Colin continued to wheel his bike forward. He went out the other side of the customs checkpoint, down the ramp and onto the quay.

As the ship appeared towering before him, he now found himself trying to hold in check surging feelings of elation. He didn't want to be counting chickens or anything but he was beginning to think he may have made the first hurdle intact. Perhaps his scout's disguise had helped more than he had even imagined. With a little more confidence, he walked out into the sunshine on the jetty beside the waiting ship. 'What a lovely looking day!' he marvelled. It had all seemed so easy. Or '... perhaps a little too easy,' the thought occurred to him momentarily.

He had been lucky at the passport check. He would have to be more careful in future not to give himself away, he was able to discern. He wheeled his bike carefully up the metal ramp onto the boat, then along and down again, into the parking hold. Finding a space between some trucks and cars, he padlocked it up so it didn't roll around in rough seas. Colin now made his way up to the cabin deck. After locating his cabin and dumping his rucksack, he went to explore the ship a little and identify the canteen for later. Anything to keep himself busy and keep his mind off things. He wouldn't feel as though he was completely in the clear until the ship began to pull out of port.

*

It seemed to take an interminable amount of time getting people and cargo aboard. It was looking as there would be no further incidents however, until they actually started lifting the ropes that tethered the boat to the harbour wall. Colin had sat on a bench at the side of the deck towards the bow of the ship in an effort to keep his mind distracted by watching the final proceedings on the quay below, when he heard a loud shouting and commotion emanating from the customs area, directed towards the boat. He felt an uncomfortable twinge in his stomach.

A heftily built, uniformed official with a gun on his belt, was waving a clip board and calling angrily to a staff member who was beginning to lift up the final gangplank. The official ran heavily towards the staff and while engaging him in an urgent discussion, kept pointing at the boat. Colin frowned, watching from the deck. 'Send him away, send him away!' he tried to will silently to the staff member.

After a few seconds the staff member nodded and began lowering the gang plank again. Colin started to feel concerned. But surely it was nothing to do with him ... was it? The uniformed official boarded the ship holding his clipboard looking alarmed and angry. The gang plank was left lowered and the staff member made no effort to lift it again. Other staff waited by the bollards, delayed from releasing the ropes.

'What's going on!' thought Colin. He watched anxiously but nothing happened for about five minutes, then the loud speaker crackled. Colin jumped, his nerves were so jingled.

"Attention all British Nationals," it repeated in Spanish and then English. 'No!' Colin groaned inwardly. The announcement continued. "Please assemble for inspection of all customs clearance documents at the Pursers office immediately".

Surely the customs couldn't have been tipped off about him ... could they? Colin's alarm started to grow. Who else knew about what he was doing? His mind began to flit back and forth. Apart from Ana, there was just - Juan Pablo. He thought for a moment. Could Juan Pablo be a nasty snitch? He felt a flash of anger, and then a sense of fear. He searched his memory banks frantically for any evidence of slyness on Juan Pablo's part. After a moment, 'Don't be ridiculous!' he told himself and chastised himself for having such an uncharitable thought. He changed tack. If it was not Juan Pablo, then had he been set up by the people Juan Pablo had bought the stuff from? Was that a possibility? He concentrated. It was impossible to discern he concluded, and best to assume he was working himself up over nothing.

Slowly raising his eyes, Colin idly glanced around the deck near where he was sitting. A few other passengers, as well as one or two crew members were milling around, sitting or standing here and there. None of them looked like British nationals, or appeared to be responding to the announcement. Now however, they noticed Colin where he was sitting, and all started eyeballing him suspiciously. The expressions on their faces sent a shiver right through him. A tingling sensation like electricity ran across his scalp. They had such hard accusatory stares. You might have thought he were a child murderer or something. A thought suddenly occurred to Colin. Did they all know something he didn't? He glanced around anxiously. What had happened?

'Pull yourself together,' he said to himself sternly. 'It's nothing but a routine check you fool.'

Drawing a breath, he stood up and forced himself to turn and walk however mechanically towards the gangway along the side of the boat, and the door that led to the stairs. He remained completely cognisant of the heavy stares of condemnation which pressed into his back from behind, and seemed to physically weigh on his shoulders, causing him to hang down his head in shame. His paperwork clutched so tightly in one hand that his knuckles were white, Colin heaved open the heavy wooden door with the other hand. Stepping through, he walked as if wading in treacle towards the stairs and down to the purser's office. When he finally got there the armed official was already standing outside the office door checking documents furiously on his clipboard. The Purser and a ship's crew member stood solemnly a little to the side. 'The games up!' thought Colin, and then, 'No! Pull yourself together man!' he chided himself.

Two or three other people had arrived before him. Colin moved reluctantly forwards to join the short queue, as a condemned man might approach his last few steps to the gallows. Papers rustled in his shaking grasp and his knees trembled visibly beneath the hem of his short trousers. The documents of each person were checked quickly and now it was Colin's turn. The official snatched the papers from Colin's hand and glared at them, and then back at Colin, staring hard at his eyes. Looking up, the official said to one or two others who had arrived after Colin, "Is ok, you can go." He shook his head, waving them away with his hand, and then hunching his shoulders and bending forward slightly, he peered long and hard at Colin. 'He knows,' thought Colin.

The official looked back to the papers and studied them with fury. Finally he looked again at Colin, who was fighting to keep his legs from quaking as his pulse began to race. "Foot passenger?" barked the official in English, incredulously as he stubbed a large index finger at Colin's hand written entry on the form.

Colin swallowed and shook, then nodded, then shook his head. "I had a..." His mouth had suddenly gone dry, and the words had got stuck on his tongue. He swallowed again, "I have a pushbike," he managed to articulate.

"Where?" The official demanded to know.

Colin pointed to the steps, "Down ..." he swallowed, "in the car hold."

The official scowled at him impatiently. "Show me!"

Colin paced stiff legged towards the steps, trying his hardest to walk naturally, but he had become aware of a sharp pain in his stomach. He gulped. Forgetting the official for a moment, he was now extremely anxious he might be in imminent danger of losing control of his bowels. That wouldn't look very good, especially with his short trousers on. Concentrating with all his might on maintaining control of his stomach, and beginning to sweat profusely, he led the way to the top of the steps and pointed down towards where the bike was secured. The official looked down into the barely lit well of the hold. Colin perspired and shivered as he tried to keep his mind on steadying his stomach and controlling his breathing.

Finally the official glared at Colin, his eyes full of judgemental condemnation.

Colin looked at him guiltily. He felt nauseous. "How did you know?" he asked weakly.

The official's expression had relaxed into a smile, as he held Colin's papers out towards him. Now though, as Colin reached forward to grasp them, the official withdrew them again, and his smile evaporated.

"Sorry, what?" he asked.

Colin stared at him dumbfounded. The question hung suspended by the neck, dancing in the air. The official looked at Colin curiously, his expression becoming increasingly pained as he tried to decipher what he had heard. Colin gaped like a stranded fish until, "Now can I go!" he said at last, raising his voice slightly above the hum of the rumbling engines.

You could almost see the thought process working its way downwards behind the official's face like a pachinko ball as he tried to disentangle this phrase, in a second language. Finally, he broke into a smile again and handed the papers over. Somehow Colin's documents had not been processed correctly at the inspection check in, he explained in imperfect English. Feeling giddy, Colin retrieved his papers with gratitude. The Purser and crew member were nowhere to be seen, so politely as possible he excused himself from the official, and walking as quickly as he could while keeping in a straight line, he minced off in pursuit of the nearest men's room. To his immense relief, he was able to find one just in time.

Fifteen minutes later Colin was feeling a little better. He stood on the deck again as they finally pulled out of the harbour and even smiled back at one or two of the other passengers as they ambled by. Slowly he drew a deep breath of fresh air and held it. He smiled at the open ocean as it reflected the sun onto his face. He would not need to deal with any more border guards for a couple of weeks. He breathed out. He could relax for a little while, and even perhaps begin to count his money. He had successfully completed phase one of his plan. 'Time for some refreshments,' he thought, and he headed towards the canteen.

*

It must have been a very interesting and enjoyable experience crossing the Atlantic by ship in that age of air travel. Colin did his best to keep his own company on the boat, with his head buried in his bible, or focussed on making notes in his notebook. He had a sketchbook providing a further excuse to spend many hours alone. He cultivated his image of pious scout traveller. This also enabled him to excuse himself from the occasional late night drinking sessions with the other passengers. There were only a half dozen or so other passengers, apart from the truck drivers and ship's workers who did not attempt to interact at all with the civilians. Colin did not wish to get drawn into conversations and risk tying himself in knots with his story over such a lengthy period as two weeks. Therefore he kept himself to himself as much as possible.

One night as they were crossing the equator he had a dreadful nightmare that he was visiting his new-born baby and Ana, who had been incarcerated in a remote prison miles from anywhere in some vast, hot and windswept wilderness. He couldn't understand why they were behind bars and it was excruciating to see them but not to be able to draw close and comfort them. Eventually he awoke utterly drenched in cold sweat, his bedsheet strewn on the floor beside his bunk. The memory of the dream lingered with him for several days but other than that his mind was relatively undisturbed during the crossing.

After several days without seeing land as they traversed the hemispheres, it must have been a great relief to finally catch sight of the coast of Morocco as it emerged on the starboard horizon. Except perhaps for Colin. For most it would have been a wonderful voyage along that coast, in the sparkling blue waters and then through the Straits of Gibraltar. The Spanish coast would have looked marvellous in midsummer as they continued on through the Mediterranean Sea; then along the coast of Southern France and finally into the Italian port of Genoa.

*   *   *

On the fourteenth day at 2.30pm they were finally pulling into the harbour. Looking over the harbour wall, Colin was relieved to see a relatively informal operation. Collecting his rucksack he made his way down to the hold and located his bike.

It seemed undamaged on inspection, so he un-padlocked it and wheeled it towards the back of the hold to wait for the ramp to be lowered. He nodded hello to the other foot passengers as they gathered to wait and he tried to relax himself. One or two of the other passengers had cars or motorbikes and were waiting in the separate traffic queue with the cargo trucks. Eventually the ramp was lowered and they filed out into the sunshine. They walked along a platform for a little way and were joined by a larger group of foot passengers who had just disembarked from a ferry. This made Colin feel a little less conspicuous.

At the end of the platform they were ushered through into a building that looked like a warehouse. At a table sat a couple of uniformed officials wearing sunglasses. They were leaning back in their seats and smiling, looking very relaxed.

Some of the disembarked passengers had suitcases on wheels, carried holdalls or shouldered rucksacks. Colin positioned himself with his bike more or less in the middle as the procession approached the checkpoint. As he walked towards the seated customs officials, Colin tried to maintain his focus on not bumping his bike into anything or anyone. Even still he couldn't help but be fully aware of the two officers' presence. He felt it was imperative not to accidentally make any eye contact with them as he drew close, even behind their dark glasses.

They didn't seem to be paying attention to anything however, and simply waved everyone straight through, including Colin. Not even a passport check.

Colin walked clean through the customs checkpoint and as he continued on towards the sunshine, he became elated. He smiled and waved at his fellow travellers as they went in different directions, suddenly feeling sociable for the first time since he'd met them. Through the other side of the building, he now stood alone on the pavement at the edge of the plaza, in the sunshine in Genoa. On his back was a rucksack. On his khaki socks were tassels and he looked for all the world just like a Baden-Powell scout. One hand that was clutching the handlebars also held onto his bible. He was so close to home he could almost smell it. He smiled at the passers-by and they smiled back at this friendly and pious looking scout with his unflashy utilitarian mountain bike. "What bouncy looking wheels it has," some of them may have mentioned admiringly as they glanced at the fat tyres on his bike.

His sense of elation however was premature. He still had two more border checkpoints ahead of him. Girding himself, he set off again, wheeling the bike. From here it was a short walk to the train station. The bike was stored in the luggage car on the train, and Colin located his seat.

It was not long before they were approaching the border crossing into France. Colin noticed two ticket inspectors working their way down the carriage towards him. Again he felt an uncomfortable sensation in his stomach. You must focus on staying relaxed, he kept telling himself as he concentrated on calm breathing and a disinterested gaze. He had his ticket ready. When they arrived he handed it over. They hardly looked at him, perhaps only saw the scout's uniform. Colin chastised himself for being so jumpy about ticket inspectors. He was handed his ticket back and soon he was in France. One border to go, he was nearly home. Leaning his head back on his seat, Colin watched the French countryside roll by. He was feeling quite pleased with his progress so far.

About twenty four hours later Colin got off the train at Calais, and wheeled his bike along through the customs buildings. From Calais on the French coast it was a one hour ferry ride across the English Channel to Dover in England. From Dover assuming he cleared customs, it was a ninety minute train ride to central London. Despite any apprehension he may have had there were not more than perfunctory checks at Calais. Again they didn't even ask to look in his rucksack let alone consider what his bike may be concealing. Less than two hours later he disembarked at Dover. At Dover he was stopped by Customs.

An official looked at his passport while he stood by the Nothing to Declare section holding his bicycle.

"Anything to declare sir?" the official looked up at him.

"No." Colin shook his head trying not to think about his bike tyres.

"Can I look in your rucksack please, sir?" The official held onto his passport.

"Sure," said Colin, flipping the bike stand down with his foot and slipping off his rucksack. His pulse quickening.

He handed the bag by the straps to the official.

"Did you pack this bag yourself, sir?" The official stood the rucksack on the table and unbuckled the flap at the top.

"Yes, I did," said Colin, nodding.

As the inspector worked through his belongings, picking out various maps, guide books and bibles he asked, "Travelling on business sir? Or pleasure."

"Pleasure," said Colin, "and education," he added. He was beginning to enjoy himself, perhaps too much.

"Are you carrying any illegal substances today sir?" The official suddenly stopped what he was doing with one hand in the rucksack, and stared directly at him. He had locked Colin's eyes, giving Colin no time to think or avoid the penetrating gaze.

Colin stared at him blankly, then "No, sir" he said , shaking his head slightly, and trying to prevent his eyes widening. He couldn't afford a single flinch, not even the slightest flicker of recognition.

The official gave him a hard stare. Colin managed to hold a fixed gaze.

"Very well," he said at last, standing up straight. "Enjoy the rest of your day sir," he handed back Colin's documents. Then leaving Colin to repack his rucksack alone, the official turned to search for a new quarry.

Colin quickly stuffed everything back in the backpack, as he tried to control his excitement and remain cool. He suddenly found himself having to concentrate to suppress an ecstatic smile, which seemed to almost have a mind of its own as it kept trying to appear on his lips. He was technically through onto home turf. Hoisting the straps of his backpack over his shoulder, he grabbed the handlebars of the bike and kicked the stand up. Careful to avoid forgetfully glancing over his shoulder at the officer, he wheeled the bike out towards the train station at the back of Dover ferry terminal.

Once he was on the train, Colin left the bike in the luggage car again, and made his way to his seat. When he had first touched foot on English soil again, after having, it seemed, successfully negotiated all borders, he had expected to feel ... at least pleased. All the sights and sounds had appeared completely ordinary and normal, even after having been away for so long, and strangely he had felt ... well, nothing. As he sped towards London, he gazed out of the window at Kent as it flew by and occasionally looked up at the leaden sky. Dark clouds hung seemingly just a few hundred metres above, blocking out most of the daylight even on a midsummer afternoon. It should still be broad daylight but at six pm it already seemed like night was falling. Usually, such a dull grey British summer's day might have depressed him, especially after so much time spent in sunnier climes. Today though, inside – secretly, it thrilled him.

Chapter 4

Colin still wasn't home and dry yet however. While he had the merchandise still safely hidden in the bike tyres and had successfully negotiated all the border crossings, he now had to contend with converting it as fast as possible into money. He needed to sell it before he was, through some mishap, caught in possession of it and subjected to Her Majesty's pleasure for several years. More urgently even than that, he needed to locate somewhere discreet and secure to spend the night and it was already gone eight pm.

He disembarked the train at Victoria, a major junction in central West London. Collecting his bike from the luggage car he wheeled it carefully along the platform then handing his ticket to a guard, walked out into the large square arena that connected the different train lines. Looking around he spotted a circular aisle in the middle of the arena with several phones, not all being used. Wheeling his bike over, he kicked open the stand. Heaving off his rucksack he put it on the floor and crouched down then unzipped a pocket on the top and fished out a black phone book. Flipping through it he found a number, then standing up again, walked a couple of paces to a pay phone. Looking at the book he dialled the number. 'Ring ring. Ring ring.' It rang six, eight, ten times. On the twelfth ring he was about to hang up, when he thought he heard an answer. He put the phone back to his ear. 'Ring ring.' "Where are you Brendan?" he muttered as he hung up the receiver.

As he turned back to his bike he noticed a child of about eleven was absent-mindedly caressing the handlebars and about to wheel it away. "Oi," Colin barked and darted forward. The child let go the bike and skipped back a couple of steps. "What?" he said, injured. "Yeah, yeah. Scarper!" said Colin waving his arm at the boy. He would have to be a bit more careful, he thought.

Now he had other problems though. What to do about Brendan? He had thought this through on the train in France, and had decided that his friend Brendan was the best person to call on, with the hope of having a place to spend the night. But now Brendan wasn't home. It wasn't entirely unexpected but a bit unfortunate on a week night, thought Colin. Brendan had a two bedroom apartment to himself close by in Camden, and had a spare room. Moreover he was quite keen on the occasional line of cocaine so wouldn't call the police or anything when Colin told him what he had done. Colin had been rather looking forward to seeing the look on Brendan's face. Brendan was one of his best friends from college days.

Colin had known that there was a small chance Brendan might not be home, and he had a couple of back up ideas. It had to be someone Colin felt he could trust completely. This was really vital. Yet now that push came to shove Colin suddenly felt that the only person he really could trust, was Brendan. Now the thought that he might not be able to contact Brendan started to concern him. He had spent nearly all his money on the trip and had very little left. £10.82, he confirmed after a quick check. Not even enough for a cheap hotel. For the first time since he had begun his planning, he suddenly didn't know what to do. He looked round at the cafes. He didn't want to spend his last few pennies on expensive station coffee. It was about

8.30pm, late July it would start getting dark in about an hour. The last thing he wanted was to spend the night on London's streets with so much cocaine in his possession, well-hidden even though it was.

One bonus at least of being in the station arena was that he did not look out of place standing around not going anywhere. Not yet anyway. For another two or three hours anyone might think he was simply waiting for a train - plenty of other people were standing and sitting around the place. Much later than that though and people would start to wonder what he was doing. He needed to find somewhere to go.

Colin waited by his bike and watched the clock creep round the wall. Even if Brendan was not out of town but was simply at the pub, he might not get home for another three hours. By then it would be too late to explore his other options. Colin was getting hungry now as well. Eventually the clock was showing almost nine o'clock and he went back to the phone. This time he was careful to keep one hand on the bike. If Brendan didn't answer now, he would have no choice but to start trying some of his back up options.

He dialled Brendan's number again. 'Ring ring.'

"Hello?" It answered at the first ring.

"Whew! Brendan. It's Colin."

" ... Colin?"

"Thank god you're home."

"Are you calling from Columbia?"

"No, I'm in London."

"London? What happened? When d'you get back?"

"Just off the train. Listen Brendan, I want to ask you a small favour."

"What is it?"

"Can I maybe crash at yours for the night?"

There was a pause, then, "Yes of course you can! No problem. Come right round. I'll be pleased to see you."

"Brendan, you may have just saved my life. See you in an hour!"

It was a four mile walk to Camden. Wheeling the bike slowly on the side walk Colin recollected how he had been friends with Brendan since they met at college more than ten years before. Colin had seen a poster on the wall in one of the college buildings offering holiday work as a motorcycle dispatch rider: motor cycle provided, full license required. He had ridden motorbikes before college and had a full license so he was eligible. The money looked good, so it seemed the perfect holiday job for him. There was a note on the poster to register at 10am on Saturday in the student union. That was where he met Brendan for the first time. Brendan was the only other person who had turned up to register. Colin was from South East

London and Brendan was from Basingstoke, which was Eastwards. In a north of London campus, studying interior design or similar, they had almost felt they were family.

About an hour after he set off, Colin started to recognize Brendan's district. Still wheeling the bike he worked his way through the familiar streets of houses. He knew the way well. At one point, about half a mile away from Brendan's house, Colin paused, and under the light of a street lamp that had just come on in the dusk, he made a mental note of the road name, which he read from a sign post. He walked a little way down the street, then looking up and down at a few doors, he identified one and chose a number. He repeated the street name and door number a few times as he walked on, pushing the bike.

Brendan lived on the second floor of a small Victorian terraced house. At shortly after 11pm Colin knocked on the plain red, wooden door, his bike leaning beside him his rucksack on his back, still wearing his scout's uniform.

He heard thumping of feet as Brendan bounded down the stairs. The door flew open. "Col..." Brendan stopped in mid speech, gawping at the scout that looked like Colin in front of him.

Colin laughed and put his finger to his lips. "Shhh," he said. "Let me in, I've got a story to tell."

Brendan's eyes lit up and he grinned. "Yes," he said. "Park the bike at the bottom of the stairs next to mine."

Colin wheeled the bike up the step and into the hallway. Leaning it against Brendan's pushbike which was propped against the wall, he closed the door behind him and followed Brendan upstairs.

*

They were seated in Brendan's front room, Brendan in an armchair, Colin facing him across the coffee table from the couch, half-drunk mugs of tea stood on coasters. They grinned at each other, having established Colin had had a good time on his travels, since they'd last seen each other perhaps a year or more ago.

But they still hadn't got round to the scout's uniform. "So when did you join the Scouts?" said Brendan.

Colin looked him in the eye for a moment. "Brendan, it's a disguise!"

"What for?"

Colin leaned forward and said quietly "For smuggling cocaine."

Brendan's eyes widened and then started to dart from one of Colin's pockets to the other looking for a sign of it. "That's brilliant!" he said, laughing loudly and clapping.

"Sshh," said Colin putting his finger to his lips.

"I didn't say anything."

"I know but y'know, let's keep our voices down discussing this."

Brendan looked doubtful.

"Do you ever hear your neighbours?" said Colin.

Brendan continued to look at him blankly. After a moment he said, "Yeah, I s'pose, if they're shouting sometimes. Can't usually make out what they're saying though."

"Yeah well, you never know. Just to avoid getting excited and shouting something inadvertant."

Brendan looked at his watch. "Well are we going to do up a line!" he looked to Colin's pockets. "But I still don't get the scout uniform," he continued.

"It's not in my pockets," said Colin, following Brendan's gaze which now darted to his rucksack, which had been dumped in a corner. "It's not in the rucksack," said Colin. Brendan's eyes whipped back to Colin. "Shoes?" said Brendan, looking at Colin's feet.

"The bike," explained Colin.

Brendan's jaw slowly dropped and his eyes widened. "The bike. Where ... I didn't see anything ... In the bike?"

Colin leant forward over the coffee table and lowered his voice. "Two kilo's. Hidden in the bike."

"Two... Kilo's! Are you kidding me?" Colin shook his head almost imperceptibly. "You could get *twenty years* for that," said Brendan.

Colin thought for a moment. "Only if they catch me. Listen, before you say anything else, is it alright if I just call my folks, let them know I'm ok."

"Yeah, of course," Brendan nodded.

Colin was holding the receiver to his ear. "Dad? It's Colin. ... I'm back home. I'm in London.... No I'm not coming up yet. Dad! I've got a job interview in London tomorrow. Listen I'll tell you all about it when I see you. It's a great opportunity. I'm staying at Jack's."

Brendan frowned. Colin fixed him a hard stare to warn him not to speak.

"Let me give you the address. Ready? ... " Colin started to read off the house number and street name he had memorised earlier. "... Yeah, it's in Camden. Ok, great to speak to you. Glad you're well... I'll be in touch... Thanks... Bye."

Colin hung the phone up and Brendan looked at him inquiringly.

"If the customs were on to me, which I don't for one second think they are, they would find my parents address listed as my home address. If they happen to call on my parents asking about me over the next few days, my dad will give them another address, not your address." Brendan nodded. Colin continued, "So they won't turn up here unannounced. I will ring my dad every couple of days and he will tip me off if any customs or police came looking for me."

Brendan nodded. "Nice one," he said.

They looked at each other in silence. After a moment, Colin said, "You got any tyre irons?"

Brendan nodded. "Ah. The tyres!"

"Sshh!"

"I... Yeah ok, I'll keep my voice down."

"You fetch the irons then, I'll bring the bike upstairs."

Shortly afterwards the bike was upside down in the middle of Brendan's living room floor, the coffee table pushed out of the way to the side, the wheels taken off, and one rim of each tyre removed. Picking up the first wheel, Colin carefully grasped a piece of the black plastic and began pulling the first rolled package from the wheel. He noticed small amounts of powder had escaped into the tyre cavity, settling inside it and on the black plastic wrapping, mixed with water condensation. Colin frowned, that didn't look good. He reached his finger forward and felt the plastic. "It's wet!" he said.

"It's not meant to be wet?"

"No of course it's not meant to be wet," he said.

"How'd that happen?"

"I don't know," said Colin, puzzled, adding miserably, "Maybe on the boat or something."

Carefully he carried the wet package, laid across his upturned hands over to a small dining table at the side of Brendan's living room. Brendan skipped along in front clearing any chairs and furniture from his path. Gently he lay the long package on the dining table and they went back for the second one. It had also leaked slightly and more escaped cocaine mixed with condensation.

They stood and looked in wonderment for a moment at the two packages. Finally, "Got a Stanley knife?" asked Colin solemnly.

Brendan nodded and went to fetch it. Colin brought a couple of straight back chairs over from the wall to the dining table, and sat on one waiting for Brendan. Brendan returned and handed the sharp knife to Colin, as he sat down next to him.

Carefully Colin cut a slit along the length of the first package. Inside were four sausage shaped packages weighing quarter of a kilogram each, completely wrapped in masking tape. Colin lifted the first one out of the black plastic. Quickly Brendan reached behind him and grabbing a broadsheet newspaper from the coffee table laid it on the dining table in front of Colin, under the package. Colin laid the masking taped package onto the newspaper, then carefully inserted the tip of the blade into one end of it. Immediately there was a musty or mouldy odour. Colin and Brendan glanced at each other. That was not a promising sign. Leaning over the table top, Colin began to cut through the package a bit further. He cut about two inches, then put the knife down and pulled the sides apart with his fingers. They both leaned forward to peer into the opening. Something was amiss. Not only was there a bad odour, the cocaine was blackened and looked wet.

At that moment a police siren sounded in the distance. They both paused instinctively. Police sirens were common at night time in London. Gradually it grew louder. Soon it was apparently at the very end of their street. Behind the curtains they could see a glimmer of blue flashing lights. Brendan stood up and walked urgently towards the window, drawing back the curtain an inch and peering out.

The siren continued to crescendo, the lights brighter and brighter. The siren cut suddenly but the lights were flashing so brighter than ever. Colin sat transfixed at the table, looking up at Brendan. Brendan turned round to face him. "They're outside," he mouthed, incredulously. Colin let go the parcel of drugs, stood up and walked over to the window. He peered over Brendan's shoulder and through the gap beside the curtain. Sure enough, directly outside a police car had stopped, its lights flashing blue, its siren switched off now. "Oh my god!" gasped Colin.

"What's happening man?" Brendan whispered.

Colin just stared at the scene below.

"Colin, don't tell me you've brought the police here. This is my flat man!" He looked at Colin who didn't return the gaze and simply said, "Shut up Brendan," as he continued to peer out of the window, through the small gap beside the curtain.

"Right, please flush everything down the toilet." Brendan demanded, still in a low voice, staring at Colin. "Now!"

"Just wait a minute, Brendan!" Colin hissed, still watching out of the window. Brendan continued to glare furiously at Colin.

The police remained seated in the car, and the lights continued flashing. Soon after more sirens approached and flashing lights appeared at the end of the road. Now the doors of the police car opened and two uniformed officers got out. By this time Colin's chest was starting to heave as he tried to catch a breath. His pulse was suddenly racing, even his legs were trembling.

"They're all over the place," he said, over the noise of the additional approaching sirens. Ok I'll flush it," he hurried back over to the table.

He quickly gathered up the packages careful to avoid spilling anything, then started quickly towards the bathroom door. Just before he followed, Brendan peeped through the window again. Colin burst through the bathroom door then stopped and stared at the toilet as he considered how to lift the lid with all the drugs he was holding in his arms. Still looking through the window Brenday watched as one of the policemen walked up the path towards the front door of a house opposite, on the other side of the street.

Brendan gasped. "Wait, Colin! They've got the wrong door number," he called in hushed tones. "Colin wait!" Colin had heard him the first time. He didn't need to hear it twice. In a moment he had returned the packages to the table top and was back beside Brendan again, peering through the gap beside the curtain. The police officer was knocking on the door across the street as another flashing vehicle drew up. It wasn't a police car however, this one was an *ambulance*. The door of the other house opened and the police officer entered. In the street two of the ambulance staff had slid a stretcher out of the rear and were wheeling it onto the pavement and up towards the open door opposite.

Brendan breathed in slowly and deeply and then exhaled. "False alarm," he said as

Colin slowly drew the flats of his palm down his face.

"Oh my god, that was close!" said Colin, breathing quickly. "I was about to flush the lot."

After their breathing had returned to normal and they were a bit calmed down, they continued to wait a further ten minutes or so to keep an eye on what was happening outside. Eventually all the vehicles drove away and after determining there was no more drama about to occur outside, they made their way back towards the dining room table. Another siren sounded in the distance, and they both stopped in their tracks and held their breath. The siren faded gradually and they exchanged a glance. Sirens were something Colin would simply have to get used to. Approaching the table they regarded the opened package. It wouldn't have mattered if Colin had flushed it. There was no question it was ruined from the smell alone. As he sat down again, Colin grabbed the Stanley knife and drew it the whole length of the package. Opening the slit the full length he could confirm that the entire batch was rotten. Colin was devastated. This was a disaster. He rubbed his hand over his mouth and closing his nostrils with his thumb and forefinger for a moment.

"What's wrong with it?" said Brendan putting a hand to cover his nose and mouth.

"I don't know. It must have leaked." Colin pulled the bag apart with his thumbs to inspect the whole contents. There was not a hint of white to be seen. It was all damp, grey and black.

"Is it all like that?"

"I don't know. I hope not. How should I know?" Colin reached out and picked a second package from inside the black plastic wrapping. He lifted it over using his fingers and placed it on the table in front of him.

He took the blade and carefully poked it through the end of the second package. Instantly again there was another wave of the now familiar noxious odour. Their hearts sank. Colin drew the blade down the package but even before he pulled it fully apart with his fingers again, it was clear the merchandise was entirely spoiled.

"I can't believe it," said Colin, looking thoroughly perplexed. Such a turn up had featured nowhere in his brilliant plan.

"Can you fix it?" said Brendan.

Colin shook his head. "I wouldn't think so," he said. He felt as though he was about to start sobbing. Tears were even welling in his eyes.

"Oh, man!" Brendan wailed.

Reaching forward dejectedly, Colin picked a third package from the black plastic and laid it on the table in front of him.

The evening was not turning out to be anywhere near as much fun as they had first imagined. Brendan had retreated and was watching suspiciously from a few paces away. Colin pierced the bag. This time a tiny puff of fine white powder shot into the air. There was no foul odour. Colin looked at Brendan. Their eyes sparkled. Quickly Colin wrapped up the spoiled bags to trap the mouldy smells, and Brendan after drawing back a curtain and opening a window to allow some fresh air in, came back and sat down at the table. Colin drew the knife down the length of the package, and their spirits began to lift. As Colin pulled the bag apart with his fingers you could see the whole length was full of perfect looking beautifully pure, almost luminescent white crystals, tiny snowflakes that seemed to cling magnetically together, retaining the shape of the inner tube. Brendan gasped. He had never seen anything like so much cocaine and had certainly never come across anything so pure.

Most cocaine in London would have been little more than thirty percent pure, even for societies' 'elite' which paid the highest prices. It was such a lucrative trade, and such a moreish drug that at each level of distribution just a little would be taken out, and replaced with some crushed paracetamol perhaps, or baking soda. It was virtually impossible for anyone to purchase anything much purer than perhaps thirty four percent at any retail level. Ninety eight percent was off the scale in the UK, even for major players. To Brendan, just the thought of it was mind boggling.

Colin reached into the package and dabbed his finger tip into the crystals, picking up a small coating which he then rubbed on his gums under his top lip.

"May I?" asked Brendan.

"Go ahead," said Colin.

Brendan did the same thing. Immediately he felt a powerful numbing sensation shoot into one front tooth, then the next. He tapped his finger round his front teeth and gums. They were completely anaesthetised. He found this amusing and surprisingly not at all unpleasant. Certainly it was infinitely more pleasurable than the needles Brendan's dentist used to deliver novocaine into his gums. In fact as far as he could discern the overall effect of the legal and illegal versions was pretty much identical, just without the pain or injections. 'Thank the law for those needles,' he thought. The numbness in his teeth increased. He felt a flush over his whole body. His scalp tingled mildly and he realised how wonderfully healthy he felt and how poised he had become.

"Nexsh time I have a toose pulled," said Brendan with a wide grin, "I'm going to pud thiz on my gumz jusht before I go in, an' tell him no indjecshionsh thank you."

"*Very* good idea," Colin grinned.

Turning back to the table Colin pushed the opened good package carefully to one side, and picked out the next package. He pierced the end with the knife. A small puff of white powder escaped. He looked at Brendan and nodded. "I think that means the package is good," he said. Brendan nodded. Colin put the package to the side, extracted the second batch of four and took the first of those to open. It too, seemed fine. One by one he worked through the remaining three packages. They all seemed fine. Just the first two were spoiled, twenty-five percent of the batch.

"Not a complete disaster then, by any means," said Colin. "One and a half kilos in pristine condition."

Brendan nodded, wide eyed. "Of the best quality," he said.

Brendan fetched a roll of masking tape and some aluminium foil, and a razor blade and a small mirror from the bathroom. He sat back down and polished the small mirror thoroughly with his sleeve while Colin sealed up the bags. Before sealing up the final bag, Colin tipped out a quarter gram or so for personal use onto the newly polished mirror which Brendan had placed on the table top in preparation. While Brendan looked on he then wrapped the sealed bags in silver foil including the spoiled packages, and took them to place in the freezer compartment of Brendan's fridge. They had agreed that if there was a bust, Colin would take all the responsibility and Brendan would deny any knowledge. His freezer compartment was otherwise empty apart from a half empty and frosted up ice tray. If the Police uncovered the cocaine stash, Brendan would simply say he never used that compartment and hadn't even opened it for months, and Colin would take full responsibility.

After clearing up - which included washing the tyres and bits of plastic bin bag wrapping under the tap in the bath to remove any residue, and binning them, as well as wiping the rims of the wheels - they sat back down in the front room. Colin extracted his last £10 note from his back pocket and rolled it into a tight tube. They had agreed to allow themselves just a small line each this evening as Brendan had work to go to and Colin had a lot to get done as well. Using a razorblade, Colin separated a small amount of cocaine from the pile he had poured onto the mirror. This small amount he chopped one way then the other with the blade. There was something exciting about the whole preparatory ritual itself, it seemed ever so sophisticated and exotic. They both watched as Colin worked the magic alkaloid into finer and finer crystals, the razor blade clicking and clacking on the mirror.

Eventually, using the blade he divided the chopped portion into two equal amounts and drew each into a long thin line along the mirror surface. Holding the rolled £10 note tube to his nostril, he leaned forward, being careful not to breathe out and blow the powder everywhere. Now he "snorted" or sucked into each nostril half of one line. He then handed the still rolled note over to Brendan and slid the mirror along the table top towards him.

Holding the rolled note tube to his nostril with one hand Brendan brought his face down towards the mirror. He sniffed in, as he moved the end of the tube along the line. The whole line disappeared. Brendan felt only a mild sensation in his nose; it was an agreeable feeling and there was a slight smell of chlorine perhaps. Then... Zing! Suddenly he sat bolt upright as a pleasurable wave of energy ran up the length of his spine and set his scalp tingling with the most splendid sensation. Instantly the pair were launched into an enthusiastic, seemingly vital and fascinating conversation for half an hour or so.

"I forgot to mention," said Colin after a while. "Also, while I was in Colombia, I met a girl and we're having a baby."

Brendan spluttered with surprise. "Well you have been a busy boy scout.

"Congratulations!" he said when he had finally caught his breath.

Ordinarily with cocaine in London, people found themselves feeling very excited, even ecstatic for say twenty minutes. Then inexplicably they found themselves feeling very awkward, uncomfortable and irritable.

When the drug wore off, conversations were left suspended in the air, like the cartoon *Roadrunner* suspended over a cliff. Suddenly the motor of the conversation disappeared, and the subject matter it was now apparent, was insufficient to sustain the sense of excitement with which the participants had hitherto engaged. This condition left users feeling strangely empty and hollow, even foolish for being so over enthusiastic about a mundane topic of conversation. Now they were ready for a top up.

Another line of coke would alleviate the irritation, for twenty minutes. In this way they could stay up all night taking the stuff.

However with Colin's batch, owing to its purity, this wearing off of effect was a smooth glide with a gentle touch down. Colin and Brendan were able to take a smallish line, become very high and over enthusiastic for thirty or forty minutes, then go to sleep a little while later, and wake up the next morning feeling extra specially refreshed. By about 2.30am on the night that Colin brought the cocaine back, they were both safely and soundly asleep. Colin was in the spare room with the biggest smile of the two. His plan seemed to be working out reasonably well for him so far.

Chapter 5

The next morning Brendan went to work at about 8am feeling surprisingly alert after so little sleep. Colin had a busy day planned: shifting his merchandise. He did not want to hang onto it for a moment longer than was necessary. Also, the sooner he got some money and a flat to rent, the sooner he could call Ana and arrange for her to come and join him in London as they had arranged. Very responsibly, he did not wish to make the telephone call before he had shifted the gear, just in case there were any hot connections anywhere along the line.

The sort of people Colin planned to meet today were unlikely to be awake yet, so he simply relaxed watching morning TV for a few hours until about 11am. Then he could finally switch off the television and get to work.

Sitting on the couch with the phone in front of him on the coffee table, he flipped through his black phone book.

A few of the entries had the note, Friend of Dorothy, in brackets. The first one in his book that he came to said Steve (Friend of Dorothy). Dorothy Lamour was a co-star of a famous mid twentieth century US movie star and stand-up comedian called Bob Hope. Bob Hope was a contemporary slang term for 'dope' - that is cannabis or cannabis resin. Any entry in Colin's book with the words Friend of Dorothy in brackets was a cannabis supplier.

He dialled the number and Steve was apparently up and about. A cheerful voice answered almost instantly. "Yup?"

"Steve? It's Colin."

"Alright Colin? What's happening?"

"Is it alright to pop round for ten minutes?"

"No problem."

"See you in half an hour."

"See you in thirty." And they hung up. This had been a standard double speak which usually would have meant that Colin wanted to come and make a purchase. At any rate it meant that Steve was home and it was ok for Colin to pop round and see him.

Flipping on through his little black phone book, he found two other names with Friend of Dorothy written in brackets.

He would follow these up later, he decided. He had a good feeling about Steve this morning.

Going to the kitchen he tore a couple of plastic zip lock freezer bags from a roll he found in a drawer. He fetched one of the silver foil parcels from the freezer. Using Brendan's kitchen scales he weighed out about an ounce. An ounce was around 28 grams. He carefully tipped this into one of the freezer bags, and thoroughly wiped out the bowl from the scales, for Brendan. He shook the bag so the powder collected in the bottom, then laying it on the counter, rolled it up like a big cigar, pressing any air out of the bag, and closing the zip lock at the top. He then dropped this into the second freezer bag, replaced the silver foil parcel in the freezer drawer and went back to the living room carrying the small plastic bag containing the ounce of cocaine. Laying it on the coffee table he went into his bedroom and fished around in his rucksack until he had found a safety pin. Taking it with him he returned to the living room and sat on the couch.

Unfastening the safety pin, he picked up the plastic freezer bag containing the second rolled freezer bag with the cocaine, and threaded the needle through the top of the bag in several places. Finally he undid the button on his trousers and pulled the elastic band that held up his boxer shorts away from his flesh. He had to stand up for this bit. Next he dropped the bag into the boxer short and threaded the needle through the elastic band at the top several times before closing it with the safety clasp. He buttoned up his trousers and patted his belly. Short of a full strip search, no-one would ever know.

He had £10.82p in his pocket. He had not wanted to ask to borrow money from Brendan. He could hop on the bus to Steve's which would cost about 90p.

He hadn't been to Steve's for a year or two as he had gradually lost interest in smoking dope, but he remembered the way. Shortly before midday he was approaching Steve's house. It was in a cul-de-sac of small semi-detached socially funded housing. None of them looked like they had had any external maintenance work done for at least a decade. In front of Steve's house was a tiny overgrown garden with a privet hedge that almost blocked the entire window.

He knocked on the door which could really have used a fresh coat of paint.

The door opened and a young man in his early twenties with long hair and a goofy grin stood gawping at him.

"Oh. Steve home?" said Colin.

"Come on in man," slurred the hippy with smiling but bleary eyes.

Colin followed him in through the front door and then through a door on the left of the hallway into Steve's front room.

It took a moment for his eyes to adjust. Most of the light was blocked by the hedge outside the window. In the centre of the room was a long coffee table with couches facing it on either side. At the end of the table Steve was sitting in an armchair. In front of him on the table were several blocks of dark brown cannabis resin, and a set of brass penny scales in a velvet box.

Three or four other young men slouched on the couches, where the fellow that answered the door had re-joined them. One or two were smoking spliffs, another was rolling a spliff. The air was thick with cannabis and tobacco smoke.

Steve looked up from his scales. "Y'alright Col? Not seen you for yonks."

"Y'alright Steve. Actually, not sure if you've got a moment? Something I wanted to run by you."

Steve looked up at him for a second. "Oh ok," he said. "Gi's a mo'." He focussed his attention back on the scales. In one of the small brass dishes was a copper two pence piece. This had weighed the scale completely to one side. To rebalance it he was selecting small chips from the brown blocks of resin on the long coffee table in front of him, having fractured them with a small sharp hammer blow previously. Now he added small chips to the other dish of the scales, trying different sizes to get the balance right. A two pence piece weighed close enough to a quarter ounce. In fact it was marginally over but in those days it was standardly used to weigh quarter ounces of hash and the many dealers were prepared to accept the margin of difference as the whole sale price was generally low and there was plenty of profit.

Cannabis dealers also often slightly *over* weighted the scale with the goods as a further bonus for their customers. Where it was tricky to get the balance exactly right they would generally veer in favour of the customer. This was all part of the social veneer that was painted over the illicit cannabis trade. A pretence of camaraderie, perhaps born of the alleged criminality or their behaviour. People did not usually even consider the person they scored dope from to be a dealer as such. Rather he or she was a mate who helped them out sometimes; more akin to a sociable landlord at the local pub, than an evil drug pusher. Similarly the dealers often saw their clients as genuine friends, and therefore there was a tradition in the illicit cannabis trade of giving the benefit of the balance to the customer; and at least the pretence of generosity.

When the scales were balanced, Steve picked up a plastic coin bag such as the banks supplied over the counter, and tipped the chips of resin into it. Folding the end back in to the bag to close it he threw it like a lopsided Frisbee over to one of the young men on the couch. The young man pushed two ten pound notes along the table top towards Steve, who just left them there untouched.

"Right, Colin. I'll follow you into the kitchen," he said. He gathered up his blocks of resin and put them into plastic bags which he brought with him as he traipsed after Colin out of the door and down the hallway towards the kitchen. However sociable his relationship with his customers, he did not apparently wish to leave them unattended with his stash of merchandise. The two tenners he left on the table. Presumably he would easily notice when he returned, if someone had taken a piece of one of those.

At the end of the hallway was a narrow galley kitchen. In the far wall a windowed door led to an overgrown garden.

There was no table, Colin turned and stood next to the counter worktop that ran one down one wall.

"What's going on," said Steve grinning, as he approached.

"Just calling round to see if you wanted any 'Charlie'."

"Cocaine?"

"Yeah. Good quality." Colin nodded.

Steve put his plastic bags on the counter and rubbed his eyes momentarily with his fingers. "What's the deal," he said at last.

"I got a little bit of cocaine to shift. It's through a direct contact from South America, I am telling you, it is 98% pure."

"How much is it?"

"Well, only because I know you, I can maybe stretch to forty sov's a gram. Obviously it's worth more considering the quality and purity. I'm really looking for sixty even in bulk."

"Forty's the standard rate anyway."

"Yeah, for street coke. But this is 98% pure. You could cut it three times if you want and triple each gram."

"I don't know, I don't really want to get into cutting 'Charlie,'" said Steve, looking a bit doubtful.

"You don't *have* to cut it. Instead you can just give your punters a really good deal."

"Mm." Steve appeared to be considering it.

"I'm telling you Steve, this is a good deal."

"Ok, I'm in. Let's do it." Steve started rubbing his hands in anticipation. "Where is it?"

Colin fished the bag out from his trousers. "How much do you want to take?"

"Mm." Steve mulled. "Forty a gram, you say?"

"Yeah."

"Ok, it seems like a pretty good deal I guess. If it's as good as you say it is, I'll probably take a whole gram."

Colin looked at him. "Eh?"

"I'll definitely take a gram. For forty. I'll need to dab a bit first, not that I don't trust you or anything, but you know, habits of the trade and that."

"One gram? Don't you... I mean... I thought... I was looking to sell a bit more than one gram ..."

Steve looked at him. "More than a gram? I don't think so mate. I would normally just buy a quarter. I don't have much demand for it. I mean, the people who come here are mostly unemployed. They spend like ten pounds a week on a bit of hash and that's it. I can cut an oz' up into £5 bag deals and it will keep me going till Christmas."

Colin stared back at Steve, at a loss. Damn it. He was wasting his time here. "Oh, jeez. ... Oh alright then, you can have a gram. Have you got any electronic scales?"

Steve nodded and opening a kitchen draw took out a small set of black plastic electronic scales that measured accuracy to .01 grams.

*

As he walked back out into the daylight ten minutes later Colin felt a bit dazed. He was forty pounds richer which was almost as much as Brendan would earn in a day, and more than many of Steve's punters would receive in state handouts constituting their entire income for each week, but he had been expecting much more.

He walked back down the residential streets to the high street where the shops were. He popped into a sandwich shop and bought a sandwich, then spied a telephone box. Fortunately it worked. He dialled the next 'Dorothy' tagged number in his book, arranged to visit then went and sat at the bus stop while he ate his sandwich. Occasionally he padded his belly gently below his belt, just to check the safety pin had not popped open on its own. The bus arrived after twenty minutes.

Chapter 6

Colin managed to visit both of the remaining tagged names in his book that afternoon but it was a similar story at each one as he explained to Brendan, later back in his front room. Brendan had just got home from work. It was about six pm.

"John took six grams and Stu took four. So that's eleven altogether Colin was saying. "And that's all my contacts, and none of them think they'll want any more before Christmas!"

"What'd they pay?"

"Steve paid forty for one, John paid sixty a gram and Stu paid forty. So that's five hundred and sixty quid."

"I don't think that's at all bad for a day's work, Colin," Brendan admonished. "I got sixty pounds for ten hours hard graft today … so why are you always wearing black?" Brendan was a carpenter.

"You're kidding right?" Colin was mildly irritated by Brendan's response. "At that rate it'll take me five years to shift it."

They looked at each other.

"Well maybe you should come and work for me then, Dr Chekov." Colin joked, breaking the tension. "I'm in mourning for my fortune." They both laughed.

"I was quoting Hamlet's mother," said Brendan.

"I think that was a misquote then."

"Speak for yourself!"

"OK then. Make a cup of tea, Gertrude."

They were showing off the fact that they'd sat through an English literature course together at college. In both Shakespeare's *Hamlet* and Chekov's *The Seagull* black clothing was used to represent a character's state of mind. 'Gertrude' was the name of Hamlet's mother. Brendan felt unduly sensitive these days about what he saw as a lack of high level intellectual stimulation opportunities at work owing to the nature of his job. It was a sense he had felt ever since he started going out with a young woman who was a graduate, with a master's degree and who held a relatively senior management position in a large corporation on a considerable salary.

Brendan got up to put the kettle on while they pondered Colin's dilemma. Brendan knew two further small time dope dealers.

That evening they were able to track one of them down who was walking distance from Brendan's house, but he wasn't interested at all although they stayed for a couple of hours drinking wine and smoking hash with him and a few of his mates.

As they walked home in silence, it was dark, around 10pm and Colin was decidedly moody. This was not what he had anticipated. He did not want to spend the next half a decade shifting his two keys of coke. Then a thought occurred to Brendan.

"What about Susan?"

"Who's Susan?"

"Sally's mate Susan." Sally was Brendan's girlfriend.

"What about her? I don't think I've met her."

"Yes you have. At that party at Sally's last year."

Colin couldn't picture her. "Anyway, what about her."

"Well, you know how she likes to powder her nose ..."

"Look Brendan, individual punters are no use to me. It's just wasting time."

"No, I was thinking more about her mate, Tim Peach."

They had arrived at Brendan's house and he was pushing his key into the lock.

"Tim Peach ..." Colin may have heard that name before. He followed Brendan up the stairs, past his reconstituted bike, shutting the door behind him.

"I'll put the kettle on," said Brendan. "I'll tell you about it in a minute."

As soon as they were sat down in the front room with a fresh cup of tea, Brendan picked up the phone. "Sally! It's me. Give me Susan's number.... Because I want it. For a mate... No, he's gonna do her a favour. What's her number? Nothing. I'll tell you tomorrow." He gestured to Colin to pass him a notepad and pen on a small side table next to a standard lamp. Colin passed him the notepad and pen.

"Yep, OK," Brendan began taking down the number. "Thanks. It's not too late to ring her now is it? I'll tell you tomorrow! Alright, thanks. I'll call. Bye, love." He hung up the receiver then started dialling again.

"What's going on?" said Colin.

"I'll tell you in a minute," said Brendan. "It's ringing.... Susan? This is Bren... Sally. Oh sorry, love. I must have dialled your number again by mistake. Can you forgive me. Yeah, ok. Bye." He hung up the phone again. "Shit," he added under his breath. Re dialling he managed to connect this time to Susan.

"Susan? This is Brendan. Good! Thank you … and you? Excellent. Listen are you busy tomorrow?" He covered the mouthpiece with his hand and said to Colin, "she's a teacher… summer holidays." Then uncovering the mouthpiece again, he chatted to Susan for a few moments before he arranged for her to come round the next evening to meet Colin.

"Susan is a friend of Tim Peach, and Tim Peach may be able to help you." Brendan explained to Colin after he had hung up.

"I don't want to meet cocaine dealers," complained Colin. "They have their own hierarchies, and it's basically gangsters." Colin was convinced that the cocaine industry was run by dangerous gangs. As he was keen to explain to people at parties when he had had a bit too much to drink, prohibition was solely responsible for the rise in organised gang culture in the 20th century. People would sometimes laugh at this assertion, and then Colin would drone on about how the Italian Mafia did not exist prior to alcohol prohibition. That Sicily was a poor island, where half-starved chickens scrabbled in the dust for a peck of grain. That in the nineteen twenties, as he insisted, Italian immigrants were confined to poverty-stricken areas of New York and lived on the breadline. Yet within a decade or two, alcohol prohibition had given birth to the largest, most powerful and brutal gang families in world history, and that the Mafia was now richer than the ten biggest organisations on the planet. By the time he had finished all this, whoever he had been in conversation with, had usually already wandered off.

"Tim Peach isn't a cocaine dealer," explained Brendan. "He's more of an up market cannabis dealer."

Tim Peach, also known as 'Peachy' to his friends as Brendan explained, was a highly educated senior management level careerist in the civil service. In his fifties he had a good income from his job but supplemented it by selling good quality cannabis to a small select group of his connoisseur acquaintances. It was very rare to be granted introductions to this type of dealer. They were not really in it for the money, more because they liked the drugs as did some of their friends, so it was a way of getting access to the drugs. Also it lubricated a social network for people such as Tim and his wife. Tim would often invite his punters who were actually his friends to lavish dinner parties that he and his wife held, where there would be perhaps a dozen educated successful people, some of whom, may have been held in high regard by the establishment – those in power. At such parties not only alcohol, but also cannabis and even cocaine would often be consumed without restraint, and without any sense of guilt or concern for the law.

Susan carried on the story the following evening as she sat with the two of them. "Not only does Tim have dinner parties," she said, "also he has a friend named Wendy. Now Wendy," Susan carried on pointedly, "originally comes from Canada, and now is a top accountant. No, wait, she is the chief accountant at ITV… or Sky maybe. Anyway, she is the actual Chief Accountant. I mean she earns like quarter of a million or something. She got whatever is the equivalent of a first from Toronto uni, and scored the highest marks in her year in Canada in the post grad accountancy exams. Anyway the point is, she now lives in the UK, and has this top job, and she has these dinner parties with all her posh friends. They are all like, people with really high level jobs and careers, some of them even well known.

"So they have all these big dinner parties, and some of these people are like, complete coke fiends. So at these parties, I've heard about it, some of them are like, sitting around snorting a line of coke every second breath. So Tim's plugged into this network. Although he doesn't sell coke, these people are connoisseurs. If what you've got is all the same quality as this," Colin had given her a small amount of coke on a mirror to test, "then he will want to try it. Now, I don't know where Wendy's mates get their coke, but I doubt they deal with gangsters if they can possibly avoid it."

Colin, slightly wide eyed, agreed that this was definitely a lead worth exploring. Brendan passed the phone to Susan, who dialled Tim Peach's number. After a few moments she spoke into the receiver, "Tim? It's Susan... Well, I've got someone here you will definitely want to meet... Ok, thank..." She lifted the receiver from her ear, they could hear the dialling tone. "He hung up already," she laughed.

"What did he say?"

She put on a deep voice, "Dinner. Tomorrow at eight. Arrive at seven."

*

At six fifteen the following afternoon, Colin ran down the stairs to answer the door. Brendan was off out with his girlfriend Sally for the evening. He turned the latch and pulled the door open. "Come in Susan," he said.

As soon as they were upstairs Colin picked up the receiver from the phone on the coffee table and dialled a number he read from a business card he was holding. "I'd like to book a taxi please," he said into the speaker. "Ten minutes," he said to Susan after hanging up.

Then going into the kitchen, he weighed out some cocaine into freezer bags again. He didn't want to carry around more than absolutely necessary, especially at night time. Going on his experience so far he reckoned that six grams was likely to be more than enough for a sample, as tonight was more about acquiring contacts for the future, than selling. He pinned the bag into his boxers as before, and joined Susan in the front room again for a chat, until the taxi arrived.

It was about a half hour's drive across London in the evening traffic. Soon Colin paid the taxi driver, and they clambered out of the car.

Standing on the pavement they paused for a moment to admire the large Georgian house in front of them. It was a big square box of a building with a huge black glossed door and a double sweep, gravel driveway. Parked on the driveway was a very expensive looking Jaguar behind which there was a more ordinary looking four door saloon. The crunched up the gravel driveway and climbed five or six steps to stand in front of the enormous front door. There were three electronic buzzers, presumably the building was made into three large apartments. Susan read the bell numbers and pushed one of them. As she did so Colin noticed a small

44

rectangular box connected to the wall above the door, inside which was a security camera directed right at him.

The door opened. Tim Peach was a large man. Six foot four and about the same round the waist. He had wreaths of charm and a rich charismatic voice.

"Susan!" he said. "I thought you'd emigrated." He was immaculately dressed and manicured in smart casual attire with black leather shoes brought to a shine you could literally see your own reflection in.

"Hello Peachy," she laughed, handing him a bottle of white and a bottle of red wine that Colin had purchased at her suggestion, on route. "This is Colin." At that moment Tim's wife Melanie appeared beside him. She was also very well dressed. In complete contrast to Tim she was absolutely tiny. They both stood smiling delightedly, in the entrance to the beautifully presented communal hall way. Both Susan and Colin were glad to have thought of bringing the wine. Even so they suddenly felt a little under dressed in their jeans and casual t shirts.

Tim didn't seem to pay attention to their attire however, and introductions were jovially made as they entered and followed Melanie and Tim into the ground floor flat. Melanie disappeared straight away into the kitchen taking the bottle of white with her to put in the fridge. "She's the best Chef in the world," said Tim in a loud voice, to Colin and Susan. "He wishes," called Melanie from the kitchen, sounding amused.

Tim led them to a large room, the size of two rooms. One half looked like a sitting room and the other, a dining room. Decorated to a very high standard with high ceilings and expensive looking carpets and furniture. Small chandeliers hung in place of light bulbs in the centre of each half of the double room. One wall of the whole room consisted of glass and ceiling to floor curtains, with sliding doors in it, leading onto a paved terrace and then a perfectly landscaped garden. Some of the sliding glass doors were half open allowing direct line of sight to the lovely summer evening sky.

Tim placed the red wine bottle on the dining table with one or two others, then walked over to a drinks cabinet and picked up four wine glasses and a half drunk bottle of white wine covered with beads of condensation and invited them to sit on large puffy modern armchairs upholstered in high quality linen, arranged around a large square coffee table. As they sat down and Tim started pouring some wine into the glasses, he said to them, in a loud voice while he nodded his head towards the kitchen indicating Melanie, "She cooks like a chef, and goes like a hooker!"

He burst into laughter at his own joke. Slightly inappropriate shrieks of laughter could also be heard emanating from the kitchen. Colin and Susan glanced at each other a bit askance. However Tim was so full of charm and bonhomie that they had soon forgotten the crass remark.

He seemed to love talking, Colin thought, as Tim regaled them with stories of his amazing exploits. Each of his stories invariably involved a scam of some kind and at some point Tim always emerged as the crafty winner. This man loves a fiddle, thought Colin. He was beginning to like Tim enormously. Melanie seemed to spend most of the time in the kitchen, but Colin quickly discovered that for all her diminutive stature and occasional social awkwardness, she had the biggest heart, and only ever had good things to say about anyone.

Within ten or fifteen minutes Colin felt sufficiently comfortable to un pin the plastic bag from inside his trousers, and tip the inner bag containing the cocaine, onto the coffee table. "That's six grams," he said.

Tim's eyes lit up and he grabbed hold of the bag greedily. He pulled it open and peered into it with glee, then reached in a finger and dabbed it into the powder. He rubbed it on his top gum, and waited a few seconds. Colin and Susan watched, awaiting his verdict.

Tim had never tasted cocaine anything like it. This seemed close to 100% pure. Genuinely uncut cocaine: this was simply unheard of. "My *word!*" he said. "You *have* done well, Master Colin. I'll *take* it. How much *more* is there?"

"One and a half keys," said Colin.

Tim looked at him. "Wow! Forty a gram, you want for it?"

Colin nodded hopefully. "I've also got half a key that is water damaged."

Tim thought for a moment. "I may know a top chemist who will be able to help you with that," he said. "He's in charge of the chemistry department at Edinburgh University. Complete genius.

"So anyway, I'll take a hundred grams right now if you've got it," continued Tim.

Colin shook his head. "I only brought six with me."

"Where are you based?"

"Camden."

"You got the gear there?"

"Yup."

"One moment," Tim held up a finger. He got up and walked to the phone on a side table. Picking up the receiver he dialled a number from memory. After a few moments he said into the speaker, "Ed? Tim. Got a job for you. Are you busy? ... Ok, be here in five." He hung up.

"That's Ed," he said. "He's my personal taxi service. I've known him for decades. Absolute salt of the earth. He'll be here in a minute to run you home and back again. Melanie!" he called in the direction of the kitchen.

"Yes darling!"

"Serve dinner eight thirty. Is that alright, love?"

"Yes it is darling."

Tim returned to his seat at the coffee table. "Tomorrow," he continued to Colin, "I'll have a couple more people here. Be here at six. Bring half a key. We'll discuss the remainder then."

Colin stared at Tim for a few moments. This was all perfect, he thought. Like it was just falling into place. This was exactly what he had hoped would happen. Here was a man who clearly understood the meaning of '98% pure, from Colombia'.

'Now we're talking!' thought Colin. 'That will be nearly twenty five thousand pounds within twenty four hours. This is precisely the kind of deal I was looking for. Well done Brendan!

"Melanie!" Called Tim again.

"What!" Melanie appeared almost instantly in the doorway.

"Bring my mirror and razor blade will you?"

"Oh! ... Ok."

Moments later Melanie reappeared carrying a small mirror and razor blade and wearing an eager expression.

Joining them at the coffee table she quickly descended into an argument with her husband. Repeatedly insulting her, Tim criticised her every single action, and Melanie was compelled to keep loudly defending herself and deflecting the blows, while together they started chopping up lines on the mirror.

First Melanie scooped some powder carefully from a small plastic bag onto a mirror using a razor blade.

"Darling! What are you doing? You're going to spill it all! Why don't you think?"

"I didn't spill anything. I am thinking." Unnerved though, now she fumbled with the bag and a tiny amount of powder fell beside the mirror onto the table top.

Tim didn't miss a beat. "Look what you've done. I can't believe you. How can you be so clumsy? You have the brains of a cat."

It wasn't a big deal in fact. Melanie quickly scraped everything up with the blade and deposited it back on the mirror again with the rest.

"Well... cats are intelligent creatures," she said. "Anyway, what sort of cat do you mean?"

They both started chopping and manipulating the cocaine, on the same mirror.

"I don't know... let's say... a dim-witted cat."

"No! That's not what I said... Oh dear, you do make me laugh. You are a very funny man you know Peachy."

The doorbell rang, and announced the arrival of Ed. Immediately breaking away from his bickering and chopping, Tim led Colin to the door, informing him on the way that Ed was very useful. Opening the door, he invited Ed to step in and introduced Colin to him in the large hall way. Tim and Ed, a mild mannered West African man in his late forties, with a round face and boxer's shoulders, had known each other very well for over twenty years.

"Guess how old he is," said Tim, abruptly.

"Oh!" said Colin. "Really?"

"Yes, just take a wild guess."

"Well, I don't know. Perhaps ... thirty eight?"

"He's forty-eight!" exclaimed Tim, delighted. "Doesn't he look young, Colin! He's ... how old is it Ed? What? He's ... you're nearly fifty aren't you? Forty-nine next birthday. That's it. Isn't it."

They all admired Ed's remarkably youthful appearance for a few moments. "You've got plenty of grey hairs coming through now though. Right? Ed? Eh? I thought that was you. Mm ... really? But that's what you told me. Are you absolutely sure. Show me the top of your head. Why not? Just tilt your head forward. Come over here, under the light. Oh don't be so silly. For god's sake, just show me ... Oh alright, have it your way. Hmm, very strange. Well, I don't know ... maybe it was Melanie then." Neither Colin nor Ed knew, unfortunately. Now in a booming voice, Tim instructed Ed to take Colin, "wherever he wants to go, bring him back in one piece, and treat him as though he is Royalty!"

Chapter 7

When Colin arrived at Tim's the next day at six as arranged, he still had over one thousand pounds in cash left in his pocket. Also he was the proud owner of a second hand midrange and low mileage maroon Rover that he had purchased with almost three thousand pounds in cash that very afternoon, from a car dealership in Camden, having pocketed £4000 in used notes the previous evening from Tim. He drew his car up onto the gravel driveway and parked it behind the classy looking Jaguar. He had enjoyed the drive last night, and liked Ed a lot, a happily married family man with a great passion for all kinds of sports, but he wanted his own car. Not a driver, as Tim had kept on advising, even while Ed was still there, until it had started to feel awkward keep having to say no. Eventually he was coerced into conceding at least to consider it.

Colin reached his hand down and pulled a lever beside his seat, before opening the door and climbing out of the car. Pushing the door closed he walked round to the opened trunk, and withdrew a black briefcase. Lifting out the briefcase, and shutting the trunk again, he crunched a few paces of gravel, then climbed the steps to the door and knocked.

As he was shown into Tim's front room by Melanie, he saw that Tim, and three strangers were already in there, seated. Tim and two of the fellows sat on the armchairs at the large coffee table. The third stranger had pushed his armchair to the side and was sitting in - what in Japan they call - the seiza position. That is kneeling with legs folded flat, tops of feet flat to the ground, and back held perfectly straight and upright. Hands held in lap. It was a disciplinary seating position in Japan, and was also adopted by some martial arts types in the west as a health promoting sitting position, which perhaps it is.

In any case such was the belief of John, who now sat in this position on Tim's floor. John had a haircut like William the Conqueror in the Bayeux tapestry, except his mop was tightly curled and ginger. He was not excessively tall but was extremely sturdy and generously built. He was wearing martial arts style white cloth shirt and loose fitting trousers with bare feet. There was an aura of peace and tranquillitys about him.

Tim introduced Colin to John, and to the other two strangers sitting on the arm chairs.

They were extremely interested to meet the fascinating young man that Tim had been telling them about. An enterprising and remarkable individual indeed, they all agreed, if he had found a successful way to smuggle two kilograms of finest quality Colombian cocaine into England, all on his own. And really, it was the very finest quality, they were unanimous.

The second man was a neighbour of Tim's, a friendly if ordinary looking fellow, named Pat. Colin could trust either of them with his life, explained Tim sincerely, indicating Pat and the final fellow.

This was Colin's concern: to be certain he could trust them. There was a level on which ... he distrusted everybody.

The final stranger was a wiry little man with short cropped hair wearing a worn-in black suit and John Lennon wire framed spectacles similar to Colin's. He was introduced as Todd, 'he's a friend of the Chemistry Professor.'

Colin put his briefcase on the floor beside the table and sat down.

Tim sat and allowed Colin to chat with John, Pat and Todd for a little while about this and that, until he started to feel comfortable that they were probably trustworthy and decent people, conceding of course their flagrant disregard for contemporary drug laws.

John made a living selling Moroccan hash soap-bars to a loose social network, and sold cocaine occasionally to a circle of people he knew like they were friends. Generally, he sourced it himself from people perhaps doing something similar to what Colin had done. Pat, was a self-employed painter and decorator and, in his spare time, a cannabis dealer to rich and sometimes famous or creative types. He lived a few doors down from Tim and believed he could find a ready market for such top quality cocaine amongst his affluent cannabis clientele.

Todd was friends with the research chemist, 'Dr Bill', who had a tenure at Edinburgh University and, who also had a secret laboratory hidden in the back of his house. There he experimented with and produced various illicit substances. Todd did not think it would be a problem for Dr Bill to clean the tainted coke, for what Colin thought was a very reasonable fee.

After some time Colin invited them to question him about what he had accomplished with the cocaine, and how he had achieved it. He told them the gist, but not all the details at this time, as they were newly acquainted. Nevertheless they were all duly impressed.

Finally Colin picked the briefcase up from the floor and placed it flat down on the table. Then he opened it to reveal two of the good quarter-kilogram packages, and the two spoiled ones.

"These are the tainted packages," Colin lifted out two of the packages and held them out to show the others. They nodded respectfully. There was almost a sense of the religious, they held the product in such high esteem. If they had been wearing hats they would have now removed them, in a display of mourning at the sight of god's beautiful harvest so sacrilegiously tainted. After a moments dignified and reverent silence Colin held the packages out for Todd to take. He picked up the two packages from Colin's outstretched hand and placed them lovingly in his own briefcase which he then snapped shut.

Now it was the turn of the good stuff. Colin slowly and gently lifted the two good packages out of the briefcase, making sure to avoid any daft accidents, such as catching the wrapping on the latch of the briefcase so it tore open and whole lot was entirely swallowed up by the thick pile carpet before their very eyes. Pat and John were on tenterhooks, following Colin's every move and quite literally licking their lips in anticipation.

They both wished to open and lovingly inspect their 250 gram packages, as well as check them carefully on some small electronic scales. It was extremely exciting for John and Pat, not to mention Colin. The quality was superlative. The weight was correct, the price was more than right. Once fully satisfied - in fact they were more than satisfied, they were ecstatic - they gave ten thousand pounds each in bundles of cash to Colin, who placed these in the briefcase, with equal love and care. He closed the briefcase and returned it to the floor beside the coffee table.

They all arranged to meet again at Tim's in a fortnight, Pat and John for another quarter key each, and Todd with whatever Dr Bill could manage to salvage from the spoiled batches. Then they all shook hands. Paul, John, and Todd left, however on Tim's invitation, Colin stayed for a delicious cold chicken, ham and salad supper created by Melanie, which they ate together, sitting round the dining table.

*

A fortnight later Todd returned to London with what Dr Bill had been able to salvage, which was miraculously almost all of the spoiled coke. Colin paid Todd a reasonable fee for the work, and sold the cleaned coke on again to Pat and John.

By this time Colin had rented himself a nice flat through a friend of John's who was happy to take cash. He had called Ana by now. She had a standby ticket prepared, and flew over to join him very quickly. Within six to eight weeks, he had very nearly shifted his entire stock.

He had cleared over seventy thousand pounds in cash, tax free in under three months. It was enough money to pay for tickets to their wedding reception in Colombia, and to treat Ana to a luxury honeymoon in Greece, as well as to fund a comfortable lifestyle for a year or so, and to provide some nice gifts for their soon to be arriving baby.

This was the end to a fine little story. Sorry, this should have been the end to a fine little story. It would have been very well for Colin and his friends perhaps, if it had stopped right here. A windfall like that would no doubt have been plenty for most people to get a head start setting up a family and a home. For unassuming and modest folk such as you and I, perhaps. Not by any means, for Colin however. His sense of ambition was not yet remotely satiated. He had tasted 'blood' and he liked it. He had already set his sights onto far higher things.

Chapter 8

For the next few months Colin and Ana enjoyed a work free lifestyle in their modest rented accommodation while Ana's pregnancy came to term, and until Colin was almost halfway through his money. Now he started to consider how to step up a gear. During this time he had taken to visiting Tim Peach on a weekly basis for a couple of hours most Wednesday afternoons. These were purely social visits. Colin enjoyed Tim's company, and over time learned to feel he could trust him a great deal.

On one particular Wednesday afternoon about nine months after he had first returned to London from Colombia, Colin walked out of his front door and down the garden path. He went through the little wooden gate at the end, and climbed into his Rover, as usual. This week however, he did not drive to Tim's, instead he drove to the local motorcycle store.

It was a large store with dozens of gleaming new motorbikes lined up on the sidewalk outside. After looking around at some bikes outside for a while, and then several more inside, he approached a staff member.

"Can I help you sir?"

"Yes, thanks. I'm planning a solo motorbike tour, I'm looking for a good road bike."

"Wow! How much fun is that! Where will you be going to?" The staff member appeared to be a keen motorbike rider himself.

"South America" said Colin. "I'm planning to perimeter the entire continent."

"Wait a minute now. You're going to make me jealous." They both laughed.

"So you want something reliable, economical, dependable, never stops."

"Exactly. I like fat tyres."

"What size range?"

"400, maybe 600."

"My first thought would be the Honda CB400," he led Colin over to a motorbike with a large petrol tank, and fine looking expansive tyres.

Colin looked at him. "I was thinking more the 600," he said.

"Excellent choice," the shop assistant walked towards to a 600 cc bike.

*

The following Saturday morning, the same bike was delivered to Colin's home address. Colin, Ana and the baby were still in their rented place. That afternoon Colin took his new bike out for its first spin.

It was marvellous to ride a brand new bike that was well balanced and handled like a dream. The gleaming pristine tank and glistening polished chrome flashed beneath him in the afternoon sun. The engine purred softly. The seat was wide and comfortable and the riding position just right for the long haul. Back home, he parked it carefully in the street outside his house. He padlocked both wheels with a heavy duty chain, then gently threw a rain cover over it.

Over the next few weeks he took the bike out most afternoons to put a few miles on the clock and because it was enormously enjoyable. Usually he took scenic tours around the countryside on the outskirts of London. Once or twice he took Ana on pillion if there was someone to look after their baby for a couple of hours.

One Friday at 10am, Colin came out of his front door, walked down the path, turned right into the street and uncovered his motorbike, just as usual. He folded the cover and put it on the sidewalk, then un-padlocked the large chain. Picking up the cover, chain and padlock, he carried them back inside, and emerged again after a few more minutes. Now he was fastening the strap of his crash helmet under his chin as he walked down the path He had left the front door wide open. As he climbed onto the bike Ana came out from the house. Shut the door behind her, then followed Colin down the garden path. She walked out through the small gate at the end, and turned left, away from Colin on his bike. Colin lightly pressed a red button underneath his gloved thumb and the bike burst into life, as Ana climbed into the Rover. When she was ready, Colin slowly pulled a U turn then set off in the opposite direction as Ana pulled away from the kerb and accelerated after him.

Within twenty minutes Colin delivered the bike to a local shipping company. Ten minutes after that he climbed into the passenger seat of the Rover next to Ana, and she drove them back home.

About three weeks later, carrying his crash helmet in one hand Colin strolled down the path that led to the shipping port in Colombia - where not more than twelve months previously he had wheeled his mountain bike. He signed the paperwork at arrivals, then rode the motorbike through customs and out onto the road, turning towards Juan Pablo's house. On his arrival a few hours later, they stored the new bike in the workshop for the night, and strolled into town for a beer or two.

For the next six weeks, Colin hung around at Juan Pablo's parents', and had a generally relaxing time. Every day he would take the bike for a ride lasting at least six to eight hours.

Then one evening Colin and Juan Pablo disappeared into the workshop.

Juan Pablo had been working as an apprentice at his father's car and motorbike repair shop, therefore he had some knowhow already, and they had access to all the necessary tools. Before long they had removed both inner tubes from the motorbike. These had about ten times the volume of the mountain bike inner tubes, and they had purchased ten kilos of 98% pure cocaine to fit in the wheels.

This time, to avoid any leaks, the cocaine was vacuum sealed in kilo packages made of heavy duty plastic, using a machine that Colin and Juan Pablo had bought second hand for about US$100. They put about six or seven keys into the rear inner tube which was about thirty percent larger in volume, and the remainder into the smaller, front wheel inner tube. They sealed the inner tubes in a similar way to the last time, using motorbike puncture repair kit glue. They then put the bike back together and pumped some air into the tubes. Colin sat on the bike and bounced a little bit, not too much. The tyres held.

They tidied up, and locked up the workshop with the bike secured inside. Then went into town to play billiards.

Later that night, as he lay in bed, Colin concluded that he had noticed a change in Juan Pablo since a year ago. When they first met this time, he had found himself chuckling at all the new tattoos Juan Pablo had accumulated. He had also grown much in confidence as a young man.

His confidence had shown itself over the game of billiards at a billiard hall in town earlier that evening. Juan Pablo and Colin were relatively evenly matched as players. The first couple of games had gone one each way and then on the third game they were down to the last ball, the black which would be the decider. Somehow neither of them could get a clear shot on it and the game kept going on.

There was no money on it, yet they both had their own reasons for a seemingly equal determination to win. Juan Pablo considered himself something of a hotshot with the billiard cue. They were in his home club, and a lot of his peers and competitors, were watching out of the corner of their eye. He had expected to show everyone else, including Colin who was several years older than he, and his competitors, who was on top.

Colin on the other hand wasn't particularly bothered about billiards, or even this particular game. They had had a pool table at home in the piano room when he was a child and he had become very proficient at pool, although not piano. He was not particularly proud of his cue skills. With Colin, it didn't matter what game it was, he simply had to win it. There were no exceptions. This evening, Juan Pablo had arranged to shoot a few rounds of eight ball on a pocket billiards table. On their fifth and final game, as they each in turn failed to sink the eight, they each became more and more frustrated, and determined. It was a fine match and as well as a couple of Juan Pablo's mates, some other people also started gathering to watch.

Eventually Colin hit the cue ball with such vigour at an almost vertical angle, for a curve shot he was convinced would work, that he catapulted it clean off the table.

Now a huge row blew up between the pair of them. Juan Pablo and all the onlookers were certain the rules stated that Colin must forfeit the game. Colin was under the impression that Juan Pablo simply got a free shot, which wasn't available on the black, so he should just carry on with the next shot. Things were beginning to become a bit heated when finally Juan Pablo had to send one of his mates to fetch a hall manager to explain to Colin that according to house rules, Juan Pablo was correct.

This had infuriated Colin, who was now convinced they were ganging up on him and stitching him up, as the outsider. He was stunned that Juan Pablo should take against him. If in doubt, he asserted, the guest's rules always took precedence. Though he knew he was wrong about the rules, he was still very upset about it all and extremely irritable as they walked home afterwards. He didn't care how he won, just as long as he did ... otherwise he would be in a thunderous temper that sometimes lasted days.

As he fell asleep Colin went over a few things in his mind. In some ways he felt more confident than this time round, having personally observed that smuggling cocaine successfully was in fact feasible. However he was also aware of now stepping into more dangerous territory regarding a potential prison sentence, that is, if he accidentally made any error.

Another thing he was aware of, was that a portion of the cocaine he and Juan Pablo had hidden in the motorbike inner tubes that evening, was even superior to the 98% pure variety that made up the rest. About ten percent, two point six seven zero one kilograms to be precise, was what was termed 'flake cocaine'. This was the very best quality available anywhere, and was a rarity even in Colombia. So much of a rarity in fact that the only other existence of it known to anyone in Juan Pablo's town, was co-incidentally also precisely 2.67401 kilograms - that had been confiscated by the local police in a recent bust, as reported in the local newspaper. Colin was appalled at the apparent corruption. And the absurdity of the drugs situation, where all sides it seemed had their fingers in the illicit pie.

The police in his own country with its supposedly advanced civil institutions, were - according to the national press - themselves not immune by any means to corruption by the prohibition of cocaine. Was there, he wondered, a single country where it was any different? By prohibiting such powerful substances, leaving no grounds to educate people about them properly, was society simply persecuting human nature?

It wasn't Colin's fault that there was such an overwhelming demand. He didn't create that. It pre-existed him. With such an economic in-balance someone somewhere was *bound* to fall into such a role, as he had. It was inevitable. Couldn't they see that? Regardless of punitive admonishment and the risk of social excommunication the whole routine was inherent in human nature, in all societies, in all places at all times. It was all part of the same single process. The whole contemporary relationship between society and recreational drugs had got out of whack, and it would always cause someone to fall into a gap. Similarly the situation left all credible drugs' education in the hands of the pushers, who were as often as not, among the most charming people you could ever hope to meet.

Consider that 'Bootleg' Joe Kennedy had made his fortune as a booze runner during prohibition, it was one of Colin's favourite anecdotes. Wasn't it time they recognised the cops and the drug smugglers were just two sides of the same coin? They were the same person, they could even switch sides, (as we might see). If it wasn't Joe, or Colin it would always be someone else.

All the while the laws remained unchanged, there would always be other Colin's following in his tracks and doing the same thing. Yet the persecution of human nature - would no doubt continue unabated.

In his deepest sleep Colin even dreamt that the very establishment maintaining the modern day institutions of society may even have had fundamental flaws going right to its foundations. Flaws that if they did exist, would surely have been better addressed at the root cause, rather than the symptom. Perhaps there was some universal psychological flaw that drew so many to drug use. All that was required was the sharing, through education, of a more enlightened understanding of the way to use such drugs beneficially, and of people's psychology, and of the relationship between the two.

Colin was upset that certain police forces were engaging in the same pursuit as he was, and may even have been supplying the market as well as policing it, yet he was the one that stood to get into big trouble for it. Held to account by the very people that had supplied the product to the market. On a deeper level perhaps Colin's subconscious was railing against his decision to involve himself further in such an industry. In his heart of hearts - whatever the ins and outs, the rights and wrongs - maybe he had recognised that he was approaching some invisible point of no return.

*

His distemper hung over the following morning. He couldn't find his motorbike keys on the counter where he thought he'd left them and started shrieking at Juan Pablo hysterically assuming *he* must have taken them.

"Alright! Keep yer head on!" admonished Juan Pablo. "You left them in the ignition remember? They're still in the bike I would imagine. It's all locked up so stop freaking out. You gotta start taking it easy, man."

Colin knew Juan Pablo was right. Calming himself down, he managed to get some breakfast inside him. That made him start to feel better. 'I was just hungry,' he thought. He always got upset when he was hungry.

At 10am Juan Pablo drove one of his father's motorbike pick-up vans, along the track to the workshop. Juan Pablo climbed out of the driver's seat, and walked round to the back. Pulling open the rear doors, he slid out an aluminium ramp that was laying on the floor inside, and propped it against the back of the van so that it ran at a gentle angle to the ground. Then he walked over to the workshop door, unlocked it and lifted it up to the ceiling. Colin walked in ahead of him and went straight up to the motorbike. Sure enough the keys were sitting in the ignition where he had left them the previous evening. He undid the steering lock, and pushed the bike forward off its stand. Wheeling it round and back out of the door, he lined the front wheel up with the ramp, about a meter away.

Juan Pablo now went round behind the bike and grabbed hold of the metal seat rack. Together, on the count of three, they pushed forward and heaved the bike up the ramp, and into the van. Colin put the stand down and then clambered out, so that Juan Pablo could get in and fasten two or three canvas straps to each side of the bike, which were permanently fastened to the inside of the van. By pulling the ratcheted straps he was able to secure the bike firmly in place.

They then both walked round and climbed into the cab at the front. Juan Pablo started the engine. As they drove by the house, Colin hopped out and collected his rucksack and crash helmet. He was wearing the shirt and long trousers of a scout leader. He had thought tassels and short trousers on a motorbike might arouse unnecessary suspicions from customs officials. In his rucksack was a green, scout's beret to complete his disguise.

As soon as he had climbed back into the seat next to Juan Pablo, they pulled out onto the lane and drove towards the main road. When they reached the junction however, instead of turning left towards the Pacific Ocean and eventually the port, Juan Pablo turned right. Soon they were on the main highway heading inland, towards the Amazon Jungle, and the border with Brazil.

Chapter 9

Before long they were on a dual carriageway with music blaring. Colin was able to leisurely watch the Andes mountain ranges roll by. An old 'Steppenwolf' song was on the radio, "Get your motor running..."

Colin sat up in his seat and, listening to the music found himself smiling again as he looked out of the window at the sun drenched alpine scenery. Finally, his spirits were beginning to pick up again.

It was an eighteen hour drive to Bogota. They stopped for the evening at a guest house on route. Very early the following morning they set out, arriving in Bogota by late afternoon.

After spending another night in a hotel in Bogota, at around mid-morning they drove to the airport. It was an internal flight so there were no customs checks. The bike was taken to be put on board by the staff at the airport. Juan Pablo and Colin shook hands, thrilled by the adventure, and Colin set off in search of the departure gate.

From his window seat on the small aircraft Colin could see the last of the Andes giving way to relatively barren tropical plains. Then the tropical plains gradually became encroached by the edges of the Great Amazon Jungle. The immensity and sheer scale of it was staggering. Even with the extended view afforded by the 20 or 30 000 foot altitude of the aircraft, which seemed to reveal the very curvature of the earth, still the rainforest stretched to the horizon in every direction.

As they started their descent, cutting through the deep green of the jungle he could see a gigantic caramel snake that also stretched from horizon to horizon. It was the Amazon River, in some places a kilometre or more in width, where tributaries joined it for example. The mighty river visibly marked the border between Colombia and Peru.

The forest below was now thick with trees. He could see here and there that small areas had been cleared to make a few acres of farmland, and occasionally he saw small settlements made of sometimes just two or three thatch roof houses; tiny islands in the midst of the jungle.

Now he could see, up ahead the isolated town of Leticia consisting of several thousand houses perhaps, on the banks of the river, right in the middle of the jungle. With the closest highway stopping more than five hundred miles short of Leticia, the only access to the remote jungle outpost was by air or river. One side of the town was in Colombia, the other side was in Brazil.

On the edge of the town as they made their final approach, Colin could see a single, wide tarmac strip that was Leticia Airport. Indeed, he thought it was starting to look very wide indeed, and much too short; when thankfully the aircraft began to circle at the last moment, and changed its line of approach by ninety degrees before finally touching down to safety.

It was mid-afternoon by the time they had landed in Leticia. Soon afterwards Colin retrieved his bike on the tarmac outside the plane where it was rolled backwards down a ramp by a couple of airport porters. Without starting the engine and with his rucksack on his back, he wheeled the bike out towards the exit and then into town. Once outside the airport bounds, he pressed the start button to fire up the engine but still did not climb onto the bike. Instead he used the throttle and clutch to power it gently alongside him as he walked. It was not much more than a kilometre, about a twenty minute walk to Leticia town centre.

Once or twice friendly local people passing on small motorbikes or in old cars stopped to ask if he needed any help. No thank you ever so much, he assured them, touched by their generosity. He was simply stretching his legs, he explained.

In the town centre, there were various shops, restaurants, bars and supermarkets, and plenty of tourist guest houses. He parked the bike at the side of the road, near a small café which had some tables and chairs laid out on the pavement. Sitting at one of the tables with a clear view of his bike, on its stand a few metres away, he ordered a draught beer when the waiter appeared. Colin enjoyed sipping the cool and refreshing lager in the afternoon sunshine, as he watched the people passing by. Many were tourists, a lot of them students on gap years he suspected. Many wore colourful loose fitting ethnic shirts and long pants, made from light linen cloth, purchased for a few cents at local markets, which looked ideal attire in the jungle heat and humidity.

He didn't see anybody that he thought might also be an international cocaine smuggler. If any people looked at him, they too did not realise he was a drug smuggler and instead saw an adventurous but straight laced looking scout leader.

Three young tourists, one woman and two men, all in ethnic garb had sat at a close by table and also ordered beers. The young woman appeared to take a shine to Colin.

"Is it your bike?" she enquired, smiling at him across the tables and nodding towards his motorbike.

Colin nodded but didn't smile. He wished to avoid being drawn into unnecessary conversations.

"Wow!" she said. She was impressed, her two male companions perhaps less so.

"Where have you been?" She asked.

"Rio," Colin lied, "Argentina, Peru, Colombia."

"It's fantastic, the young woman enthused. She was very pretty, noticed Colin. Her two companions had started their own quiet conversation. Colin smiled.

"How long have you been on the road?" she asked.

"'Bout three months."

"Has it been fun?" Colin nodded and smiled again. She was sure to be with one of her companions, he was wasting his time and running unnecessary risks. This smile was an attempt to end the conversation.

"Will you take me for a ride?" she said.

Her two companions stopped their conversation and both looked towards Colin.

"Oh please take me for a ride," continued the woman. "I love motorbikes. My ex had a motorbike."

"I would usually," said Colin, "but it's broken down at the moment."

"Oh," said the woman, disconsolately. "Tell you what," she said, brightening up again. "Do you want me to get someone to look at it for you? I know a mechanic literally there, across the street. He's ace. He can fix it whatever for you. He'll do it as a favour to me."

Now her two companions turned to look at the young woman. "Who is a mechanic?" one of them asked.

"Don't worry," Colin interrupted them, "I've already spoken to a repair shop in Manaus, on the phone. I'm taking it there on a boat leaving tomorrow. Specialist Honda mechanic. Gotta be."

"River boat." One of the young woman's companions confirmed.

Colin nodded.

"We've already done that," said the companion, nodding slowly to demonstrate his complete familiarity with Colin's imminent travel plans. "If there's anything you want to ask us ..."

Colin stood up and fishing some paper money out of his pocket, put it on the table for the waiter. He weighed it down against the blusters of hot breeze, using the small glass ashtray, and walked slowly towards his bike.

"Buy your own hammock to take with you!" advised the young woman as he walked away. "They'll charge you ten times what you'll pay here in town, once you are on the boat."

Colin turned. "Thank you for the advice," he said sincerely. Then hoisting on his rucksack and taking care not to knock the start button with his thumb by error, he rolled the bike round the corner as quickly and slowly as he could manage.

From Leticia town centre he wheeled the bike the few hundred metres down to the dock. It was slightly down-hill all the way so he did not need the engine anyway.

Here's what the **Lonely Planet Guidebook** has to say about Leticia.

*Leticia lies right on the Colombia– Brazil border. Just south across the frontier is Tabatinga, a Brazilian town of similar size. The towns are virtually merging together, and there are **no border checkpoints** between the two.*

From Leticia he could walk right through into Tabatinga in Brazil. He could get an exit and entry stamp in his passport voluntarily, at a nearby kiosk, and then simply board a boat down the Amazon to Manaus. At Manaus he could wheel the bike about one kilometre to the airport from where he would be able to take another internal flight to Rio.

There were several boats at the dock. All pretty pale pinks, and white and baby blues. Adorned with orange candy and peppermint lifesavers, to fend off collisions, they looked for all the world to Colin like giant multi-tiered wedding cakes bobbing about on the river. Rose petal reflections dappled the caramel water, as though handfuls of floating confetti. The giant jostling cakes were two, or sometimes a precarious looking three layers high. Some of their decks were opened to the air, and trimmed with dainty painted wooden balustrades. These were traditional Amazon River explorer boats. It was an atmospheric and picturesque moment for Colin, set against the jungle backdrop and the blazing tangerine sky. He was sufficiently moved, to take a photograph of the scene as the afternoon shadows grew long, on the bustling dock, deep in the Amazon Rainforest, just before he booked his passage on an old fashioned river explorer.

He managed to book himself onto a vessel which could also take his motorbike. It was to leave that very evening. "Here's a card," the booking agent said as Colin purchased his ticket in the small travel office nearby the small pier. "Show me the card to get a discount. If you ever plan to come this way again," the man said. Colin took the card and looked at it. It had a stencilled drawing of a wedding cake on the front. He nodded before he put it in his pocket. "I do," he affirmed. He glanced nervously through the window to check on his bike with its tyres stuffed quite full of cocaine, as the man counted out his change. It was parked on the sidewalk outside, with the steering locked but with no chain and padlock.

After loading the bike safely from the pier onto the boat, and having carefully overseen proceedings as the straps were fastened to secure it; following the young woman from the café's advice he set off to wander round the town and buy himself a hammock.

*

Following a light supper in one of the local food markets, eating on tables in the open air under lamp light surrounded by a cloud of circling insects of all shapes and sizes, he returned to the boat with a new hammock swinging from his hand in a white plastic carrier bag.

He boarded his boat, checked his bike was still in position, and then went along to the lower deck to string up his hammock as far away as possible from the rarely cleaned toilets and shower section. The boats were nowhere near fully booked, and there were only about half a dozen hammocks or so hanging laterally towards the middle of the lower deck. A person appeared to be sleeping in one, the others were empty. He walked to the front most end of the deck, and hung his hammock as far as he could from the other passengers'. Hopefully they would register the statement that he wished to keep himself to himself. He climbed in and pulling his cap over his eyes tried to go to sleep.

Colin was awoken the following morning, by the gentle swaying of his hammock. He kept his eyes closed for a few moments and listened to the sounds around him. Distant squawking birds and screeching monkeys punctuated the sway of the tree tops in the breeze. Splashes in the water could be heard every few seconds, some close and some maybe hundreds of feet away. Some splashes were small, some huge. In the background was the gentle hum of the engine that droned beneath the deck. Opening his eyes he saw that no-one else had slung a hammock at his end of the deck and he felt slightly relieved.

Swinging his feet round out of the hammock, he sat up and from his perch, which was closest to the bow, drank in the view forwards of the vessel. Towering trees crowded to the banks on each side of the caramel serpent, several hundred yards wide. They were navigating about 30 yards from the shore on the left. As they moved down stream they would sometimes disturb brown and orange pheasants, or red and blue parrots which squawked panic stricken as they flapped blunderingly into, or over the trees.

Occasionally a large red monkey could be seen swinging through the higher branches along the river banks, whooping loudly as it escorted the alien boat through its territory. On the river, small and large rafts of flat leaved bright green weeds floated by silently. At almost every moment some thing somewhere in the water was splashing.

Mysterious and monstrous creatures appeared momentarily above the surface, again and again taunting, then disappearing before anyone could identify what they could possibly be. Some were so huge they set off huge sprays of water with each jump. Other times it was much smaller creatures, fish perhaps, giant frogs, red eared terrapins the size of dinner plates sliding down the bank, or diving kingfishers flashing blue silver and gold.

Here swimming with determination upstream, was a great leatherback turtle's head and the mound of its soggy looking brown shell sticking out of the caramel water like a brandy soaked plumb pudding. There trailing the boat aft of the bow, downwind, was the enormous snout, sharp white teeth and black nostrils of a giant alligator. It cast a long 'v' shaped wake that spread out across the river behind, as it sniffed Colin's scent in mouth-watering anticipation and watched him with hungry eyes. It stared at him ceaselessly with its gleaming yellow, glowing, luminous bulbs, waiting for him to somehow accidentally fall overboard, helpless into the soup.

"Not today, Mr Crocodile!" Colin grinned and gnashed his own ivory chisels at the beast, which metamorphosed into a log of chocolate and melted before his eyes.

Far above the marzipan trees, the candy lemon sun itself seemed to smile as it sparkled, and shone its sugar dust rays onto the whole continent from the highest and freshest of sapphire skies, cool enough to freshen gums and flint enough to clean teeth.

*

Back beneath the canopy, as the boat trundled slowly onwards, yet another blood curdling scream pierced the jungle hubbub, only this time it was human. Colin span round terrified, and looked aft. A young tourist woman was standing on the deck beside her hammock, which had become all twisted up on itself. She was in an advanced state of semi undress, not to mention panic, and was hopping crazily yet still somehow gracefully from the delicate ball of one bare foot to the other, peering down at the deck around her feet. She determined it was safe to stand still, then looking up, caught Colin's eye. "Spider!" she wailed at him from under a large mess of wavy straw blonde hair.

Colin sat there blinking and staring for a few moments until a boat staff member appeared, a serious looking but tiny young woman in a uniform of black nylon knee length skirt and white, starched collared shirt, her lovely mahogany hair pinned loosely back in a bun. She looked about twelve but insisted she was seventeen.

Apparently the tourist had awoken to find a giant hairy spider with nasty pointy fangs crawling along her leg as she lay in the hammock. Entirely unprovoked, she said, it had begun attacking her leg ferociously.

"Did it bite you?" asked the staff member urgently.

"No, I don't think it actually bit me," said the tourist, quickly hitching the hems of her short pants, and inspecting the inside and outside of her thighs. 'Very nicely tanned thighs,' thought Colin. She was otherwise wearing just a loose fitting rather skimpy cotton vest, Colin also noticed.

"Is it still here?" the staff, laughed and started untwisting the hammock.

"Yes, it is still in there. Is it dangerous?"

"Of course it is dangerous."

"Oh dear," whimpered the tourist, taking a few steps back, clutching her fists to her mouth and flashing her big blue eyes at Colin.

Without much ado the staff quickly finished untwisting the hammock and holding it open, inspected inside. The tourist, apparently squeamish was looking through her fingers from a safe distance. Unable to see the spider, the staff took the corner of a blanket that was in the hammock and lifted it slowly, shaking a little and twisting it round to get a good look.

Suddenly a large black spider with fat and very hairy legs shot out of a fold in the blanket and ran up towards the staff member's outstretched hand. The tourist renewed her screaming and Colin as well this time almost jumped out of his skin for a brief instant, although he managed to disguise it.

The tiny staff member however retained her composure entirely, and waited as the huge arachnid scuttled up the blanket, until it almost reached her fingers. It was the size of her face. With one fluid motion, she dropped the blanket, crouched to the floor bringing the enormous spider downwards, and held it upside down on the deck by pinching her fingers. With her other hand she swiftly withdrew a long pin from the bun in her hair, and brought it down pushing it quickly through the swollen silvery belly of the giant arachnid. Instantly its thick black hairy legs curled up tightly around her slender childlike fingers; and it stopped moving. It had all happened in an instant.

Smiling triumphantly she stood up holding it aloft, like a prize fighter stretching up her arm to show Colin and the tourist, who had finally stopped screaming, that it was dead.

Colin and the tourist burst into applause.

"What was it?" begged the tourist.

"Tarantula!" announced the staff member, completely matter of fact.

"Uyggh. It's so revolting," wailed the tourist.

The staff member shook her head. "Uh-uh," she said, "it's so delicious."

"Arrggh!" said the tourist pretending to gag. "You're not going to eat it! Please tell me you're not going to eat it. Oh, oh, oh!"

"Mmm. Toast it and eat it. You want some?" She held it out towards the tourist.

"Noooo," the blonde woman howled with laughter and ran round in a dainty circle once or twice flapping her hands and screaming. One or two others poked their head round the corner to see what all the commotion was.

"For you, sir?" the staff member held out the dead tarantula towards Colin.

"No thank you," he graciously declined.

"Very good toasted," she asserted. "And very lucky," she explained. "It is a symbol for Very Good Luck."

"Not for the spider," Colin winked at her. But he had made the two women laugh, which he immediately regretted. He did not wish to appear more sociable than was absolutely required.

He grabbed his towel and toothbrush out of his rucksack, and trying not to smile encouragingly while at the same time trying not to appear insultingly aloof he made his way past the tourist and followed the staff member alongside the wheel house. She disappeared upstairs and he simply checked that his bike was still there quickly, then walked back alongside the wheel house but not all the way back to the hammock deck Instead, this time turning right into the washroom area.

When Colin returned to the hammock deck, he was a little surprised to see the blonde tourist balancing cross legged, sitting in his hammock. She was facing the front of the boat, with her back to him. He was about to shout something to get her to move, then he thought better of it, and approached, saying. "Oh, hiya."

She turned round and smiled. Perhaps, thought Colin, if he made friends with one passenger, it would give him cover from interacting with anyone else. Her, and her currently absent companion were the only other two westerners on the boat. Plus, she was 'very cute'.

Chapter 10

The boat wound slowly down the wide caramel river at a relaxing pace. Every half an hour or so, they would pass a small jetty on one side or the other. Some of them had a couple of forest dwelling people waiting for a ride to another jetty further along. Small foot paths led from the jetties up into the forest. At the top of many of the foot paths were small patches of cleared flat ground with full sized white painted goalposts. Also often a handful of thatched roofed jungle homes.

Occasionally they saw jetties that were much larger, floating platforms tens of meters square. Here sometimes the boat would stop to take on supplies and they could stretch their legs on the foot paths for ten minutes.

It was about three day's boat ride to Manaus, during which time Colin became friendly with "Helen", and was able to avoid most other conversations. The other tourists were local people and a couple of gap year students, like Helen and her friend from college she was travelling with. They drank the occasional beer with a couple of local students who spoke English, and they generally all ate meals together. He didn't have to explain too much. He was a scout leader on holiday, testing routes and adventure excursions for his scouts.

On the morning of the fourth day they arrived in Manaus. Colin said goodbye to Helen and her travelling companion and the others at the main harbour pier in front of a bustling fruit and vegetable market. Manaus was a large jungle town of two million people built on the wealth of the rubber industry in the nineteenth century. It stood at the junction of several Amazon tributaries; and it had a domestic airport.

However Colin did not disembark straight away with the other travellers. Instead he remained on board, for the final leg of the journey. It was another ten minutes ride, up a small tributary beyond the harbour market. This led to a terminal pier which was the actual end of the line for the boat. Apart from Colin, one or two local passengers had also remained on board.

The terminal pier happened to be about one kilometre from Manaus Airport. He wheeled the bike off the boat, and starting the engine, wheeled it up the hill to the airport, and into the departure area.

He checked in the bike to be loaded on an internal flight to Rio. He boarded the same flight and was in Rio by early afternoon.

At Rio airport he collected the bike once more and wheeled it out of the airport.

He turned out of the airport and onto a busy high street. He switched off the engine to take advantage of a sidewalk sufficiently wide that he didn't upset the passing shoppers too much, pushing his bike alongside him. Suddenly he thought he heard his name being called out.

"Colin ... Colin!" He *had* heard it. He turned round. A few dozen yards away he saw Helen, with her college companion. They both looked stunning with skilfully made up faces, wearing a bikini and a flowing silk sarong each, tied on coquettishly at the hips, sliding a bit low where the knot had started to work loose.

Then Helen started running towards him. Putting the bike on its stand he turned round to say hello. Helen embraced him, pressing against his chest, and kissed him eagerly on the cheek, then more softly on the lips. He didn't want to get an accidental pull for indecent exposure, of all things. He thrust his hands deep in his pockets.

"What are you doing?" she said giving him a quizzical look.

"I'm... mm... sorry. It's just... it's a bit... awkward to... "

"What are you doing with your bike?"

"Um... yes exactly. Just taking it down to the Honda mechanic, over there for repairs.

"Well maybe if you happen to know where to get some good coke, I might invite you back to my hotel room for a party." Helen looked at him quizzically.

He started at her blankly.

"Oh well, tough luck you," she said, then leaning forward, grabbed his shirt lapels with one hand and pulled his face down to meet hers and kissed him on the mouth again, more slowly this time.

Then she skipped back and joined her friend, now pulling her in close by the arm. "You should learn to take some risks, you square!" Helen called to him turning round to look at again. They both laughed at him. Then Helen winked at him before they turned and walked away.

After a few paces Helen looked back once more, waved her free arm, and blew him a kiss. "Maybe come anyway, you know which hotel we're at," she reminded him. Then off they sauntered, clinging onto each other, caressing satin sun kissed arms.

They each sure had a unique hypnotic sway Colin noticed, as he watched their long swinging legs in their high heels, and gracefully snaking hips in sliding down sarongs. Flowing manes cascaded over exquisite shoulders, tumbling down perfectly tanned backs. Colin, and even some of the strolling shoppers too, kept on watching them long after they had disappeared out of sight.

A lesser man might have given in to the siren call of temptation and skipped his booking on the boat that evening, on the off chance, and waited like a buffoon for five or six weeks until it sailed back round. But Colin was bigger than that. With a shrug and a heart-felt sigh, he heaved the cocaine laden bike forward once more, the engine still switched off. On parts of the journey where it was convenient or necessary, he put the engine back on again for a few moments. After around two kilometres he arrived on the quay side where he had booked passage on a cargo vessel to Genoa once more.

Chapter 11

There were no further hitches, until he went through customs at Rio. He was ordered to the side by a uniformed official who asked in broken English about the purpose of his travel and to see his papers. He handed over his documents and explained his scout story.

After a few minutes an official in a dark grey suit approached. He repeated the same questions in fluent English. Colin gave him the same answers. Now the suited man fixed Colin's gaze. "What's in the petrol tank, sir?"

Colin was on the verge of saying, 'Nothing,' when he switched tracks.

"Unleaded. It's running very well. I can clean the plugs if it's smoking again." "Please remove the petrol cap!" instructed the suited man. Colin obligingly inserted the key into the cap lock and removed it.

"Allow me, please," the customs officer took the handlebars from Colin, and shook the bike side to side, then looked into the tank.

"Ok, sir. Thank you," he said, standing up again and passing the handlebars back to Colin.

Colin experienced an ecstatic rush of adrenalin, as he rolled the bike forward. He was through.

It took about two weeks on the boat. Disembarking at Genoa he had to get on and ride the bike up the ramp from the boat. It was only a couple of hundred yards and he could take it at walking pace. However even at that speed the weight of the cocaine had a gyroscopic effect on the bike, which seemed to tug one way and the other beneath him, so that he had to fully concentrate on his riding to hold it in a straight line. Before he could exit customs at Genoa however he was stopped again.

This time, by two Italian uniformed officials. He dismounted at the side of the traffic lane, after being flagged down by the uniformed officials. First of all they asked for him to remove his rucksack. Standing it on the table they took each item out one at a time, and placed it on the table. Colin felt relatively calm so far. Currently they were miles off target. Every now and again, as one or other revealed a certain item from the depths of the sack, he would suddenly turn and stare at Colin, checking for any reaction. Colin knew that all the time they were looking in the wrong place such as his ruck sack, he had nothing to worry about but it was a bit unnerving. His could only hope they would not think to look in the tyres.

When they had exhausted the main section of his rucksack, the officials moved onto the pockets in the flaps. One by one they searched through them. Again nothing. Colin looked on trying to remain impassive. Leaving his belongings scattered on the table one of the officers barked something in Italian and they both turned to look at the bike. Once more they looked at Colin, this time he nonchalantly didn't bother making eye contact and surveyed instead his belongings on the table. Although his pulse threatened to quicken he was almost immediately able to gain control and portray an outward sense of calm. Out of the corner of his eye he noticed the shorter, squatter of the officers walk towards the bike. He stood beside it, his back to Colin, stroking his chin and perusing it.

Next he walked a deliberate circle round it inspecting it all the time. Inside, Colin was anxious, outside it was a struggle but he was so far maintaining the appearance of composure. When the officer had completed three hundred and sixty degrees he stopped again with his back to Colin. After a couple of moments, he suddenly span round at the waist, twisting his knees and spinning on the balls of his feet, trying to catch Colin's expression. Colin was pretending not to pay attention, and was cleaning his fingernails. He was secretly aware of the eyes upon him. His anxiety was building inside, reaching a pressure point. He knew he had to fight it, but it just kept building. Where would it stop? Something had to give ... then suddenly a switch flipped inside Colin's head. He had entirely forgotten he was anxious. He just knew he loved the sense of winning against these two. He glanced at the taller official and smiled when he saw he was being scrutinized.

The squatter man strolled up to the bike. This time be took a flexing rubber rod with a small weighted bulb at the end and lightly tapped the tank, cocking his head to listen, then spinning triumphantly again back towards Colin.

The smuggler had begun to indulge the notion that the officers were some kind of joke act. This notion appeared to make complete sense to him now. What increasingly nonplussed Colin, was the officials' somehow altered behaviour. They were acting in a strangely exaggerated manner. Or at least that's how it appeared to him as his mind started to warp, under the strain he was forcing himself to endure. 'They are like melodramatic comedy actors,' he thought. Maybe it was some kind of double bluff to catch him unawares. Or... suddenly the idea occurred to Colin that he must have been caught in some hidden camera comedy or fly on the wall documentary set up. This idea too suddenly made complete sense. His eyes began to search round curiously for the hidden cameras. He could see the security cameras but that's not what he was looking for. If there was a clandestine film crew, he couldn't see it, it was very well camouflaged. Colin looked at the taller man again, to see if he was laughing. He was not. He looked very serious.

'I don't know why *he's* looking serious,' thought Colin to himself, visibly waggling his head. 'It's not *his* liberty at risk.' He wanted to say it out loud for the secret microphones, it was a great joke, it should be captured for the TV show. He should say it out loud, he knew he should, it was too good an opportunity to miss. He faintly mouthed the words certain that there was an invisible camera pointing straight at his face, getting the close up and that some TV expert would be able to read his lips. The cameras had started to make him feel a bit self-conscious, and he couldn't quite bring himself to voice the words.

Finally the official by the bike demanded Colin unlock the petrol tank cap. Nonchalantly, playing it up again for the viewers, he was convinced this was being filmed for a live entertainment show, but that it was some big secret. Colin sauntered over, unlocked, span open and removed the cap with a flourish. Pretending to ignore Colin's over acting, the official stuck his rubber rod into the tank and waved it about inside, banging the walls of the tank. He then gingerly withdrew it, and wiped it dry with a tissue drawn from his pocket and then thrown in the bin.

Finally they let Colin through onto the streets of Genoa again. He was still half suspecting he had cameoed to enormous laughter and applause on a TV programme somewhere.

He paused on the street as he gradually came back to his senses. While he had thought he was suppressing his anxiety it had apparently found another outlet through a kind of surreal imagined perception that had at the time seemed completely real. He suddenly remembered with horror that he almost told a joke out loud in what was nothing but a fantasy experience. Thank god he had controlled the impulse. He had allowed his imagination to run away with him, he realised. He must keep his feet on the ground in future, he determined, and keep a better grip on reality. As he pondered it, he realised that there was a positive to draw, that in fact he had just received a good lesson. This made him feel a bit pleased with himself and he relaxed. As he relaxed, his mind started to wander. 'That's the second time they've searched my tank,' he thought with a small laugh of mirth. Then another thought struck him. Why do they keep stopping me this time? Are they on to me? Or is it coincidence? He reflected on this for a moment. He wasn't sure what to do. If they were onto him, he would need to take drastic action. Get rid of the bike? No, somehow just cut open the tyres and dump the coke in a drain somewhere. Or better still, dump the bike in a canal and report it stolen. Wait, he told himself. Get a grip, he insisted inwardly. His train of thought stopped and after a few moments he was able to reflect more calmly again. It has to be coincidence, it now became obvious to him, and he suddenly relaxed. Nothing to worry about. He chuckled at his own foolish overreaction.

Feeling much better for a moment, he wheeled the bike round to the station following the same route as previously, and at last had it placed on the car train. He found a seat and sat down to relax, alternately still amused at his own foolishness, and horrified by what he almost said out loud, which recollection always seemed to lead him to the suspicion he was already known to some crack international customs unit.

He repeated the twenty four hour or so train ride to Calais, this time in a sleeping compartment. He finally managed to settle on amusement in his mental dichotomy and fell into a sound and comfortable sleep. But when he awoke, he could only think about the customs unit that might be following him, and a sense of fear and dread started to creep up on him. Rubbing sleep from his eyes, he turned his attention objectively on this notional crack unit. Who could they be? Where had they come from? As he pondered these questions he realised there was no evidence to support the idea that anyone was secretly following him, at all. It was nothing but ridiculous paranoia. Now that he examined the idea, he realised it was not one worth considering. In fact, where had the idea come from anyway, he now started to wonder. He couldn't quite remember. It was ... Oh well, it didn't matter. With his paranoia exposed to reality, and some self-assurance reclaimed, he turned his thoughts instead to breakfast in the restaurant carriage.

He collected the bike at Calais train station around lunch time. After wheeling it a few kilometres to the ferry, he rode it slowly into the car deck. This was on a lower deck of the ferry.

*

The channel crossing was calm. Colin avoided company as usual, and spent most of the time in the dark of the small cinema, watching an old movie called Ghostbusters. It was a very funny movie about... ghost busters.

It was dark too outside by the time he drove the bike slowly back out of the car deck and onto the English side of the Channel, at Dover. There had been no problems at any borders since Genoa, and Dover was no exception. Until he drove off the ferry ramp.

He was following the line of cars in front, sitting on the bike, moving at walking pace with the flow of traffic. He drove off the metal ramp, and onto the actual concrete of the harbour at Dover. That is to say, he was finally home on British soil. He was driving slowly and carefully up the steep incline of the concrete ramp that led away from the boat. He could sense a slight mishandling of the rear wheel, which was now starting to slide from side to side on the sloping surface beneath. He was concentrating on balance, and clutch control when a shout came from behind.

"Gentleman on the Honda motorcycle!"

Colin tried not to flinch, and continued at the same slow speed, pretending he hadn't heard.

"The man on the motorbike! In Scout Uniform! Pull over to the side please!"

Colin's blood ran cold. There was no way out of it. Instinctively he checked his mirrors, flipped on his indicators using his thumb, and then glancing over his shoulder, pulled over and stopped to the right hand side of the traffic flow. A uniformed customs officer was running from the car hold of the ferry, up the slope towards him. Colin remained seated on the bike and pulled off his crash helmet. As he did so he found himself start to glance round for any hidden TV cameras. Then with a jolt he remembered what had happened before. Don't say he was descending into temporary insanity again! At this thought, he suddenly sensed panic sweeping towards him. He bit his bottom lip hard and ordered himself to get a grip just as the officer pulled up slightly out of breath.

"Can I help you?" said Colin, trying to portray a relaxed expression.

"You're tyre, sir." The officer spoke between breaths. "Your tyre is flat,"

Following the officer's gaze, Colin looked down at his rear tyre, alarmed. It did look flatter than it should be, however it was not completely flat. He stood up and climbed off the seat of the bike, standing beside it, then crouching down and feigning an inspection of the tyre.

"Didn't you feel it sliding sir?"

Colin stood up again. "Yes, I did. I knew it was a bit flat but didn't realise quite how bad. I thought there was also oil on the ramp," he pretended to look back at the ramp surface."

"No. You've got a flat rear tyre, sir. A slow puncture perhaps. Don't worry too much, sir. These things do happen. If you'd like to wheel it back down, we can inflate it quickly for you.

"Thank you, officer," said Colin. He had to continue to think fast. "Um. There's a petrol garage at the top is that right?"

"Yes, that's right, sir. Just at the top of the slope turn right, then a quarter of a mile further up the hill, again on the right."

"They should have an air pump, I expect, shouldn't they? I don't want to take up your valuable time."

"Yes, that is correct, sir. They have air."

"It's no problem, I'll wheel it up there quickly. Thank you very much," said Colin. Using the throttle he started to wheel the bike up the slope again. The cars slowly overtaking on his left. He switched his hazard lights on so all four indicators were flashing.

"One moment, please sir!" the official called out behind him.

"Colin swore under his breath.

He turned round to see the officer approaching him again with a doubtful expression. "Would you mind just opening your petrol tank for me, sir?"

"No, not at all," said Colin trying to hide his shivering. In an attempt to appear jovial, "I'm getting used to it," he just about managed to prevent himself from saying. Just stay quiet, he told himself. Now removing the key from the ignition he unlocked and removed the petrol cap lid. The customs officer fished a small but powerful flashlight from his inside jacket pocket, and bending over peered carefully into the tank, shining the light all around inside it. Colin waited trying to appear patient.

After a few moments the officer stood up.

"Thank you very much, sir. We never can be too careful, as you know."

Colin smiled weakly and nodded. "I understand," he said as he replaced the petrol cap. Trying to contain his sense of wanting to sob, he turned and started to wheel the bike up the hill.

"Ah! One more thing, sir!"

Colin screwed his face up in frustration. What was it this time? Once more he pulled on the handbrake lever and squeezed in the clutch.

Relaxing his expression, again he turned and looked back over his shoulder, trying to control his growing frustration. "How can I help you, Officer?" he said as evenly as he could.

"Be very careful and mind the traffic please, sir," called the customs officer. He turned to wave past the following vehicles, which overtook them and pulled ahead. Then he gave a final wave come salute, and turned to run back down the slope.

As Colin turned away again he was finally unable to stop his lower lip quivering wildly even though he was finally left in peace to wheel the bike up and onto the road out of the port entrance. His face crumpled and he suffered a mini nervous breakdown while he walked. By the time he reached the top of the hill he had allowed it through his system and was over it and his eyes stopped streaming. At one point he paused briefly to blow his nose using up about five man size tissues as he shifted endless amounts of mucous. Finally after he had wiped his eyes dry with his sleeve, his vision cleared again and he could continue up the hill once more. "Never again!" he told himself.

The motorbike and scout's uniform perhaps allayed any suspicions anyone may have had about him. If there was nothing in the tank there was no-where else it could be. The significance of this was not lost on Colin. His initial suspicions that tyres would fall below any customs' official's radar seemed to be bearing out. From the top of the slope, he looked round behind him. Seeing no sign of the customs officer, he turned left instead of right. A quarter of a mile further he turned right. There was Tim Peach was waiting for him in a car park with a motorbike pick up van. They loaded the bike and started on the drive towards London.

As they were pulling onto the motorway, Colin turned to Tim who was driving and said, "Did you notice anyone following us?"

"No," said Tim, glancing at him then back at the road. "Why? Did you?"

"I don't think so."

"Did you get stopped?"

"Not really." Colin told Tim about the customs officer on the ramp.

"Did he ask you any questions?"

"No."

"I think there's nothing to worry about."

"I hope you're right," said Colin as he angled his head to watch the headlights in his passenger side wing mirror.

For the rest of the two hour drive, if he wasn't looking in the wing mirror, he was turning round to look through the back window.

"I think we're alright," said Tim. as they entered the London suburbs.

"Yeah, I know," said Colin.

"Look," said Tim. "If they were onto you, they wouldn't let you go through customs."

"They might want to see where we're taking it."

"I doubt that. But even so we'll know as soon as we get back, in that case, right?"

"Yeah. I guess you're right."

"Not guessing. I am right."

"Yeah ok, you're right."

They stayed in silence for most of the remaining journey. Colin slumped in his seat and looked out of the window at the glistening reflections of the lights from the shops and traffic, and street lamps, bouncing off the dark and black, wet and shining roads and pavements, in the pouring rain.

Chapter 12

Tim had rented a built in lock up unit which he could use as a mechanics garage, underneath a railway arch in Deptford, South East London. It was well off the main roads, and very quiet at this time of night. It was not the sort of place police would even drive through after dark, if they could possibly avoid it. There was a row of units built under the arches housing obscure businesses; small chemical factories for example, screen printers and such. There was a high wire fence separating the arches from the public road, creating the impression of a private area although it was not actually gated. It was dark and the few other businesses had already shut for the night and the people had all gone home. The whole area was deserted. They unloaded the bike and wheeled it into the lock up, shutting and locking the door behind them.

Inside the walls and ceiling formed a large arch way of whitewashed but otherwise unsurfaced Victorian brick work. The railway track ran along the top. A train rumbled in either direction every ten minutes until about midnight. Each arch had a unit built into it, along a stretch of a dozen or so arches. The small ungated but fenced in lane ran in front providing car and van access to the workshops.

It was around 9.30pm. About a third of the units were still vacant, scattered between the occupied ones. Inside Tim's unit, in one corner was a cubicle containing a sink, and kettle. In the rear corner was a round wooden coffee table and three, old armchairs. By these, against the wall was a small two bar electric heater plugged into a mains socket. Against the right hand wall was a square formica table and some wooden chairs.

The floor was bare concrete. Ed, Tim' s driver was waiting with tools and set to work straight away removing the wheels and then one rim each of the tyres on the motorbike, while Tim made Colin a mug of tea from the plastic electric kettle. They sat in the small armchairs smoking cigarettes while they relaxed and watched Ed struggling to extract the inner tubes.

Eventually when he was done, Tim stood up, and walked over to the square table. Sitting down, he took a set of electronic scales from a briefcase on the floor beside him. Colin joined him at the table. Then Tim took out a newspaper and covered the table top with sheets from it. Finally he took a hobby scalpel, and a household desert spoon from the case and laid them on the newspaper.

"The scales weigh up to ten kilograms," he explained to Colin, "but only accurately up to one kilogram, to within a gram," Colin nodded, "so we'll have to weigh it in batches," concluded Tim.

Extracting a pile of freezer bags from the briefcase, Tim placed one on the scale and weighed it showing Colin the result. Taking the scalpel, Tim grasped one of the packages Ed had unwrapped from the black plastic bin liner and put on the table, and cut it length wise. Holding the freezer bag open with one hand on the scales, Tim slowly began to shake and tip cocaine from the package into the freezer bag with his other hand. All the time he kept his eye on the digital scale reading. When it reached a little over one thousand grams he stopped. He glanced over his shoulder to check Colin was paying attention, then began to spoon small amounts of cocaine back out of the bag into the package again, using the desert spoon, until the scale read 1000g. He looked at Colin again. Colin nodded. Tim zip locked the bag and laid it at the back of the table, then started with the next bag.

Colin now reached over to the pile of freezer bags and picked one up. Reaching across Tim, he grabbed the spoon and ladled half an ounce or so, about fifteen grams perhaps, into the freezer bag, then laid it beside Tim's elbow on the table. He tapped Tim on the shoulder and said, "a tip."

Tim nodded acknowledgement, and said, "Oh, that's terrific. Thank you very much."

Now Colin returned to his armchair while Tim proceeded to weigh up all the merchandise and Ed stood watching, amazed at the sight of so much cocaine. Every now and then Colin would wander over to check proceedings. This irritated Tim who had been hoping to pilfer a little of the powder as he worked, however Colin was highly suspicious of everything and watched him like a hawk, even from his armchair.

By the time Tim had finished, a fine layer of white powder covered the square table and upright chairs and most of the floor around them.

Tim packed up the last bag, and started to notice the fine layer of powder that had somehow appeared. It would have altogether amounted to only half a gram perhaps, but Tim did not like to see it lying around.

"Do you want to sweep that up," he said to Ed.

"I've got 10026 grams," Tim said turning to Colin. Actually it had been a thousand and twenty eight, but about 2 grams appeared to have found their way into Tim's jacket pocket despite all the scrutiny. The deal had been slightly generous. It had been forty three grams over. Colin had already given Tim fifteen grams, then Tim had swiped a couple more and it was still twenty six grams more than expected. Now as he looked at the scales, Tim could have kicked himself for not pilfering a further couple of dozen grams. Next time he'd know better. He was extremely irritated that Colin had been watching so closely. "Sound about right to you?" he asked Colin, gruffly.

Colin nodded and smiled. "Very good Mr Peach!" he said, rubbing his hands together with pleasure. "Add an extra twenty six grams to your tip if you will."

"Oh! Thank you very much, sir. Very kind, I'm sure." said Tim, touching his forelock, and bobbing up and down in his seat. He quickly weighed out twenty six grams from the last bag, and added it eagerly to the freezer bag, with the fifteen grams Colin had already given him. 'I'll just have to get him next time,' he thought.

As Ed was walking over to fetch the broom from the cubicle, they heard the sound of a car pulling up outside. They all stopped what they were doing and looked at each other. The engine cut. They heard the car door open then slam shut. Then the sound of footsteps moving quickly across the tarmac lane outside, towards their lockup. Tim looked at Ed and frowned, then nodded, questioning. Ed shook his head. They didn't expect anyone to be around this time of night. They were not anticipating any visitors. The footsteps stopped outside their door. Bang! Bang! Bang! There was a loud and stern knocking.

Tim looked at Colin, and frowned, then put his fingers to his lips to keep him quiet. He waited a couple of moments then shouted aggressively. "Who the *fuck* is that?"

"Hello Tim! It's Jim here."

"Jim," Tim gasped incredulously. "Oh, hello mate. One moment." Then to Colin, "It's the caretaker, Jimmy" he articulated quietly. Then shouting again through the door. "What is it Jimmy? I'm in the middle of something 'ere. Can it wait?"

"Sorry about that, just wanted to let you know you left your lights on, on the van."

"Oh! Ok. Thank you Jimmy. Gimme two sec's." He looked around him to see how much incriminating evidence was still on display. It all was on display. He couldn't open the door now. Tim shouted again through the closed door. "Soon as I've finished in here I'll come out and switch them off."

"Is the door open on the van? Do you want me to switch them off for you?" Called Jimmy through the closed lock up door.

Tim looked at Colin, who shrugged adamantly. Tim heaved an exasperated sigh. "I can't remember. Can you check for me, Jimmy?"

The footsteps went, and returned. "It's open Tim, shall I turn the lights off for you then."

"Yes, thanks Jimmy," Tim called. They listened to the footsteps again. "It's like the fucking Goon show," Tim whispered to Ed, who laughed as quietly as he could.

Eventually they heard Jimmy's voice once more. "I'm off for the night now then, Tim. I'll leave you to it."

"Thanks, Jimmy, all the best." Tim called. They listened to the sound of Jimmy climbing into his car again then driving away.

Colin glared furiously at Tim.

"Ed, do you want to go and fetch the others?" said Tim.

"No problem, boss," Ed said. He let himself out of the doorway, shutting it behind him and disappeared. Tim walked over and locked the door again. Colin exploded.

"You left the *lights* on?"

Tim, large man though he was looked startled. "Sorry Colin. It must have slipped my mind."

"Jeesus Christ!" said Colin, putting his hands to his head. Leaving the van lights on had been asking for attention.

"Don't blame me," said Tim, gathering up to his full height and towering over Colin. "You're the fucking manager. It's your job to keep an eye on things," he reprimanded sternly. He put his hand to his chest momentarily then, almost as though to himself, "Can't you see that your bad temper just hurts *you*," he muttered. "Every time."

Colin drew back. "Yeah, ok, you're right." After a few moments, he added, "Sorry." Tim didn't seem particularly put out by it now, anyway.

They returned to the armchairs to sit and wait for the others to arrive. Tim put a small amount of the cocaine from his tip bag onto a small mirror and chopped up a couple of lines. He offered one to Colin, who declined, then rolled up a twenty pound note and hoovered up both lines, one up each nostril.

Instantly his eyes cleared and shone brightly. He began to emit a healthy looking glow. Sitting up straight, he breathed in slowly and deeply, holding one hand to the bridge of his nose. Then dabbing the tip of his index finger onto the traces of powder remaining on the mirror he rubbed it onto the gums under his top lip. "Mmm!" he said to Colin, approvingly. "Spectacular!"

Soon they heard the sound of another car draw up outside.

"It's Ed and the others," Tim assured Colin. He got up and walked over to the door. Unbolting it, he opened it an inch and looked out. Then leaving the door ajar, he walked back to his seat and sat down again. A few moments later, the door banged open and in walked Todd, John, Pat and finally Ed. The first three were looking at Colin, wide eyed and with big grins. Was it true? Had he really made it back safely, with all the 'Charlie'?

"Colin!" they said as soon as they saw him, smiling with wonder, and walked straight over to greet him. Shaking his hand and patting the shoulder of the great man, "You're a bona fide genius! You're a star!" they told him.

Colin stood up to bask in the glory and shake hands.

"Any contamination?" asked Todd.

"Nope," said Colin.

"You remembered to turn your lights off. Didn't you." Tim said to Ed. Ed nodded.

Then Tim began to take the other three one at a time across to the square formica table to do business, on behalf of Colin. Ed who had locked the door again behind him was holding another briefcase. He approached the table and handed it to Tim, who opened it to check the contents. Inside were one hundred and twenty five thousand pounds of sterling bank notes. Tim didn't bother to count it. He just wanted to check it was in there. "Take it over to Colin," he instructed Ed, handing back the brief case. He called over to Colin. "Count it now please Colin. You'll get the rest in four weeks." This had been arranged previously. Tim was responsible for making sure the rest of the cash would materialise as promised. Colin knew Tim well by now, and trusted him a great deal. The price was set at twenty five pounds per gram, to shift all ten keys at once. This was the going rate for bulk deals, Tim explained to Colin.

The rate for buying up to about half a key was around forty pounds. Punters purchased up to a gram for around sixty to eighty pounds per gram from retail dealers. The official street value according to law enforcement and media agencies was about one hundred and sixty five pounds per gram, which was about six or seven times more than Colin was in fact receiving.

Of course cocaine was never actually sold at the officially stated price except perhaps on street corners to gullible strangers, in five or ten pound wraps which would contain just a fraction of a gram consisting of perhaps 30% actual cocaine, if you were lucky. Colin knew that the pushers operating such markets were often just kids or youngsters, who hung out on the streets, and who would get maybe a dozen wraps on 'tick' (credit) from a dealer on the next level up from them, who worked from a car, or in a local flat. If they did well and avoided arrest they may ascend to the dizzying heights of the next rung themselves within six months to a couple of years or so. Such supply networks were of no interest to Colin and his associates. John and Pat for example supplied more sophisticated markets of professional and affluent people who could easily afford the drug, and sought the best quality available regardless of the rate.

Todd was on hand in case there was any contamination again, and also to collect some of the cocaine. Dr Bill, his chemist friend, planned to convert this portion – the largest share at five keys, into crack cocaine in his secret chemistry laboratory at his home in Edinburgh. Dr Bill and Todd had associates in Yorkshire who had a ready market for this concentrated form of the drug which was smoked in a pipe. The high was so accelerated, even supersonic, and just so pleasurable and completely moreish that the instant anyone took a puff on a crack cocaine pipe, they reputedly could think of nothing else but where their next hit was going to come from for about three weeks afterwards.

Crack cocaine was so mind altering that lifelong friends and even lovers or spouses who started using it, sometimes quickly fall out as they suddenly found themselves seething with uncharacteristic envy, thinking the other had taken more than was fair or reasonable, from the perpetually dwindling supply to be shared.

Todd, Pat and John had pooled their money in the briefcase for convenience as per Tim's previous instructions, in time for Ed to collect them from Tim's house, where they were waiting. By now Colin had counted his money, it was correct. Tim was careful to lock everything up securely, the bike still inside, then Colin followed Ed to his car for a lift home. Dr Todd and John climbed in beside Tim in his van, while Pat climbed into the back of the van, and Tim took them back to his place where their cars were parked.

Colin sat in the passenger seat of Ed's car, his rucksack on the back seat, and the briefcase full of cash on his knees. Ana was waiting up for him at their rented flat. They hadn't seen each other in over three months. In the kitchen he opened the briefcase on the table and showed Ana the cash, which completely amazed her. She fed him supper, then they went to bed.

The following morning Colin returned to Tim's locker at 10am. He parked his car behind the van which was also outside, and walked up to the shut door. Inside he could hear Tim shouting. He tried the door. It was unlocked so he opened it and walked in.

Tim was standing over Ed, jabbing his finger and yelling loudly. He was berating Ed for forgetting to sweep up the dust. Colin looked around, there was still a fine layer of cocaine dust everywhere. Ed was due to run the bike down to a dealership with Colin in Tim's van, but now Colin had to wait while Ed hosed down the inside of the lockup.

Finally they were able to thoroughly wipe the bike clean, and wheel it into the van, without the inner tubes. They took it down to the local dealer, who gave Colin a reasonable deal in cash. Ed then drove him back to the lockup. He gave Ed a hundred quid, said goodbye to Tim, climbed back into his Rover and drove home.

Colin received the remainder of the money from Tim as promised four weeks later. His proceeds amounted to two hundred and fifty thousand pounds in cash. He still had maybe ten thousand left over from his previous trip. I was a large amount of cash, and could be considered a life changing sum. Very few people in late twentieth century Britain would ever see such an amount of money in one pile. Colin's plan was becoming highly lucrative.

Nevertheless Colin and Ana, after Colin's relentless insistence, did not start spending money with no regard. They stayed in their rented flat for the time being, which was a very modest place. Ana bought a few nice clothes and accessories. They bought lots of toys for the baby. Colin did not upgrade his car or alter his upgrade his wardrobe. He wished to maintain a low profile and not to advertise his money.

To keep themselves occupied, Colin began visiting antique fairs, and took up golf with Brendan who was already a keen golfer, while Ana enrolled on a foundation course for an undergraduate degree at a local university, to get her English up to speed.

Colin continued his weekly social visits to Tim over the next twelve months. It was about a year since his first motorbike trip, and he still had about two hundred thousand pounds in cash hidden underneath his and Ana's mattress. Colin and Tim were sitting in the lounge half of Tim's front room, in the big puffy armchairs, looking out of the half opened French windows at the garden. There was a half drunk mug of tea in front of each on the big square coffee table and they were both smoking cannabis 'joints'. They didn't share their joints like teenagers, they made and smoked their own.

"Who do you most trust out of all the people you know that I have met?" Colin asked Tim after a lull in the conversation.

"John," said Tim without thinking. "John is the most loyal person I have ever met."

"Does he know how to ride a motorbike?" asked Colin.

"I don't know. Probably. I'll get him to come over next Wednesday. You're planning on coming next week are you? You can ask him yourself."

The following Wednesday afternoon, as promised, John joined Tim and Colin for a chat. They shared a bottle of wine and smoked cannabis for a little while. At an appropriate moment Colin asked John, "Do you know how to ride a motorbike, John?"

John did, he had a full license in fact and had ridden a lot in his youth.

"I'm putting a team together," said Colin, "for another run to Colombia."

John knew the amount of cash Colin had made from his previous trip, also how easily he seemed to have come through customs, and was immediately eager to become involved in the project. "I'm definitely in," said John. It was a no-brainer for him with the amount of money concerned. "How many people do you need?"

"This time," explained Colin, "I want to do another test run first. So I'm looking for two riders. I've got someone in mind for the other bike. I need to check with him, otherwise we may need someone else."

John probably knew people, he said. Colin said he preferred it to be someone he already knew.

Colin then ran over some details with John, and arranged to meet him again on Thursday evening in Tim's lockup at 7pm for an initial group briefing.

The following evening, as arranged, he called round on Brendan's flat in Camden at about 8.30pm, and knocked on the door.

They went upstairs, Brendan fetched a bottle of beer for each of them, and then they sat in his front room together. The talked golf for a few moments, then Colin said simply, "Wanna work for me?"

"Work for you?"

"Yeah."

"Are you serious?"

"Yeah. Look I didn't come to pressurise you or anything because there are genuine risks, as you know. I just want to offer you first refusal."

Brendan didn't dismiss the notion outright but was hesitant. "I'm interested to hear more. What would I have to do? How safe is it?"

"Listen, first of all," Colin looked straight at Brendan's eyes, "Brendan, don't forget, I have already done this myself. Honestly, I promise you, it is so darned easy. Not only that. My method is completely fool proof. It's inconceivable to them that there could be any drugs hidden in inflated tyres. It's why they never looked at the tyres at customs. They can only imagine we would use the petrol tanks; which makes a nice little red herring in some respects.

"It wasn't because of the scout uniform, it was the tyres. I guarantee you, they will never ever guess that it's in the tyres. Ever."

Brendan stared at him. Colin seemed so certain, so confident that it made it seem possible. They would never look in the tyres, he mulled the notion. "Ok," Brendan said at last, not committing to anything yet, still considering, "tell me how we would do it."

By the time Colin had explained some main details, Brendan was willing to consider coming to the meeting next Thursday with Colin and the other rider in Tim's lockup for the initial group meeting. Brendan still hadn't fully committed himself. He would let Colin know after he had thought about it.

The fact was however that Colin's method looked very clever to Brendan, whichever angle he analysed it from. It had already demonstrated itself to be so.

Also, the prospect of more people that he knew becoming vastly wealthy overnight, like Colin seemed to have done, gave him a very dissatisfying twinge of envy. He was pretty sure that it was partly because he didn't have much money that his girlfriend had dumped him. That he might spend the rest of his life, slogging at a low paid nine to five while increasingly his acquaintances made fortunes and raced ahead of him in leaps and bounds he could not hope to keep pace with, was not a comforting thought to Brendan. Unquestioning adherence solely to the nine to five option might in fact prove to be the un-intelligent route, he mulled.

If this system of Colin's continued to be successful, he would in all likelihood end up getting involved at some point down the track, if he was to be honest with himself. In which case, better (even more intelligent still) to do so at the beginning perhaps when there would be less heat.

Finally Brendan was not going to be in this for the long haul like Colin seemed to be. If Brendan were to 'sign-up' it would be for one trip only. That was the single most intelligent option, it was obvious, to reduce the risk. If he could make a clean quarter of a million sterling as Colin was suggesting, that would be enough to set him up for life because he would continue working afterwards, but at his own pace. He could live on his proceeds for ten or twenty years, and save all his wages every week over that time and have enough for a comfortable if modest retirement.

Brendan was beginning to agree that it may well only be fools that turned down such opportunities. He was being invited into a hidden dimension of reality that nobody else even knew existed, let alone could perceive. Nobody else could even see what Colin was doing. No-one knew about it. Colin had discovered a secret world, a pristine, untouched landscape. A place which no-one had ever even heard of, which was waiting to be staked and claimed by whoever had the nous to do so. Perhaps only a fool would turn down an opportunity like this. Whichever direction Brendan viewed it from, it was starting to look for all the world like this could be a very intelligent thing to do.

Reaching over to the coffee table he picked up the phone receiver and dialled a number. After a few moments he said into the mouthpiece, "Colin? You can count me in."

Chapter 13

On a dark winter's evening, in late 1994, Brendan stepped off the 18:48 train to London and Cannon Street, at Deptford station, and walked to Tim's lockup under the railway arches, which address Colin had given him last time they had met.

It was about five past seven when Brendan knocked on the lockup door. "Come in," he heard Colin's voice. He opened the door and walked in.

Already there was John, and Colin of course, and also Tim, who Colin had invited to stay and listen when he had arrived to unlock the door for Colin an hour earlier.

On the left side wall at the rear, beside the sink cubicle area, Colin had arranged the armchairs in a semicircle facing the wall. A projection screen had been set up, and a projector sat on a small table with a stall beside it for Colin to sit on.

Now that Brendan had arrived, Tim made a cup of tea and the others sat in the armchairs to wait.

"Alright John!"

"Alright Bren."

All they knew was that they were the two new riders.

Tim emerged from the cubicle carrying a tray with a large china tea pot, a jug of milk, four tea mugs and a couple of packets of chocolate biscuits. Tim poured out the tea using the coffee table which had been moved beside the projection screen, and passed the mugs and biscuits to John and Brendan. Colin took his seat on his stall beside the projector while Tim took the third armchair and lit up an enormous hand-rolled Cuban.

"Before we go any further," Colin announced, "I want to talk about money."

John and Brendan nodded.

"Last time, as you know," Colin continued, "I put five keys in each tyre of a Honda CB600." He looked at Brendan, "I was able to offload this for twenty five a gram."

Brendan nodded again.

"With a bigger bike, we could double the amount of coke. Therefore I propose bigger this time, with ten keys per wheel."

Brendan and John nodded again, to show they were following.

"That will net half a million per bike."

Brendan and John whistled. Tim grinned widely and puffed on his cigar.

"This is how we will divide it up. You each get half, I get half of all the cocaine carried in the bike you are riding." He looked at John and Brendan in turn. Their eyes widened.

"Quarter of a million each," said Brendan, thinking out loud.

"Half a million for Colin," chipped in Tim.

"This is very generous of you," said John to Colin.

"Wait," said Colin. "There's more."

John and Brendan glanced at each other then back to Colin.

"I want you to invest your own money."

There was a stunned silence. Then Tim laughed.

"You want *us* to invest the money?" said John, disbelieving.

"Correct," said Colin. "I want you each to pay for your own bikes, tickets, passage, and spending money for three months, and for the coke you carry."

"How much?" said Brendan frowning.

"Probably fifteen thousand each."

"Why?" asked Brendan. He didn't even have that much in his savings. He maybe had about eight thousand in a saving scheme, which had been left to him by his grandparents.

Colin thought for a moment, then said, "Several reasons. One, I want to engineer for you, the same psychological pressures that I had. Just in case any particular aspect contributed to my success which we didn't realise yet." He looked at them both, examining intently.

John and Brendan both looked highly doubtful.

"Secondly," Colin continued, "I want you to become invested in it psychologically, and I think this is the best way to achieve that. I wish for you to have a personal stake in it. If you have your own money invested, you will be less fixated on the risk of getting banged up, thereby giving off fewer signals for customs to pick up on. Your psychology is the main variable. I guarantee they will never look at the tyres. Unless you give the game away ... by glancing at them at the wrong moment for example."

This was beginning to sound a bit complex to John, but he felt that Colin was devising everything with his i.e. John's own best interests in mind, therefore was at this point prepared to defer to Colin's superior intellect. Also coming up with the capital would not be an issue for himself, as he already had some, which he used to buy his cocaine and cannabis wholesale. In fact even after such expenses, and aside from the money he would earn as a smuggler, this would also be a cost effective way for John to get some stock when he returned, which he would be able to sell retail at about sixty pounds per gram, netting himself at least six hundred thousand eventually.

John was happy to let Colin keep half the load on the grounds that Colin knew how to do the smuggling, and John didn't. In fact fifty percent was a very good rate for courier work. As a social drug dealer, John was already a career criminal and had no qualms about that side of things. Indeed, a move into smuggling seemed to be a logical step for him. He looked upon this as a kind of promotion.

"Colin, I haven't actually got fifteen thousand pounds," Brendan confessed. He was feeling devastated.

The other three looked at him pitifully for a few moments, then Colin said, "Ok, Brendan." To John and Tim, he explained, "I've known him a long time." Then back to Brendan, "How much have you got."

"At least eight thousand. Definitely over eight thousand."

Colin thought for a moment. "That's good enough Brendan. I'll see you for the rest."

"Really? Are you sure you about that?"

"Yes. I prefer to keep you on team than a stranger who I don't know. I want you to put in every penny you've got though. I'll make up the rest."

Brendan nodded. "Thanks Colin. I *really* appreciate it." He turned and grinned at John, beaming.

"Right then," said Colin switching on the projector and pressing the key on a lap top next to it. "do you want to turn the lights off, Tim? This is how we are going to do it."

The projector warmed up after a few moments and a map of Colombia began to emerge on the screen.

*

The following Saturday at 10.30am, Colin met Brendan and John outside a large motorcycle showroom near central London. He had considered allowing them to choose the bikes themselves, then had wondered if he better make the effort to show up and supervise. In the event he was glad he did. Left to their own devices John especially would have probably bought an extreme Harley or something.

In the end at Colin's insistence they both opted for the new '95 Honda CB 750's. These had massive bulbous petrol tanks with which to distract the attention of customs officials, as well as decent sized tyres and superbly reliable engines. As Colin had explained during the slide show, there would be two riders. Colin would be overseeing the operation on location, in the background.

They stocked up on accessories such as helmets, boots, gloves, chains and locks. Delivery of the bikes was arranged the following week. On the pavement again Colin reminded them of the next step of the plan. "Remember to start putting some miles on the clock on a daily basis," he instructed. "Try and do at least a couple of hours per day, for the next few weeks. Keep it up until I contact you again for the next stage."

They both said they understood and then each set off in separate directions.

After three of four weeks, Colin contacted John and Brendan to arrange the date and time for Ed to collect the bikes in Tim's van and deliver them to the London based depot of the shipping company. It was the same company in Rio that he had used before. They were required to attend with Ed to provide proof of ID and vehicle ownership.

*   *   *   *

Three weeks after the bikes were shipped, Brendan and John flew out to Rio. They booked into the Copacabana Beach hotel and spent a few days relaxing in the sunshine on the beach. At some point in the first few days after arrival they went to the cargo port with vehicle ownership documentation and passports and unloaded the bikes from the ship. After they had cleared customs they rode them back to their guest house. Everything on the bikes was in fine working order. After parking them up, they sat at one of the tables in the guest house restaurant to discuss what to do next.

An unresolved altercation was still hanging in the air since it had erupted in the initial group briefing at Tim's lockup. As he started going through his slide presentation, Colin had explained that from Rio, they would fly internally to Manaus, then take the river boat to Leticia, fly internally to Bogota then ride the bikes up to Juan Pablo's house over the next day or two.

They would then spend several weeks working the bikes daily around Juan Pablo's town until they were ready to load the cocaine in the tyres and begin the return trip.

However at this point during the presentation, and it had impressed Brendan, John asked a question.

"Why can't we ride all the way to Juan Pablo's from Rio?"

This had stopped Colin in his tracks. "Say what John?" Tim and Brendan also turned to look at John.

"Why do we need to fly to Manaus and take the boat and another flight? Then spend several weeks riding round in circles?"

"I'm not following," said Colin. But Brendan and Tim looking at the map, both thought it was a good question.

John explained again. "Why don't we actually make like we are on a round trip of South America. We can ride up all the way to Colombia spending some weeks, then collect the gear at Juan Pablo's and bring it back to Rio as you suggest. Like, we can do a real tour, rather than a fake tour."

Colin looked at John, then dismissed his suggestion out of hand. "No, John, I don't see they advantage of that. Now, when you arrive in Bogota..."

"Wait a second Colin," now Tim had chipped in. Colin looked at Tim, giving him quite a hard stare.

"What?" Colin demanded, imperious.

"Well John is making a lot of sense, Colin," said Tim.

However Colin was becoming quite assertive. "Listen fellas, I have this all worked out in a way that I know will work, because I have already done it."

"You shipped direct to Bogota, wasn't it?" said Tim, forgetting his grammar.

"Well, that is true," said Colin. "But this time it would be better to..."

"You don't know then?" Tim interrupted him, which stumped Colin for a moment.

Then Colin had lost his rag a bit. "Whose fucking plan is this?" This was met by stunned silence for a moment.

Then John said, more aggressively than was strictly necessary towards Colin, "Eh? Do what mate?" John got to his feet and started to square up against Colin. At this point Tim had stood up, towering over the pair of them, "Now, now boys," he asserted some dominance, "let's just all calm down for a moment."

John and Colin agreed to take a breather. "Look, there is a lot of underlying stress to these types of things," Tim had reasoned. It was agreed ostensibly that they would in that case stick to Colin's plan. However John had subsequently telephoned directly to Brendan and suggested it might be a good idea to have an independent meeting at Tim's house, without

Colin present. Brendan had agreed, thinking he would just report straight back to Colin if there was anything untoward going on.

In the event John had made a lot of sense as they discussed the situation over coffee at Tim's. Colin was under a lot of pressure, and didn't need to be concerned with all the details, he explained. "It makes more sense to me to actually make a genuine tour, though," he said.

Tim had said that he too felt Colin was burdened with many decisions, and this being a relatively minor one he had maybe not given it sufficient consideration which was why he had invited them to discuss it. "If you do get stopped and asked any questions, it's best to have a genuine story to tell," he said.

Brendan had considered all of this. He had known Colin for years and had the greatest respect for him. Moreover it was his plan, and he must know best how do achieve it. On the other hand John's suggestion and Tim's comments also made a lot of sense and Tim was clearly a very intelligent and hugely knowledgeable man. But he was reluctant to go against Colin's instructions.

In the end Brendan was half persuaded and they decided to let Colin think they were following his suggestion. After all he wouldn't know anything about it as he wouldn't even be in Colombia until shortly before the return journey was due to begin. Therefore Colin wouldn't know whether they were on a fake tour of the roads around Juan Pablo's house, or on a genuine tour of South America. If they went with John's route, they could telephone Juan Pablo from Rio and let him know they was a slight delay so he need not worry. This would hopefully stop him contacting Colin and announcing that they had not arrived as scheduled. However Brendan still had some trepidations about going behind Colin's back so they agreed to leave the final decision until after they arrived in Rio.

Chapter 14

In the bright light of a Rio morning a few weeks later, Brendan felt far happier and more confident than he had in London. Bravely for him, he now acquiesced, agreeing to adopt John's perimeter tour suggestion, despite Colin's instructions. After all, as both John and Tim had said many times, Colin would never know. They would spend about three weeks touring the continent. From Rio, they would head across the land mass through Uruguay to Argentina, across to Chile, then up through Peru to Colombia. It would make an excellent trip they both would enjoy. John called Juan Pablo and explained they would arrive in two to three weeks, and everything was fine.

The following morning they set out from the guest house on the bikes. As they pulled out of the drive way and onto the main road, they were completely unaware that they were being watched.

Across the road, opposite the guest house, hidden by the reflections of sunlight on the expansive glass window of a café, a pair of large field binoculars was trained carefully on the two bikes as they pulled into the road and set off. One hand removed itself from the large binoculars, picked up a ball point pen, and made some notes on a notepad that lay open on the café table, next to a half finished cup of Arabica coffee.

Before they left Rio, Brendan and John stopped at a large department store to buy some camping gear and motorbike panniers to carry it in. To save time, Brendan waited by the bikes in a back street while John ran inside to get some essentials: a tent, a couple of blankets and a small camping stove. After he had been waiting about ten minutes, Brendan noticed a group of three men standing on a corner fifty yards behind who were huddled in discussion and appeared to be watching him. He did his best to ignore them, but he was in the narrow back street, another fifty yards from the main road, with very few windows overlooking it, and no other people around. He began to consider if he may be in a vulnerable position.

Now they started walking towards him, and he was suddenly very nervous. At that moment John appeared out of the side door of the department store and walked over to the bikes. To Colin's immense relief, John's appearance had stopped the three men in their tracks.

"John," said Brendan, and surreptitiously nodded his head indicating the direction of the approaching men. John looked over to them. They were pretending to be in conversation again. John shook his head slightly at Brendan, to show it was nothing to be concerned about. They fixed the panniers on the bikes and were sitting in the saddles again about to put on their crash helmets, when the three men suddenly appeared next to them.

Brendan and John stopped moving, their helmets in their hands and looked at them. There was a moment's silence, then one of the men stepped forward and let them see a small stiletto blade he was holding. He was standing less than a couple of yards from John, pointing the blade towards John's stomach. Then he said something aggressively in Portuguese. Brendan recognised the words for 'money' and 'keys', in fact he was hoping it was money 'or' keys. The other two young men, for they were only around twenty years old perhaps, now stepped forward to stand almost shoulder to shoulder with the one holding the blade, and gave John and Colin sneering and dirty looks while egging their friend on.

There was barely time to think. Brendan with his heart now racing, had turned to glance at John, while at the same time, reaching for his wallet. However, with no fast or jerky movements, cool as a cucumber John swung his leg over his bike and stood up to face the young man with the blade. The young man flinched defensively in case of an immediate attack even though John hadn't made any lunges or fast moves, but he held his ground. However John had caught the young men slightly off guard simply by casually stepping off the bike. John stood still, looking quite calm and relaxed, no posture of aggression and the three men watched him. For a moment John was holding the initiative. His left hand still holding his crash helmet by his side, with his other hand he patted his back pocket to locate his wallet. Apparently it was the other side. He started passing the helmet across to switch it to his right hand, so he could check his other back pocket. The three men took a step forward. As they did so John suddenly swung his arm in a back handed stroke, sideways and upwards at lightning speed. The young men apparently never saw the helmet coming at them. Nor reckoned with the speed and force behind it. Two of them now lay flat out on the road.

John seemed to have knocked them both out cold, with a single barely considered blow, including the one with the knife. The third young man simply scarpered. Still wholly unflustered, John stepped back over his bike, and didn't even glance towards them again, even to check if they were still down. He said to Brendan, as he started putting his helmet on, "Never pick a fight with a man holding a crash hat."

'I don't think I'd every pick a fight with John, whatever,' thought Brendan. The two men on the ground were just beginning to stir, touching blood on their faces and testing teeth as the bikes kicked into gear and accelerated back towards the main road.

A little way further along, they stopped again at a supermarket to pick up emergency food rations, and water. This time, John remained looking after the bikes. Finally after locating the main highway towards Uruguay, they were on their way.

Over the next three weeks John and Brendan enjoyed themselves immensely, on the beautiful seven fifty Honda motorcycles. Sometimes they camped out under the stars in official campsites along the way, other times, they stayed in guest houses. A few roads were unmade but the bikes coped well enough on them anyway. On tarmac, which was almost all the roads, the bikes really came into their own. With wide seats, steady as a rock, and a comfortable long distance riding position, cruising at seventy mph felt like being on a gentle Sunday afternoon stroll. They were able to put many miles behind them very quickly.

It was a superb road trip with the most spectacular scenery along the entire route. Highlights, and there were no doubt many, might have included the conifer forests and mountain Lakes of Argentina. The fairy tale magical beauty of the high plains in Chile circled by snowy mountain peaks and active volcanoes. The brown mountains and snow peaks of La Paz the world's highest capital city. The icy waterfalls and mountain passes of Peru where there were some of the best riding roads in the world.

They both particularly liked Peru. Sometimes there were huge wild llamas at the side of the road or flocks of flamingos standing in the lakes. Everywhere in the spectacular scenery, the rich indigenous culture was apparent with many of the local people dressed in traditional colourful costume. There were also interesting old houses, and ancient stone carved monuments. They passed through the world's driest desert, rode by living glaciers, traversed mountain paths through luminous landscapes, over emerald hills and jagged rocky 'moonscapes'. They saw roads that looked like giant ribbons strewn carelessly across mountainsides, with hair pin bends every hundred yards. They ascended and descended 20 000 feet in a single afternoon.

After Peru they traversed the cloud forests and lush equatorial jungles of Ecuador, passing through lowland swamps in tropical heat, then a few hours later along snow bound mountain tracks frozen in the sky.

They were careful to stick to the main roads. Even John seemed a little uneasy if they ever seemed to be heading off the big highways, in some of the Ecuadorian mountains, and they would regularly retrace their steps if it seemed they had taken a wrong turn somewhere, rather than risk encountering bandits on the minor roads. It was already getting dark before they made the border from Ecuador into Colombia. Since this was well known bandit territory, they stopped at a guest house before darkness fully set in.

At altitude in the Andes, even around the equator it was chilly. There was a common area in the guest house where travellers could sit round a large log fire in a huge fireplace. That evening, Brendan and John were sitting in wicker armchairs, holding a cold bottle of beer each and watching the roaring fire. There were a few other small groups of travellers. One fellow, a San Franciscan sitting near Brendan was quite chatty, making friends with everyone. At one point, he turned to Brendan and said, "You're not smuggling cocaine are you?"

Brendan looked at him, saw he was joking, and smiled, shaking his head slightly. "Do I look like a cocaine smuggler?" he asked.

"Yes!" said the traveller. Brendan looked at John, then back at the traveller and laughed. "Really?" asked Brendan, joking.

"With bikes like that," explained the traveller, he had seen them parking their bikes earlier.

Brendan looked at him, not sure he was following the logic.

"Didn't you hear?" The traveller had realised Brendan was missing some information.

"Hear what?"

"There was a big cocaine bust yesterday, on the border crossing into Colombia." He pointed in the general direction of the high road, towards the border. "A guy on a motorbike. Like yours."

"Honda seven fifties?"

."I don't know what type of bikes, I mean with big gas tanks like yours."

"They found cocaine in his bike?"

"Yeah, in the gas tank."

"Local guy?" asked John.

"Spanish I think. So if you've got any cocaine in your tanks you'd better take it out now. They're checking all the vehicles." All three laughed at the suggestion.

"How much did they find?"

"Oh it was a lot. He'll spend a lot of years in some stink-hole jail. I think it was like, a kilo or something. Penalties are very severe round here. You gotta be what? Crazy or desperate I guess, to do something so dumb."

"Crazy if you get caught," said John. "Smart if you don't."

"Nah, you gotta be plain crazy even just to consider it," said the traveller.

"Well, to consider getting caught *would* be crazy. You are right my friend. More beers?" John offered to get in another round. They sat up quite late, drinking the beer, watching the fire, and chatting about the amazing things they'd seen, and the terrible state of the local prisons.

On the Ecuador Colombia border they did get stopped by customs as predicted, who set sniffer dogs all over the bikes and inspected the petrol tanks thoroughly. They never even considered investigating the tyres John and Brendan noticed. Even still, and although he had no drugs on board yet, Brendan felt uncomfortable. During the search he was aware that jurisdiction over his own life had been temporarily removed from himself (owing to what amounted to in his opinion nothing but religious beliefs about nature), which feeling he didn't like. He would have to psyche himself up a bit more perhaps for the real journey ahead.

By the end of the third week they had arrived in Bogota, and called Juan Pablo to inform him they would be at his place the following afternoon.

John hung up the receiver and walked back over to the table where Brendan was sitting in the restaurant area of the guest house they were staying at that evening. As he sat down John said, "Colin's already arrived."

"What, at Juan Pablo's?"

"Yeah."

"When did he get there?"

"Yesterday."

"So he already knows which way we came."

"Yeah."

"Is he pissed off?"

"No. Juan Pablo says he's ok about it."

"Mm." That was a relief.

"I don't give a toss anyway. It's my bike."

Brendan nodded in agreement then he looked through the undraped window of the guest house common room to the street outside in the dark. They had two weeks left before commencing the return journey.

It was already dark again when, the following evening they pulled up outside Juan Pablo's parents' house. They had got lost about three times trying to locate the address, and ended up arguing about the map reading, but finally they had found it.

Juan Pablo and Colin came out of the house smiling to greet them. The bikes were stored in the workshop then they gathered in the garden for a beer. Juan Pablo's parents had invited them to supper. Juan Pablo had moved out since Colin was last here, as well as gaining a couple new tattoos Colin had noticed - he felt a natural elder brother-in-law's interest in Juan Pablo's wellbeing. Juan Pablo's new place was not very spacious and the other three were booked into a decent local hotel for later.

After Brendan and John had met Juan Pablo's parents, who were oblivious of the real nature of their visit, and showered, the four of them sat round the table in the garden in the warm evening air, holding a cold bottle of beer each. John was regaling the others with accounts of the amazing and hilarious adventures he and Brendan had enjoyed over the previous few weeks.

After a while he came to relate the customs inspection on the Ecuador border the San Franciscan had informed them about. Which John thought was highly amusing considering their own particular circumstances. Juan Pablo laughed and Brendan joined in thinking he too now saw the funny side. Colin alone, looked thoughtful.

Later when Colin and Juan Pablo were alone for a couple of minutes after the other two had gone ahead into the house to eat, he brought the subject up again. "I never saw any sniffer dogs during either of my trips."

"So. You were lucky."

"No, it means I never tested the bike for sniffer dogs."

Juan Pablo looked at him. Colin thought for a few moments then said, "Have you got a hose in the workshop?"

"Should be."

"And a tap."

"Yes, what are you thinking?"

"When you wrap the coke, make sure to wipe down all the plastic wrappings with a damp cloth. When we load the tyres we also need to wipe down the tyres, inside and out, the inner tubes, the wheel rims, and finally thoroughly spray the bikes down with the hose."

"Ok," said Juan Pablo.

"That's not all," said Colin. "Now last time when I took the bike of Dover, the back tyre was a bit flat. It must have had a slow puncture. We need to make sure the inner tubes are properly air tight this time. We'll need to test them further, and we'll have to try and get the joins really solid with the glue. I want them to be able to hold full pressure, after we've loaded them. Can we do that?"

Juan Pablo nodded. "I wouldn't go with full pressure," he said, "it may place unnecessary burden on such a mission critical aspect. Mind you, maybe we can, if we change how we do the tyres. I was thinking about this anyway. We don't need to dissect the entire inner tube. We just need to cut a slit through which we feed the wrapped coke into it, working it round the tube with our fingers. We just have to make sure the circumference of the packages is smaller than the inflated tube before we put them in. Then that leaves a small enough join to use a single patch, which is going to be as strong as having no join."

Colin nodded and his eyes widened slightly. "That's excellent work, Juan Pablo," he said, patting him on the shoulder. They got up and started up the path towards the house to join the others for a very welcome supper.

After supper, they all said their goodbye to Juan Pablo's folks who had been very hospitable, and headed off to the hotel in Juan Pablo's jeep, where he dropped them off and went home. The bikes were left in the workshop.

For Brendan and John the next twelve days were a holiday, and they had the time to themselves to be idle, relax and read or go swimming, and go for bike rides if they felt like it.

Colin had conceded it was no longer necessary to stick to his original plan of regular local bike rides, as they had plenty of miles on the clock already now.

On the morning of departure, John and Brendan met Colin and Juan Pablo outside the workshop. The bikes were all prepared. Juan Pablo's van was ready to be loaded and Colin had hired a car which was parked in front of the van.

Colin wanted John and Brendan to have a little test ride on the track outside the workshop before they set off. Juan Pablo had managed to get the tyres to almost full pressure. First they tried pushing the bikes. They were so heavy and cumbersome to push, the extra weight in the wheels was not noticeable. They then sat on the bikes and rode at walking pace. The extra weight was evident but not problematic. They could get up to about 10mph before the wheels began wobbling and snaking, and threatened to wrest control from the rider.

Colin was satisfied this would be sufficient, and the bikes were loaded into the back of Juan Pablo's van, which was equipped to take two bikes side by side. Then Colin John and Brendan climbed into the hired car and set off in front of the van towards Bogota.

They stopped in the guest house in Bogota, as before, then drove out the next day to the local airport. The bikes were unloaded from the van, then Juan Pablo left to drive home. After loading the bikes onto the plane, the three of them boarded and took their seats.

When they landed in Leticia, Colin went ahead by taxi while Brendan and John rode the bikes into town at about 8mph. After Colin had bought them all a beer in a café, they wheeled the bikes down to the boat pier to find a boat to Manaus. The bikes were loaded on the boat, then they went to the food market to eat.

Chapter 15

Later that evening they boarded the boat for Manaus. Brendan and John loved it, Colin was surprised at how familiar and ordinary it all seemed. Travelling as a unit it was easy to avoid interaction with others. They formed their own little clique which kept them relatively isolated.

As before they disembarked at Manaus and flew to Rio. At Rio they wheeled the bikes down to the boat port. Here Colin said goodbye and left them to go through customs. "Remember," he said, just before they separated. "They don't know about the tyres." Brendan nodded. John grinned widely and gave Colin a thumb's up.

John who was more confident went first which allowed Brendan to follow in the psychological slip stream. Had Brendan been on his own, or been in front, he probably would not have had the courage to go through with it. With John in front however, he was able to project his whole consciousness onto John. John had complete conviction in what Colin had told him. John absolutely believed that as Colin had said, no-one would ever think to inspect the tyres. Therefore John was able to adopt the complete psychology of an innocent man, which perhaps gave off subtle signals proclaiming his innocence. In any case John was allowed straight through customs. However Brendan was stopped, which made him feel suddenly nauseous.

Perhaps he looked pale or clammy, for the official began barking at him. Brendan became flustered. He had to hand over his papers then stand to the side while they took his rucksack to pieces. Another official appeared who began asking him questions in English, about his trip, where he had been and so on. Fortunately Brendan had genuine answers, however the officials were still not satisfied. Finally they took the key from the ignition and unlocked the petrol tank. They shone torches in it and poked sticks in it. Eventually they closed the cap again, put the key back in the ignition, handed Brendan back his papers and let him pack his rucksack and continue. 'Wow!' he thought as he wheeled the bike down the ramp towards the dock. 'Colin is right, they haven't considered anyone would put something in the tyres.'

The journey across the Atlantic was straight forward, apart from the fact that John drank about twenty bottles of beer per night. They sailed up past Morocco, through the straits of Gibraltar, along the French coast and on the 3rd May 1995 they sailed into Genoa, just as Colin had done before them. They had no trouble at all with customs at Genoa. They pushed the bikes out of the port to a carpark where Ed, Tim's driver, was waiting with a bike pick up van. As they loaded the bikes onto the van, not one of them knew they were being watched. Some half a mile from the port, on the fifteenth floor of a high rise office block, a pair of field binoculars was trained on their every movement.

Occasionally one hand would release its grip, pick up a ball point pen, and jot down some notes in a notepad.

From Genoa Ed knew a local route into France, and about twenty four hours later they were in Calais. The drove onto the boat at Calais without problems, and into customs at Dover.

At Dover there was unusually heavy customs presence. Each vehicle had to be checked with sniffer dogs inside and out. When it came to their turn, John Colin and Ed sat in the cab, trying to be confident. Brendan was secretly praying he hadn't got a puncture. They sat in the cab while the dogs were let into the back. John and Brendan knew they had nothing to worry about, even with dogs. Until they head the dog start yapping crazily. The three glanced at each other in silence. There was some commotion at the back of the van, then they were invited to step out.

They exited the cab and immediately two dogs were put into it. They ran around crazily for a couple of moments, then jumped out. The cab was clean.

They could see the rear of the van was still open, and the dogs were no longer in there.

Now a suited official approached them accompanied by a uniformed police sergeant. Brendan's heart was going nine to the dozen.

"Afternoon Gentleman," said the suited official.

He wanted to know which one was the driver of the van, and what the three of them were doing. They explained that Ed was collecting John and Brendan from a road trip abroad on their bikes. The clutch and gearbox had gone on John's bike just outside Calais and he had decided to ask his mate Ed to pick him up in the van. Brendan had decided to wait with John and come back in the van rather than drive home on his own. He had decided it would be much warmer in the van.

"Where any of the gentleman aware," the official enquired, "that prohibited drugs had been found in the van?"

Brendan felt a pang of fear go right through his middle. He quickly began calculating. This meant decades in prison.

"No," each of the three intoned indolently.

Another uniformed officer appeared from round the back of the van, approached them and handed a small plastic bag to the questioning official. John, Ed and Brendan looked at it. A small plastic bag containing what looked like a piece of hash.

"Do any of you recognise this?" asked the official.

There was silence for a moment, then Ed said, "Ah, yes officer, that'll be my hash."

John and Brendan stared at Ed.

"Are there any other drugs on the vehicle?" continued the official.

"No," Ed shook his head.

"We're going to have to search your vehicle, sir."

Ed was requested to move the vehicle to a holding area. John and Brendan stood watching. This looked like it could turn into a disaster.

"Remove the bikes," the officer instructed.

The bikes were wheeled back out of the vans down the aluminium ramps and stood on their stands at the side. Then a number of inspectors boarded the van. Over the next couple of hours they searched every single inch of the van, inside, underneath, in the cab. They unscrewed the panels in the doors, and pulled the exhaust pipe off. They looked under the bonnet and even in the carburettor. They didn't give a single glance at the bikes stood at the side.

Eventually Ed was given an on the spot fine, the exhaust pipe and door panels were thoughtfully returned, the bikes graciously re-loaded, and they exited customs, carrying about forty kilos of cocaine in the back of the van, which had an official street value of over six and a half million pounds sterling.

Back in London the coke was unloaded in Tim's lockup as before. They weighed up about forty kilos as expected and none was tainted. Dr Todd was there and took ten keys this time. Pat took five, John took ten for free, and Colin had to take fifteen home which he sold to John and Pat over the next few months in five key packs.

Brendan was given two hundred and fifty pounds cash that evening in a holdall. Tim and Ed were paid off well, and Tim pilfered himself a little extra as usual.

*

These guys by now then had quite a lot of cash between them. But it was illegal cash. It wasn't marked in any way, but they couldn't really use it for major purchases, mortgages or pensions for example. As long as they didn't spend too much at a time they could otherwise use it freely. Colin was looking for a way to convert it all into legal money however. That is money he could claim came from a legitimate source, which he could pay some tax on if necessary, and put in the bank. Then he could buy property and make other legitimate investments. Until he could do that... he didn't actually feel properly rich yet. A vital inner sense he was seeking, of complete financial security, still eluded him and it frustrated him.

Over the months following the two-bike trip, Colin continued to visit Tim socially on Wednesday afternoons. He valued their chats and discussions, and Tim always had some high quality cannabis, or brandy or something fun going on. Colin was still in his rented accommodation. He was driving the same rover, and wearing the same clothes.

One Wednesday a couple of months after the trip, they were sitting in Tim's big armchairs by the coffee table, looking out of the French windows into the sunlit garden smoking some good quality weed that Tim had sourced.

"I've got a big problem," announced Colin.

"What's that?" enquired Tim.

"Well," said Colin, "the fact is, I've got all this money, I mean, I've got nearly three quarters of a million pounds in cash under my mattress in my nice rented apartment. Between me and you that is. The problem being, I don't know what on earth to do with it all."

"Ah!" said Tim, smiling. "That is the sort of problem that I know just how to solve."

Colin stared at him. "Serious?"

Tim leaned forward and explained the following.

"As soon as you leave here," Tim said, "pop into the local newsagents, and buy a local paper. Look up house auctions. Go to the next auction. Bid for a likely looking property. You want to be looking at spending about thirty or forty thousand on a place that needs a lot of work doing on it. With the current economic climate you should be able to pick up a bargain for that money. Now, you will need to pay a ten percent deposit at the auction. You can pay this in cash, it's not uncommon. When you do, offer to pay another ten percent today if they'll take cash for that as well. They likely will.

"They will usually then give you a week or so to pay the balance. What you do, is you go down there on the final due date and get to speak to whoever it is. Tell them that you are very sorry but you have run into a short term problem and you will not be able to raise the balance for another week or two. He will threaten you that you might lose your deposit. You complain, then shrug, nothing you can do, but as you are leaving you think to mention that you could pay some of it today in cash if he could accept that, and most of the rest in cash tomorrow, if that could work.

"He won't refuse it. So then you give him about ten or fifteen thousand or whatever and about the same the next day to clear it.

"Now you own the property, you use the remainder of your money to hire local tradesmen to refurbish it and do it up. Most or practically all small builders want cash for both the labour and the materials and offer no VAT. Couple of months down the line, you are the legitimate owner of a nice property. "

Colin looked at him. "Brilliant," he said.

Soon after Colin attended the local house auctions and purchased a property using cash, just as Tim had suggested. He then proceeded to engage local workmen to refurbish it. They were all happy to be paid in cash. Within a few months he had been able to use up about eighty thousand pounds on the property, which now had a value of over one hundred thousand. When the property was completed he planned to rent it out on the open market. Since it was legitimately purchased in his own name this would provide bankable income. He could then use that income, and the initial property as collateral to purchase a mortgage with which to buy a house that he and Ana could live in. It would be bigger that their rented accommodation, but still relatively modest, in a London suburb.

As the work was progressing on the house, two or three months after he had purchased it, and Colin could see that the plan was working as expected, he was at Tim's as usual on Wednesday. This time John was also there. Colin still had well over half a million pounds he didn't know what to do with.

"Just go and buy another house at auction," Tim said.

"Yeah, I can do," Colin said, but seemed doubtful, which the others did not understand.

"What's stopping you?" said Tim.

"Look," it was a great idea," said Colin, "and it seems to have worked really well. It's just that..."

"Just that what?"

"I don't know, it's hard to explain. I just don't like auctions I guess. I don't like the whole bidding culture. It always trips me up and I seem to get ripped off. I think that's partly what caught me out in the antiques business. I know it sounds ridiculous."

"Well send John to do the bidding for you."

John looked at Colin and nodded to show his willingness.

"Really?" said Colin.

"Yes of course," said Tim.

"I can do that for you," said John.

It was arranged that John would go the auction on Friday, and purchase a house for Colin using the method Tim had previously explained, and which Colin had already utilised once. Colin would get twenty grand to John in cash before Friday. Then Colin would come to Tim's at two o'clock Friday afternoon and John would join them as soon as he had finished at the auction, with the paperwork to another property for Colin.

Colin was already back at Tim's on Friday when John arrived with the paperwork.

"How did you get on?" Tim asked John on Colin's behalf, as he joined them round the coffee table.

"Ok, I think."

"You think?" Tim continued the interrogation.

"I did ok."

"Let's see the papers then," Tim was still taking charge.

"Alright," said John, "but you should know I didn't buy a house though."

Tim looked at him. "What do you mean, you didn't buy a house?"

"I bought a night club."

"You did what?" Tim was furious. "You were supposed to get a house. Are you joking?"

"Wait!" said Colin. "It's ok. How many houses do I need? A night club might be a good idea."

John nodded. "That's what I thought," he said.

"But how did you buy a night club for forty thousand pounds?" asked Tim.

"It's not a night club yet," said John.

"What is it then?"

"It's a rundown snooker hall, with no roof in South East London."

"But it's got a license for everything," continued John. "Beer, music, you name it, we can do it. We just need to spend a fair bit doing it up again, putting a new roof on and that. But as I understand it, that's part of the game, right?"

As they discussed it, even Tim started to come round to the idea. A night club could provide a very useful way to process their piles of cash once it was opened.

"We can declare money as gate revenue," said Colin. "Even if we don't sell any tickets. When you go to a night club you buy your tickets in cash, right? No none buys a ticket with a cheque or card. Once the club is opened, we can just dump cash in the bank, and keep a ledger stating it was received in return for tickets at the club door. No-one can deny that our cash could have come from tickets if we become club owners.

"Or we can just say we took the money at the bar. We can buy beer in bulk, throw it down the drain if we want, then bank a load of money, and say we sold beer at high prices in our club. It would be impossible to disprove."

Tim and John were nodding. "It's a good idea," said Tim.

Soon Colin was not only hiring workmen for his house, but also to refurbish his new club. All were happy to take cash for labour and products. He would then get them working for him on the club too. He set up a limited company to process the 'revenue' from the club with Tim as Secretary and John as Treasurer, and himself as Director.

After about six months, both the house and club were finished. He rented the house as planned and banked the proceeds, which he used to get a mortgage on another house for him and Ana. He opened the club for business, and operated it as a functioning night club. Even with the club deserted of customers it showed a healthy profit from day one.

Through the club then Colin was able to begin banking his cash. He then used the legitimate cash to set up other businesses such as an antique furniture importation business based in Lewisham, ostensibly run by Tim. Colin always maintained that this was a profitable legitimate business in its own right, however Tim said that it never earned a single legitimate penny and was nothing but a front for the cocaine money.

Twelve months after John and Brendan had completed their trip, and once again Colin and John were at Tim's, John asked Colin about Brendan.

"He's done very well," said Colin. He's still working full time, and living on his coke money. So he's banking all his earnings. I think he's getting married soon. It's worked out very well for him."

"Great," said John. Then asked, "Do you think he'd do it again?"

"No way," said Colin. "He's had enough."

John nodded.

Then Colin continued, "However, I'm ready to organise another trip John. You in this time?"

John nodded without even considering the question. "We need a replacement for Brendan then," he said.

"Uh-uh," said Colin shaking his head.

John looked at him questioningly.

Colin carried on, "We need three replacements. I'm sending four bikes this time."

John nodded and his eyes widened slightly.

Chapter 16

Over the next few weeks John helped Colin put together a team of four. These included Tommy, who was John's neighbour, Dave, John's brother in law and a couple of other friends of John from Basingstoke called Mark and Keith. Colin paid for the bikes on this trip; they were each provided a brand new Honda CBT 750cc motorbike. The bikes were shipped to Rio to be retrieved by the four once they had landed there. They had each purchased red crash helmets with microphones embedded so they would be able to communicate as they were riding. Each was assigned a code name, for fun. Red One, Red Two Red Three and Red Four.

Colin was to join them a couple of days later, to accompany them part of the way on a fifth motorbike. He would generally ride his bike either ahead or behind, catching up with them every few days.

Dave's wife accompanied him to Gatwick airport to wave him off. She had always been opposed to Dave being involved. Now at the airport as they met with the other three riders in the departure lounge she started to cause a problem.

She explained something to Dave, and after a small argument, he relayed it to Tommy, who was group leader. After another argument, Tommy went to locate a pay phone. He called direct to John.

"John?"

"Tommy? What's happening?"

"We've got a problem."

"What do you mean?"

"It's Dave."

"What about him."

"You know his missus came to the airport to wave us off."

"Yeah."

"Well, now she's managed to stop him going."

"What do you mean stop him going?"

"She's managed to talk him out of it and now he's refusing to get on the plane." Dave's wife had convinced him that if he participated any further in this trip he was probably going to spend at least 10 to 20 years in a prison in South America or Europe, and he could only pray that it would be in Europe. Eventually Dave had capitulated and was refusing to board the plane. The problem was the bike had been shipped out to Rio in Dave's name. All the paper work was in his name and only he was authorised to release the bike in Brazil.

A fair amount of swearing ensued then John told Tommy to call him back in twenty minutes, while he relayed the information to Colin.

"What are we going to do?" said Colin down the phone, as much to himself as to John.

"We could leave that bike maybe. Just go with three," suggested John.

"What? Are we having a laugh? I spent thousands on that bike. Listen mate, you brought him in. You'd better think of a way out."

"Do you want to be the fourth rider, when you fly out to join them in a couple of days?" John suggested to Colin.

"Do me a favour," Colin didn't seem to like that idea. "Now listen, mate, I've got a lot of money riding on this. You are the one that said he was good for it. This is your problem now. You'd better sort something out, son," and he hung up the phone.

In the end John decided the best solution would be for himself and Dave to fly out together to Rio, have Dave sign ownership over to him and then for John to take Dave's place on the fourth bike while Dave flew back to be with his wife in the UK, with no further connection or involvement in the scheme.

Having never been the registered owner of the bike *after* any cocaine was put in it, Dave and his wife were perfectly confident that he could never be implicated in the smuggling trip. They reasoned that it would be impossible for him to be sentenced to a decade or more in prison, in Europe or South America, should the worst come to the worst and any of the other smugglers be arrested and themselves convicted. Their clever logic was to prove incorrect.

The new group of four followed a similar route to before, across Argentina, over the Andes, up through Chile and Peru and towards Colombia. John became Red Three in place of Dave. The microphone's worked well, and they much enjoyed chasing each other through South America on four big motorcycles.

Colin flew out a few days after John, collected his own bike, and began to catch up with them. He had told them all again and again before they had left the UK, how important it was to keep a low profile. Certainly, four big motorcycles with riders in matching red helmets did attract some attention from locals in the various towns and villages they passed through. People kept wanting to know about their trip, and what they were doing. The four quickly became adept at spinning a story about a once in a lifetime adventure biking across the continent.

Colin was not that far behind them, and a couple of days after the four bikes had set out from Rio, Colin was in a hotel room in Argentina, in preparation for their first rendezvous the following day. With not much to do for the evening, he switched on the TV in his room for a few minutes before he went out to get some food. Grabbing a cold can of lager from the minibar, he sat in his chair, took a swig from the can and as his eyes focused on the screen, promptly spat his beer back out in a big spray all over the floor.

On the TV in front of him was a close up of John's face. Or someone who looked remarkably like him. Colin rubbed his eyes and blinked. As the shot pulled out he could see it was indeed John, grinning broadly at the camera. As the shot continued to pan back, he could now see Tommy sitting next to him, then Keith and Mark. All of them smiling cheerfully at the camera, each cradling a red crash helmet on his knee. It was their inane grinning as much as anything that infuriated Colin. Apparently they were sitting on some kind of sofa. Colin rubbed his hands over his face. He couldn't believe it. What was going on?

As the full shot emerged Colin could make out that the four seemed to be undergoing some sort of interrogation, or rather an interview on an afternoon Argentinian chat show. A genial looking hostess was asking questions and pointing the mic first at John, then Tommy.

"So what made you choose to ride motorcycles across the whole of South America?" she asked in accented English.

John smiled at her then at the camera, and said, "We thought it would be a lot of fun and a great way to see this part of the world."

Colin, sitting in his armchair had forgotten about his beer and was almost having palpitations where he sat. "Wha' the..." he spluttered.

The following afternoon Colin pulled up on his bike outside the hotel where they had arranged to meet. In the hotel lounge bar a little later, they sat on low comfortable armchairs around a low, candle lit table. John explained, to Colin's consternation, that they had met a rather lovely young producer in a bar the previous evening and over a beer had agreed to appear on a national television chat show. She had thought what they were doing would make a good story for national TV, Tommy had added. "Plus she was super hot," said Keith.

"Yeah," laughed Mark. "Keith only thought he was going to fuck 'er."

"I did fuck 'er," said Keith.

"You didn't fuck 'er," said John.

"Yes I did."

"Oh Yeah? When was that then?" John was incredulous.

Colin was furious. "Tell you what," interrupted Colin, "What if I broke both her legs? Eh? Then we would all know for certain that it was me that fucked her. Wouldn't we!"

"Awlright! Steady on." said Tommy.

"Do what?" said John, throwing a hard stare at Colin, and beginning to posture. He sat up in his seat and began loosening up his right arm a little. "Well what if I stopped you first?"

"Awlright! Everyone calm down now," Tommy mediated.

"I told you to keep a low f'king profile," Colin said to John through gritted teeth and also now sitting forward in his seat.

"Ok, that's enough!" said Tommy. Sat between them, he put his hands up in front of their faces. He was the smallest there by far, he couldn't even reach the ground with his toes on his bike, but one way or another he commanded authority when he felt it necessary. Perhaps because he used to be a professional boxer, a welter weight, so knew he could whip all their arses at the same time if it came to it, despite his small stature.

"You were supposed to be the team leader!" said Colin, turning on Tommy. "What the heck were you doing?"

"Calm down, Colin!" said Tommy. "It probably didn't happen exactly like it sounded. The fact is it was a bit difficult for us to turn the offer down, seeing as she knew we were staying in town for a couple of days and everything. It might've looked a little bit fishy if we hadn't played along with it."

Colin frowned at the table in front of him. "Well, ok," he said at last, unconvincingly. Over a couple more beers however the atmosphere became more jovial. They went out to a local restaurant, Colin still carrying his crash helmet, then all returned to John and Tommy's room in the hotel later that evening for a night cap. They polished off a bottle of Jack Daniel's then

Colin left. He was drunk enough that he managed to forget his crash helmet, and left it instead on the table in the hotel room.

It was about 10.30pm by the time Colin left. The other four were not quite ready to turn in, and cracked open another bottle of JD. They were only on about their second round of shots when in his absence conversation turned back to Colin.

"Who does 'e think 'e is." John was saying.

"Bit of a pillock if you ask me," said Keith.

"E's alright," said Tommy, mediating again.

"Nah, e's a nob 'ead. E's beginning to get on my tits," said John. He had stood up and walked over to where Colin's crash helmet was stood on the table. "E's forgotten 'is crash helmet," said John.

The others looked round.

"Well 'e must have noticed when he got on 'is bike," said Tommy.

"Unless he forgot he'd brought it," said Mark.

John had picked the crash helmet up and was inspecting inside it. "Oi, what's this?" he said, looking inside the helmet. Suddenly he 'shushed' the others.

"What is it?" said Tommy.

John carried the helmet back to his seat and sat down. Without saying anything he held it for the others to look inside. "What?" said Tommy.

"Look," said John, whispering. They all looked.

"Here's the microphone," mouthed John. They all looked at the microphone. "But where is the headphone," he whispered almost inaudibly.

They looked into the helmet. He was right. The earpiece had been removed. John looked at Tommy, they both understood each other. Colin had left his helmet so he could listen in on their conversation.

John walked back to the table and carefully replaced the helmet, then took a couple of quiet paces backwards.

"Y' know," John said cheerfully in a loud voice, "I *like* that Colin."

There was a pause, then Keith buckled over in an effort not to laugh out loud.

You know what, he is a *very* intelligent man," said Mark.

This went on for a little while. Eventually John tiptoed back to the table and quietly picked up the helmet. Peering inside he found the microphone switch and switched it off. He looked up at the others. "Can you believe it? He was trying to spy on us," said John.

The next morning, after they had finished breakfast and were preparing to leave, Colin knocked on John and Tommy's door. John opened the door.

"Alright John!" said Colin, smiling.

"Alright," said John curtly. "Wanker," he added, under his breath.

Colin gave John a queer look, then presuming he'd misheard, "I've come to pick up my lid," he said

John stood silently glaring at Colin.

"John! My lid," said Colin stepping forward and playfully pushing John out of the way.

"Oi!" said John sharply, and pushed Colin back out of the doorway. Colin was stunned.

"What?"

"John!" said Tommy from inside the room. "F' gawd' sake. Let 'im in."

John paused for a moment, then moved aside allowing Colin to walk in. He looked askew at John again.

Tommy walked through the middle of everyone towards the helmet on the table. "He thinks you've been spying on us," he explained to Colin.

"What?" said Colin, confounded.

Tommy picked up the helmet and carried it over towards Colin.

He showed him inside. "You see? John thinks you left the mic switched on deliberately and removed the ear piece, so you could listen in on our conversation after you left last night."

Colin peered into the helmet, dumbstruck. "Why the heck ... How would you think that?" he said to John, a look of real hurt on his face. "I didn't remove the earpiece, it fell out and got lost days ago. That's all. I didn't bother to fix it because I'm not riding with the team am I?"

John looked at him suspiciously. "How come it was switched on then?"

Colin looked at him and shrugged. "I don't know, it could have got knocked on. It could've been on for ages. I honestly have no idea. But I promise you John, on my life, I was not spying on you."

John looked at him for a few moments. "Ok," he said finally, relaxing. Convinced.

"Whew!" said Colin. "Well, good morning to you guys too."

"Sorry!" said John. Tommy shook his head at the situation, looked at Colin and shrugged.

"Ok guys!" said Colin, trying to lift morale again, "I'll wish you well, and see you next in Lima. I'll just go and say cheerio to the others." They said their farewells, then Colin disappeared to find Keith and Mark.

A short while later back at his hotel, Colin sat in the armchair in his hotel room with his helmet upside down on his lap. He reached forward to the coffee table and picked up a small earpiece speaker, attached by several wires to a miniature electronic circuit board, and fitted it all back into the foam inside the helmet. To test it he then pulled the helmet over his head, switched on the microphone and clicked his tongue a few times to make sure he could hear it through the ear phone.

The four of them very much enjoyed the riding as always. They were very pleased they would not have to meet up with Colin again before Lima, after yesterday's experiences, and there was a liberating feeling as if of children being out of sight of the parent.

On their way through Peru they made an overnight stop at a guest house in downtown Lima when disaster struck.

Chapter 17

Once again Colin was in town to meet the four riders, and was booked into a separate hotel. They had arranged to meet him in the lobby of his hotel at 7pm.

The relevant manager had not been on hand to record their passport details earlier when they had arrived at the guest house. They were invited to let themselves into their rooms, then come back down to reception at 6.30pm before they left to meet Colin. By then the manager would be back.

At just before six thirty the four gathered downstairs in the main reception area. It was full of small groups of tourists arriving to register, or meeting up to go out for the evening. Tommy had put Mark in charge of collecting the passports and taking them to the reception desk. He had a small knapsack, which he was carrying them in for safe keeping. Leaving the others in the main reception area, Mark walked over to the manager's desk and sat down, slipping his knapsack off his shoulder and hooking it over the back of his chair as he did so.

Mark smiled at the manager and they introduced themselves and shook hands. A small crowd of people hurried past behind Mark and bumped into him clumsily, as he introduced himself to the manager.

He reached round for his knapsack to fetch out the passports - but it was gone from the back of the chair. Quickly he turned round but there were just groups of disinterested tourists, involved in their own discussions.

He turned back to the manager. "My bag!" he said with a look of alarm.

"Que?" said the manager.

"Someone's just stolen my bag!" Mark started standing up. He remembered people bumping into him as he had sat down.

"No, no! You must be mistaken," said the manager, trying to placate him.

"No I'm not!" Mark started raising his voice. "Just now, some people barged into me, you must have seen it."

"Please, stay calm, sir," said the manager.

Mark stood up from his chair and started looking urgently round the room, to see if anyone was walking away, or carrying his knapsack.

He turned back to the manager. "Someone's stolen my bag!" he repeated, more desperate.

The manager was unconvinced. Mark walked urgently over to the others, and fetched Tommy.

After some discussion they were able to convince the manager that the bag appeared to have been stolen. He said he was very sorry about it, but they needed to be more careful in crowded places. There was nothing he could do to help. He would allow them to use driving licences to register at the hotel for the moment. Fortunately another of the riders was taking care of these and they could be quickly brought to the desk.

Colin could see something was up when they showed up at his hotel lobby more than thirty minutes late, by the look on their faces.

Tommy explained what had happened taking Colin to one side, away from the others. Colin listened, then looked like he was going to hit the roof. "You've gotta be joking," he said with a serious, slightly quivering face.

Tommy shook his head.

"You're supposed to be keeping a low fucking profile," he hissed, thoroughly infuriated.

Tommy looked at him.

"You've blown it then," Colin fumed.

"What?" said Tommy. "I think you're overacting a bit."

"You can't go on with new passports." Colin snarled back at him. "You'll give the game away instantly."

There was a pause, then Tommy looked at Colin again. "Really?"

"Yes!" Colin was exasperated. "Amateur smugglers always get themselves new passports, they think it makes them look clean."

"Oh shit!" said Tommy.

Colin frowned.

After a few moments Tommy said, "Look, think about it like this Colin. If we had deliberately scuppered our passports, you would be right. But in fact it was a genuine theft. If we get questioned about it we can convincingly all tell the truth, and the same story."

Colin thought about it for a moment, finally he nodded. "Yeah. Alright then," he said. "Just make sure you get police reports and don't for Christ' sake lose them whatever you do."

Therefore instead of going out for a nice meal together, Colin had to go on his own, while the other four traipsed down to the police station for the evening to file reports and get documentation required for replacement passports. It was gone 10pm by the time they were finished, and they ended up in the local McDonald's fast food restaurant, which was still open and provided some calming familiarity.

The following day they had to take the police documentation down to the local British consulate, and wait in a queue all morning to apply for new passports. There were complications at the consulate, and it was going to take some days to get new passports. This delayed the schedule. Colin was predictably irritable and went off ahead leaving them to wait in Lima. There was nothing much of interest to the riders to do in Lima. They sloped into the local bars by about midmorning most days, if not before and stayed there until bed time. They found the stay in Lima tedious and frustrating.

All four were thankful that they didn't have to see Colin again until they would meet up in Colombia as arranged. The first evening when they arrived in Colombia, as soon as Colin came to meet them at the hotel, he told them he was a bit fed up with them all. They kept letting him down, getting drunk too much, making too many errors. While Tommy, Mark and Keith seemed prepared to accept Colin's domineering attitude for the moment, this riled John immediately, and he stomped straight off in to town, to get drunk on purpose.

There was not much to do in Colombia for the next couple of weeks. Before long all of the four were following John's example, and forgetting Colin's admonishment, started spending most of the time in the local bars, drinking and playing pool. Also trying to get laid with various levels of success. In fact they were only successful with the local women if they were overt prostitutes, and even then not all the time.

Some drank more than others. John in particular was able to put away serious quantities of alcohol on a daily basis. Colin was getting increasingly wound up by all this, which perhaps was John's intention. Colin tried to remind them that he expected them to keep a low profile, but this only seemed to goad John on further.

One evening a few days before their planned departure, Colin felt he had had enough, and ordered a group meeting in his hotel room. To the four riders amazement he gave them a dressing down as though a headmaster admonishing naughty school boys.

"If you don't start bucking up your ideas," he said amidst lots of finger wagging, "I will just call the whole thing off, and send you home empty handed.

"You can sign ownership of the bikes back to me before you go. Got it?"

No one said anything.

"So if you're not sure whether you can do what I ask of you, just say so now!"

Silence.

"Go on! Now's your chance. You can sign over ownership of the bikes now. To me. And go home. Your job will be done."

Still no replies.

"Well, if you don't want to quit right now, then you'd better start following my instructions."

They were so stunned that they agreed and left in silence without remonstrating, on Tommy's recommendation. Once alone however they looked at each other astonished, and complained loudly about how they couldn't believe this guy's attitude. That evening they managed to all keep sober but they were still seething. John in particular had a big problem whenever anyone took it upon themselves to tell him what to do. "Who the heck does he think he is," he said again and again. That evening for a change, they were not drunk but were still fed up with Colin when they went off to bed.

The next morning by about eleven am however John had already forgotten his gripe with Colin, as he staggered out of a bar, back into the daylight. He had been there since 8am. Having been encouraged by a sign on the wall which read "Beer, so much more than a breakfast drink," he had now managed to sink ten large bottles of the stuff and his stomach was starting to rumble. His irritation with Colin was completely forgotten. Looking forward to a good breakfast he weaved out onto the street and up the hill towards a small café. On the way he found himself walking past a bricklayer. He had also noticed him three hours earlier when he was walking to the bar. The bricklayer had already started work even before the bar had opened at 8am. Now John was able to survey the fellow's handy work of the previous several hours.

John was a friendly chap, especially after a few beers and couldn't help himself announcing to the brick layer, who was stooped over the knee high wall he was building, "Nah, mate!"

The builder stopped what he was doing, trowel in hand and looked round to see John leaning over him. He stared up at John. "Que?" he said.

"Nah, mate!" repeated John. "You're doing it all wrong."

The bricklayer looked at him.

Grabbing up a brick and a spare trowel and stooping down beside the builder, John proceeded to give him a demonstration.

The builder was impressed with John's brick laying skills, even though he was half drunk. They also seemed to get along. After a while the builder promised to buy John lunch at the café, if John would do some bricklaying for him that afternoon. This was a plan that appealed to John. However after they had eaten, John added a new part to the deal which was that he would buy them a beer each before they started. Predictably perhaps, one beer led to six or so.

Incredibly the pair of them managed to get an amazing amount of high quality work done even after all the beers.

By the time it was getting dark, they both stood back to admire their afternoon's work. It was impressive. "Thank you my crazy English friend," said the bricklayer. "You are a remarkably skilled man."

"Thank you, Senor!" John put his arm round the neck of his new found pal.

John was really quite drunk however, and somehow tripped on something. Losing his balance he staggered backwards, and grabbed the bricklayer for support. But John was a large man by this stage and few would have had the power to hold him up. They both fell backwards onto the wall, the beautiful wall they had spent the afternoon laying. Of course the cement was not properly dry and their combined weight was enough to knock the entire wall over. A length perhaps 10 metres long and a meter or more high, came down in a kind of long Mexican wave.

"I am so sorry, my friend," wailed John from flat on his back looking incomprehensibly at the flattened wall.

His new found companion clambered to his feet and stood gaping at John still lying on the floor, and at the extent of the destroyed brickwork. "What have you done?" he cried, putting his hands to his head. "It's a whole day's work!"

"My new friend, please forgive me," John continued to wail.

"You stupid English idiot!" screamed the man in Spanish. He was not taking it well. John started to clamber onto his knees to stand up. His new friend however had lost his rag at seeing a day's work and a ton of bricks wasted. In his fury while John was still on his hands and knees the bricklayer aimed a strong kick at John's ample midriff. It winded John, and was a serious assault in his eyes. This changed the situation. John stood up and drew himself to his full height. The bricklayer stood in front of him. "You are a top grade idiot!" he screamed again at John.

Now John took a swing, struck the man on the chin and knocked him clean off his feet, and onto his back. A small group of young Colombian men happened to walk round the corner at that moment, and simply saw John knocking down a hard working brick layer. Then they noticed the flattened wall. John looked somewhat dishevelled, drunk and was being thoroughly aggressive. Assuming him to be a crazy foreigner who had simply laid out the wall and attacked the worker, they all sprinted over intent on giving him a good hiding. While perhaps not the fit young man he once was, John was nevertheless heftily built and experienced in both karate and jujitsu. He was able to give just as good as he got.

Someone across the street in a shop or a house had noticed the fracas and called the police. On hearing a foreigner was involved they arrived very quickly from a local station just round the corner while the fight was still in full swing. Outnumbered though he was, John was still holding his own. As a couple of policemen came up behind him to grab hold of him, John assumed they were more thugs trying to attack him and started taking swings at the uniformed law men. It took five of them to eventually wrestle him, subdue him and pin him face down on the ground.

John was handcuffed and marched off, put in a car and driven to some local holding cells. He was processed in an office in an old brick building, then led down a corridor and down the stairs to the cells. At the bottom of the stairs he looked at the cells and couldn't believe what he saw.

John had spent the odd night in police cells in the UK for drunk and disorderly but this was a different ball game. It was like a real life dungeon. There was a tiny barred skylight just below the ceiling which allowed only a very dim light. The walls were covered with mould and slime. The floor was three inches deep in stagnant water mixing with raw sewage. Here and there, oily looking rats ran along the edges. John could see two large barred cells. One was empty, the other had about twenty people crowded into it; local drunks, and homeless crazies, the dregs of society. Some of them stood almost ankle deep in the fetid water. As many as could had crowded onto two uncovered, rusted steel bed steads. There were no mattresses and they sat balancing on the bare springs trying to keep their feet out of the putrid water. A toilet hole on a raised platform in the corner was completely filthy. It did not seem to have any flush

...ism. The hot damp air hung everywhere with a foul stench, and the bellows and ...s of the other inmates.

...rveying this abysmal scene, John's heart sank into his toes. To his immense relief, he was at least taken into the empty cell. Thankfully the guards considered it too risky to put the foreigner in with the local lunatics and rowdies. Some in the adjacent cell began to shout to him in Spanish, which John ignored as he plodded slowly through the three inches of water, taking care to minimise splashing it on his legs too much. As the barred door was slammed shut and the bolt locked tight, John sat gingerly onto the rickety and wobbling spring bed frame, lifting his legs up carefully out of the water.

The steel bars dividing the cells were about four inches apart, narrow enough to prevent anyone invading from the other cell, but not wide enough to prevent some of them keep spitting at him. Thankfully his bed was against the far wall so they missed, mostly. He had given the guards upstairs the number of Colin's hotel, and told them Colin would post bail for him immediately. The guards told him he would have to wait in the cells while they contacted Colin. John could only hope it would not take too long.

Two or three hours later at around seven pm, the other three riders were gathering in the lounge at Colin's hotel to meet with Colin. They had arranged to go out for a meal together. It was to be Colin's treat, a kind of thank you for listening to him the previous evening and taking on board his requests. The three had now arrived and were sitting in armchairs, round a coffee table in the hotel lounge together with Colin, drinking coffee. The threat of forfeiting a quarter million pounds each had been sufficient as Colin had thought it should be, to bring them all back into line.

By the time Colin looked at his watch, it was already seven thirty. "Anyone seen John?" he asked.

The others shook their heads. "Nope," said Tommy. "Not since last night."

At that moment a waiter came over carrying a phone. "Mr Monahan, sir?"

"Yes?"

"A phone call for you." He handed Colin the phone.

As Colin listened to the phone call, his face became increasingly purple until it almost looked as though steam was going to come out of his ears.

He was in fact so apoplectic that he could barely explain to the others where he was off to, and muttered something about coming back in a little while.

Catching a taxi from the hotel, Colin was driven down the station where John was being held. He marched in absolutely furious.

He had to wait a little while before he was taken to sit at a desk with a uniformed official, who explained that John had been in a fight and was being held pending a thousand dollar bond. If Colin was prepared to pay, they would release him immediately.

"Where is he now?" asked Colin.

"He's downstairs in the cells."

"Can I see?"

Colin was taken to the top of the steps leading down towards the cells. The official gestured, inviting him to descend. Colin walked a few steps down then paused so that only the bottom part of his legs - up to his knees - were visible from below. He had seen enough. "Ok thank you," Colin said quietly, turning back up the stairs. He followed the official back to the desk where they sat down again to do the paper work.

"What happens if I don't pay the bond," Colin asked casually.

The official looked like he thought it was a strange question. "He will stay in the cell."

"For how long?"

"He will go to court after a couple of weeks," the official said.

Colin thought for a moment, then reached into his pocket, and pulled out a wallet. He began to count out a thousand dollars' worth of bills. Half way through counting, he stopped.

"Do I have to pay the bond now?" he asked the guard.

"Yes, if you want to release him."

Colin nodded. He thought for another moment or two, then suddenly closed his wallet and put it back in his pocket, with the money still inside it. "Thank you officer," he said, standing up. "I'll come back."

The guard was a bit surprised but nodded, stood up and showed Colin to the door.

Chapter 18

Back in the hotel sitting again with the others, Colin explained that; because John hadn't listened to his advice, he was now stuck in a filthy prison cell, and there was nothing Colin could do to help him. They then went to the most expensive restaurant Colin could find and under strict instruction had the most expensive items on the menu. Colin ordered plenty of very expensive wine, and said he didn't mind how drunk they got tonight. They all managed to restrain themselves nevertheless, and remained relatively sober.

Colin finally paid John's bond and secured his release at about 8am the following morning.

John was so pleased to be out of the cell, and so ravenously hungry that there was no time for any recriminations towards Colin, right now. Perhaps John considered that revenge was a dish best served cold.

Indeed, after his experience in prison, John even reduced his drinking a little, for a few days anyway. During the remainder of the stay in Colombia, all four riders were relatively well behaved and sober.

The afternoon of the day before departure, the four bikes were wheeled into Juan Pablo's father's workshop one by one. His father had another larger workshop on site at his dealership, and had rarely used his home workshop for two or three years. Juan Pablo had moved out of his parent's home into a small flat of his own, but still returned regularly to use the workshop for his own eclectic projects, and to visit his parents. So he still held onto his own set of keys to the house and workshop. Juan Pablo's mother never visited the workshop, and his father was not the prying nosey type, so it was unlikely they would be disturbed.

With four bikes to prepare, and only Colin and Juan Pablo doing the work, they started removing tyres, soon after two pm.

Juan Pablo had already bought the cocaine. They were paying a thousand US dollars per kilo. It came to a little over eighty thousand dollars, which Colin gave to Juan Pablo in cash beforehand. Such an amount was nothing to Colin these days. He still had about six hundred thousand pounds sterling in cash to his name; equivalent to about a million US dollars, plus ownership of the house and club he had purchased cheaply at auction, as well as the four big motorbikes which, while owned on paper by each rider, would be returned to him for sale back to a dealer after they arrived back in London.

Just as before, there was to be 10 kilos per wheel for each bike, however since the rear wheel was larger it could take about 12 to 14 keys. The front wheel could take the remaining eight or so. A few extra keys were fitted into the tyres using any remaining spaces that could be found.

It took several hours to pack the coke, which they had wrapped, carefully vacuum packed and masking taped in black plastic bin liners. The sealed packages were then fed into each inner tube. Unlike before when they had cut along the length of the seam on the inside of the inner tubes, as per Juan Pablo's genius suggestion, this time they simply cut a small slit on the inside of each tube. The coke packages were fed through the slit and pushed around the tube to fill it. They then sealed the slit again with a puncture repair patch, to make it airtight with the drugs hidden inside.

The inner tubes were replaced on the wheels which were then fitted back onto the bikes. After inflating the tubes to almost full pressure, each bike was tested by sitting on it and bouncing a little. Then Colin took each one for a small ride on the track outside the workshop, keeping under 5mph. Following the previous trip, John and Brendan had complained that handling was tricky with the extra weight in the wheels at anything over about 5mph, so Colin had already planned a slightly new route and arranged vehicular transport to avoid any but the most essential riding. By 8pm, he and Juan Pablo were finished. They left the workshop, locking everything carefully with the keys, and went back inside the house to have supper with Juan Pablo's entirely oblivious parents.

At 10 am on a late November morning in 1995, the four riders, who had walked from the hotel, arrived on schedule at the workshop. Colin and Juan Pablo were already there, and the bikes had been wheeled outside in preparation to be loaded into a truck sufficiently large to carry all four machines. Colin's bike was also there, on which he would follow them to Bogota.

A rental car had been hired to complete the convoy. John would drive the four riders in it to Bogota. It still needed collecting, so John and Tommy took Colin's bike, with Tommy riding pillion, to collect the car. Meanwhile, the others began pushing the large bikes up the ramps into the truck, where they were secured with fitted straps designed for the purpose.

Shortly after the four bikes were loaded, the rental car appeared, being driven by John up the dirt track which joined the lane in front of the house with the workshop, with Tommy following on Colin's bike. Now with the vehicles ready in the gravel parking area in front of the workshop, they all walked through the back garden and round the house into the front garden to sit at the garden table and have a final coffee. Juan Pablo fetched coffee cups, a sugar bowl and a plate of biscuits on a silver tray, while the others made sure they had gathered all documents and luggage correctly.

Before he had a chance to go and fetch the canteen of coffee, Juan Pablo's mother appeared out of the house, and carried it towards them across the lawn. Smiling broadly, she placed it on the table and stood hands on hips looking at them all with admiration. She thought it was a terribly exciting and noble escapade, to be touring South America on motorbikes. She was absolutely thrilled for the explorers, she said, as she helped them make sure they had organised all their belongings.

"Why are you taking the bikes in the truck?" she asked Tommy, shortly before they set off, and quite unaware her son had the day before loaded slightly over twenty kilograms of top quality cocaine into the tyres of each one.

Thinking on his feet Tommy said, "Oh, well, you know, it's a lot of fun riding in a foreign country and all, but it's also a lot of fun to drive too. You get a different perspective on the landscape. Also we thought it's a good way to include Juan Pablo in a piece of the adventure."

"That's very good of you," she said. "He's such an honest boy."

Finally, Juan Pablo's mum stood at the end of her garden path and waved her handkerchief at the departing convoy. She wiped a tear of pride from her eye for these wonderful lads who had invested their own time and money to travel such a long way around the globe. These young men, who had generously included her own son in their adventure. And yet who, in return asked for nothing but cultural enlightenment and innocent experience. They truly were angels, an inspiration to anyone. She kept waving her handkerchief until they disappeared from sight.

For the three in the car with John, in particular, it was a fascinating road trip through the Andes and into the tropical plains as they approached Bogota. That evening they stayed in the same guest house as on previous trips, with the four bikes still in the lorry. About midday the next day they drove out to the domestic airport, and unloaded the four bikes. Colin would follow on his bike. He was also travelling through Leticia, however was booked on a flight for the next day. He felt there may be a risk that if a porter were to wheel one of the other bikes with an extra 20kg in the tyres, and then his bike, which was the same model and size, they may detect the difference of weight in the wheels and become suspicious.

Therefore four bikes were loaded onto the plane. The four riders said cheerio to Juan Pablo and Colin, and boarded the plane to take their seats. There was still nothing for any of them to feel remotely concerned about yet, since they would not be crossing any checked boarders until Rio. Or so they thought. This was still very much like a holiday, or travel adventure for them, and they were relaxed and having an enjoyable time. Particularly now they were out of Colin's sight again.

They arrived in Leticia, and retrieved the bikes safely from the plane. John knew the ropes and led the way out of the airport and into town. John and Tommy wheeled their bikes on foot, while Keith and Mark rode alongside or ahead, keeping to 5mph. It was only a twenty minute walk into the town centre.

Once there they stopped for the traditional coke smuggler's beer at one of the café's, then made their way down to the port to book a boat. It was about four thirty pm and they hoped to make way that evening. There was a slight alteration to the previous trips. Instead of disembarking at Manaus and taking a domestic flight to Rio, this time they would continue in more luxurious boats with cabins,

along the Amazon to Belem, a busy port city on the East coast of the continent and situated in the mouth of the Amazon. From there, Colin had hired a removal lorry and drivers to transport the bikes by road down to Rio.

During his research, Colin had discovered that there was only one river boat from Leticia that travelled all the way to Belem and which could carry the four bikes. He had timed their arrival in Leticia so they could board that boat and depart the same evening as he didn't want them to be stuck in Leticia. If they had been bored in Juan Pablo's town, they would probably cause a riot in a small village like this. He therefore specifically arranged it so they would not have to spend time waiting for a boat there. The plan was that Colin would then arrive the next day and follow them down the river one day behind. As he only had the one bike he had more choice of boats, and would be able to change boats at Manaus to arrive in Belem actually on the same day as them. This was because the four riders' boat was scheduled for an overnight stop in Manaus.

The four riders loaded the bikes onto the boat on which they had been booked, and walked back into town to buy hammocks, on John's advice, and to get something to eat in the food market.

They had a few beers to help them sleep on the boat which they boarded at about seven pm. It was already dark, and they were quite drunk so they slung up their hammocks on the bottom deck and crashed out. It was very hot and very humid and there were clouds of insects everywhere. When they awoke they would be sailing through the Amazon rainforest and away from the insects... or so they all thought.

Each of them woke at various times through the evening and night time, and noticed the boat was still in port. They slapped at a mosquito maybe and went back to sleep. At dawn the next day, all the passengers in the hammocks began to wake up and scratch the numerous itching insect bites they had accumulated during the night. The hammock deck was about half full.

The four bike riders were the only foreign tourists. It was immediately evident as soon as they opened their eyes, that they were still moored at port.

"What's going on?" people started to say in Portuguese as they rubbed the sleep out of their eyes and swung their legs out of the hammocks.

After a little while and gathering commotion one of the boat staff emerged from the boat house, apparently to make an announcement.

Keith Mark and Tommy all looked over to John, as he made the trip before, to see if he knew what was going on. But John looked as mystified as anyone.

"Can I have your attention please," said the boat staff first in Portuguese, then again in English. Bleary eyed passengers sat up grumpily and turned round in their hammocks to face him.

"We have not yet departed Leticia," he explained carefully.

"No shit, Sherlock," said Keith, to giggles from Mark.

"This is due to a major engine failure." There were some groans. He went on in Portuguese first, English second, "We must now wait for a new engine part to be delivered from Manaus."

"How long will it take?" people started calling out questions in Portuguese. The next bit was all in Portuguese which none of the four could follow. A very friendly fellow passenger offered to interpret it for them.

"One at a time please... We expect to fix it this afternoon. However if you wish to change to another vessel we have arranged that your tickets can be transferred to a smaller boat leaving this afternoon, however you will need to change boats at Manaus in that case if you are continuing on to Belem."

People began approaching the boat staff asking various questions. The four riders thanked their interpreter, then looked at each other. "Screw that," said John, "I'm not sitting here all day with all these stupid mosquitos. If it's coming from Manaus and that's three days away it's not gonna arrive this afternoon. Let's unload the bikes and go on the other boat."

The others agreed. They couldn't afford a delay of more than a couple of days without missing the departure in Rio. "I don't know why he's cut it so fine," John complained to the others about the lack of flexibility in the schedule, as they packed up their hammocks.

John spoke to the boat staff, and arranged to leave the bikes on the boat until the other boat arrived that afternoon, then they all traipsed into town to look for something to do.

Beers at the café it was. By 8am the sun was coming up and they were already a little tipsy.

They spent the day wandering from café to bar. One place had a couple of pool tables so they shot a few rounds. By lunch time the beer had more or less stopped working and they moved onto the local whisky. At about three pm, pissed out of their heads, they staggered back down towards the port. Locating the boat with their bikes, they nodded at the guard. He recognised them and let them board. "Have they fixshed the enginnsh?" asked John. The guard shook his head and waved his hand at the stench of alcohol. "You see?" said John, vindicated. Their boat was not going to be fixed today. Clumsily they managed to unload the bikes. One at least almost tipped over the side into the river, but they managed to hold on to it, just, amid fits of giggles from the four and alternate looks of amusement and alarm from the guard.

Once on land they lined up with the bikes at the jetty where they expected the Manaus boat to appear, so they would be first in the queue. The boat still wasn't due for an hour.

They stood by the bikes in the afternoon sun, smoking rollups and sharing a bottle of whisky they had bought from a shop on the way down. About four pm, a bit ahead of schedule, the boat drew round a bend in the river, and into view. "There it is," called out John.

"Oi! You lot!" A voice they all recognised rang out from behind them.

They turned round to see Colin wheeling his bike down the road towards their jetty. Even though he was not carrying anything in the tyres, it still seemed a bit impolite to ride such a large bike through such a small town, he had considered, so he was wheeling it and the engine was not running.

"What's going on?" he demanded as he approached them, catching site of the bottle of whisky Tommy was currently holding.

"Ah! Alright Colin?" they called, a little half-heartedly on John's part perhaps.

"What's going on?" he said again as he kicked his bike stand open and walked over to where they were standing.

"Our boat's gone an' broken down, di'nit," said John at last.

"You're all fucking pissed, aren't you!" said Colin, looking at them accusingly.

"Well, not pissed," they countered, "we've been drinking a bit."

"But what are you doing with the bikes."

"That was John's idea," Keith and Mark said, almost together.

Colin looked at John. "Well?" he said.

"They're gonna take ages to fix our boat," John explained to Colin.

"But what are you doing with the bikes?" said Colin, getting annoyed.

"We're gonna put them on this boat," said John, nodding at the approaching boat. "Change at Manaus to Belem."

"No you can't!" said Colin.

There was a pause. "Why not?"

"It can't take all four bikes you stupid twerps. That's why I booked you on the Belem boat, which is a cargo boat, and it's the only one big enough with a low enough draught to take them altogether. You have to stay on that one. What's wrong with you?"

"Alright Colin," said John. "Stop having a go at everyone, will you? We can go on two separate boats then can't we, two bikes on each."

"No!" yelled Colin.

"Why not? What difference?" John yelled back.

Colin looked at him for a moment then finally said through gritted teeth, "Look! I want you to go on the cargo vessel because I want to test something for a future project. Alright?"

John looked at the sky, exasperated. "Oh, ok then. We'll just have to go and load them back on the other boat again, and wait then. So problem solved. So you can calm down now. Ok?"

"You could lose your place on the other boat couldn't you," said Colin. "And I keep telling you to stop getting pissed, and keep a low profile."

For a minute John looked like he might hit Colin. "Calm down fellas," Tommy started mediating. "I'll run down to the other boat, and make sure our places are reserved, you can start bringing the bikes over."

Tommy disappeared off to the other jetty. He boarded the bigger boat, then re-appeared a few moments later, whistled, and beckoned the others to come over with the bikes. Their places were still available.

"You see?" said John to Colin. "You get too worked up about things."

"Ok, perhaps you're right, I'll try to take things a bit easier," said Colin. "Just keep a low profile, is all I'm asking."

"Just keep a low profile," John muttered under his breath, mimicking Colin just out of ear shot, which made Keith giggle.

Soon after, they re-loaded the bikes on the first boat, even though there was still no sign of the replacement parts. "Maybe tomorrow," said the boat staff when John asked if they still expected it to be fixed today.

This was very irritating to the four who didn't want to spend another night being bitten by mosquitos.

After disembarking again, they watched Colin load his bike onto the Manaus boat, then they all went into town for food, 'breakfast' for the four riders who had been surviving all day on liquid sustenance. They returned to the port and hung around until Colin departed ahead of them towards Manaus where he would wait for them to catch up. They then went into town to find a guest house to spend the night.

Unfortunately it seemed they had left it too late to find a vacant room in a guest house. They were all full for the night with other tourists so amidst plenty of cussing and cursing they had to return to their boat to spend a second miserably hot and airless night getting bitten by mosquitos in their hammocks.

Chapter 19

The following morning, they enquired about the engine. "Not today, maybe tomorrow," they were told. This didn't lift their spirits any. All feeling rather hung over from the previous day's alcohol consumption, they felt too ill for breakfast so went instead in search of beer again. "Hair o' the dog," they affirmed to each other.

They stopped after a couple of beers however, and made sure to find a guest house for the night before all the vacancies became filled up again.

Day after day they checked on the boat, but still there was no development. Leticia was an interesting town to pass through perhaps but there was little there to interest the four riders for days on end. They went on a couple of jungle tours. They found a local brothel which they spent a bit of time at. Except for John, who refrained out of a sense of loyalty to his wife. Tommy bought a toy fishing rod and did a bit of river fishing. They played a few rounds of pool some afternoons. Mostly they drank beer and whiskey from dawn to dusk and grew increasingly frustrated.

One afternoon they discovered a bar in a shack on the outskirts of the town, in the edges of the forest, which advertised mushroom tea on a blackboard outside. These were local forest psychedelic mushrooms. This seemed like an exciting prospect and they ordered a large mug full each. The barman was a friendly local man who prepared a large brown china teapot for them, full to the brim of tea swimming with mushrooms.

It was not very pleasant to drink, but they forced it down. Soon they were all finding everything highly amusing and repeatedly collapsing in ever more hysterical fits of giggles. Except for Tommy who seemed to have gotten left out. Tommy was upset that his mug of tea didn't seem to have worked and started looking in the teapot for any remaining mushrooms. The more fed up he looked, the funnier the others found it. Scooping the remaining 'shrooms from the teapot, Tommy downed these. However perhaps he had now over done it, as he completely bypassed the giggling stage and went straight into full blown psychedelia.

Soon all four of them were in the middle of a super powerful trip. John actually thought he could smell colours. When he looked at things the colours didn't flow to his eyes so much as flowed to his nose, and when he breathed in he could smell them, he said.

Seemingly in another world entirely, Tommy lay on his back and stared at the sun high in the sky for so long that he dazzle himself and couldn't see anything. Even when he stood up and tried to walk around, he discovered he had rendered himself entirely blind and could see nothing but flashing lights, which subsided slightly over time, but never disappeared. "It's great!" he would tell people years afterwards, as he gazed into space, waving his hands about his front of him. "Really

entertaining."

Only Keith did not enjoy it so much. At one point he realised he couldn't remember his hotel room number. Then he began to convince himself he couldn't remember anything. He got so freaked out that when he came down, he still thought he'd lost his power of memory. This made him so alarmed that the very next day he went straight back and ordered another mug of mushroom tea on his own, in the hope of finding it again. Unfortunately this only made matters worse, and he was convinced for several days afterwards, that he had he'd blown his faculty of memory. "Don' worry Keith, mate," John said consolingly, "your memory was never all that anyway."

By dusk they were finally beginning to mellow out a little when they noticed some rustling in the bushes around the bar shack. Out of the trees native tribespeople began to appear. They were mainly young people with traditional decorative mud on their bodies, and exotic minimalist loin cloths, and bare feet.

At first it was a couple of people. They ignored the four tripping tourists sitting round a table outside the bar shack, and started to follow the path into town. Behind them more tribespeople followed. All young people, not children, but young adults; teenagers. More of them came through the bushes and followed the path into town. It was an amazing sight for the four men. Especially after drinking mushroom tea. It made for a spectacular visual experience. Yet the four riders were baffled by the growing procession. Their barman had long since disappeared and left them to it. Now there were even more tribespeople appearing. There were dozens and dozens, all in their native garb, emerging from the bushes and following the path into town.

The four of them, slowly coming back to their senses, looked in amazed wonderment.

After a while, the tribespeople stopped emerging from the forest and the four men watched the last of them disappear down the track.

"What was all that about?" said someone.

"It was amazing," said Keith, talking about the site of the traditional dress the people were wearing, and the sense of natural wildness that that they had about them.

"Where are they going?"

"What are they doing?"

The four were clueless.

"What's going on?" said Tommy, rubbing his eyes and testing his vision.

The four continued to sit at the table in the fading twilight and started smoking some hash that Keith had purchased in a bar in town to ease the come down from the mushrooms. Some minutes later Tommy as he regained some vision, had the fright of his life. So stunned was he that for a moment he couldn't even speak, and just opened and closed his mouth like a fish. For in the distance emerging on the track from the town direction, he could see a zombie!

He gaped and pointed but as though in a bad dream no sound came out of his mouth and the other three ignored him. Now it got worse, there were more zombies and Tommy finally managed to get the word out. "Zombies!" he uttered, pointing. The others looked round. Then John laughed. It was true, they did really look like zombies. It was the tribes' teenagers re-emerging from the town. Only now they were walking in a very slow, peculiar, stiff legged way. Each was stooping at the shoulders and looking downward. Each held a faint glowing light in their hand which shone on their face.

As they approached it was possible to see what they were doing. They were each holding a 'Gameboy' contemporary hand held computer game console. They were playing computer games as they walked. That was what they had all been traipsing into town for; replacement batteries for their consoles. It now seemed immensely funny to the four tourists.

However in the next moment Tommy was freaking out at something else. His eyes were working only intermittently as he continued to look down the track towards town where the tribespeople were re appearing, in the half-light of dusk he was convinced he saw something else.

"Look! Look!" he managed to cry out.

The others looked round again to where he was pointing. They could see the track and a few straggling tribes' people in the gathering dusk.

"What is it?" said Mark.

Tommy was almost choking in his efforts to articulate. Unable somehow to get any words out, he kept pointing desperately.

"What?" said the others, exasperated.

"I saw…"

"What?"

"… Colin!"

"Eh? Colin?" They looked at Tommy, stunned, then looked back down the track. Peering into the gathering gloom of nightfall. They couldn't see anything but the track and the last straggling tribespeople.

"Where?"

"He was there. I am sure it was him."

"Nah," said John, disbelieving.

"I am telling you, I just saw Colin," said Tommy.

The others didn't know what to make of this. None of them had seen him. They began to suspect that Tommy was still hallucinating.

Before long the barman re-appeared, and they ordered some food and drinks before they headed back into town.

*

Eventually, one morning after at least a week, and a few days after the mushroom trip, they were given the welcome news that their boat was finally ready to go. They would finally be able to continue their journey, that afternoon.

They checked out of the guest house before lunchtime, and carried their rucksacks down to put on the boat for the day. The bikes had remained on the boat the whole time. Early that evening, they left Leticia as promised.

There was not much to see from the boat in the dark, but there didn't seem to be much chance of sleeping. The top deck was semi open air, with tables and chairs where the Brazilian passengers played Dominoes and Connect Four. They chatted to each other happily and incessantly in loud voices, to hear themselves above the Brazilian techno and pop which blared from large speakers raised above the deck. The blaring music continued through most of the night. The following morning in the daylight, the sights and sounds astonished the three who had not cruised the Amazon before. For John who had followed the same route just six months previously, it all seemed very familiar.

They meandered down the river for three days. When they arrived at Manaus, to their surprise they saw that Colin was standing, already waiting on the pier. He had been able to discover the estimated time of arrival at a local travel agent, he explained.

Chapter 20

The boat with the four bikes was due to stay overnight in Manaus, so they all went into town to find some food. Later that day Colin would set off downriver towards Belem. Over lunch, he explained where he and Juan Pablo would collect them from at the port with the lorry, once they arrived. After the delay with the riverboat engine, Colin had been unable to postpone the booking he had made with the removal lorry, and instead was forced to cancel it, causing him to forgo his small cash deposit, much to his annoyance. Also he had been chatting with Juan Pablo in Bogota a few days previously about how Juan Pablo and possibly his older brother could both get a bit more involved. Through procuring ever larger quantities of cocaine for Colin, Juan Pablo had become acquainted with some relatively senior dealers who operated on the periphery of a local drug cartel. Observing the amount of cash Colin had floating around him these days, both Juan Pablo and his brother Federo had become interested in obtaining a slice of the pie.

After cancelling the removal lorry, Colin's first idea then had been to ask Juan Pablo and his brother to drive the bikes in another truck. Colin had flown back to Bogota leaving his own bike in Manaus, and met with Juan Pablo and Federo to discuss everything. As a sign of their commitment to any future efforts, they offered to provide the transportation for free. Colin was very pleased to accept this. It was agreed that if they were stopped by the police, and the cocaine was discovered, on this occasion unlike with the trip to Bogota recently, for which Juan Pablo had received remuneration, Federo and Juan Pablo would be free to deny any knowledge of the drugs, because they were not getting paid. Therefore, full responsibility for the contraband at all times lay with the nominal owners of the bikes, that is the four riders. Who, in a worst case scenario would be looking at about thirty years apiece.

They were all around thirty to forty years old so that meant; for most of their lives. They each had family and small children at home. It would probably be the children who would get hit the hardest by it. Success on the other hand would mean; pretty much never having to do another day's work again, and much improved chances for the futures of their children. A top private school: Eton perhaps. Who knew?

Each bike had twenty kilos or slightly more of cocaine. At wholesale prices that was worth £500 000 GBP per vehicle. Even after Colin had taken his 50% and he also absorbed about £15 000 costs per bike, each rider stood to net £250 000 tax free. That was equivalent to about $400 000 USD, per rider. It was a life changing sum of money. These weren't the sort of guys who might have gotten talked into putting a kilo or five in their bag by a stranger on a vacation. They were too smart to fall for that sort of trick. However this was a different proposition entirely. Colin's method was far superior to anything anyone had ever come across, and appeared to have essentially 100% chance of success. Putting the drugs in inflated tyres was sheer genius.

It seemed inconceivable that someone could get a substantial amount of drugs inside inflated inner tubes. With such life changing sums of money involved, the only question for them had been: what is the chance of getting away with it? They considered the chance of getting through was so large using Colin's method, that the risk of getting caught was negligible. Even at thirty years in prison such a low risk at such a high return was for no shortage of people, without a question worth the gamble.

Colin arranged for the two brothers to collect the bikes in Belem and transport them to Rio. Federo and Juan Pablo would be able to rent a truck locally in Belem, and drop it off at the depot in Rio, after the bikes had been unloaded at the port.

*

After lunch the five of them spent the afternoon wandering around Manaus town centre. Towards the harbour area the explored some of the local-produce open air, and covered food markets.

More or less directly in the remote centre of the Amazon rainforest, Manaus was incongruously, a large bustling metropolis. It had wide roads of several lanes in each direction full of new cars of every major make, decades old busses, numerous taxis and tuk-tuks, and hundreds of little motorbikes buzzing everywhere. The air was thick with the pollution of all the traffic.

Architecturally it was an interesting mixture of shanty town, new high rise office blocks, apartment buildings, and enormous brick colonial era buildings, painted in simple, vibrant two colour designs. Some of these big old buildings were decorated like giant Wedgewood jasperware pottery pieces, Colin thought. Here and there were the pointy spires of churches, seemingly from about every era since the Jesuits five hundred years before, until the present day.

It seemed almost every street was lined with market stalls under large faded canvas garden sun shades and awnings, selling tropical fruits, vegetables, clothes items, plastic containers, pots and pans, or touristic souvenirs.

Near the harbour was an enormous open air market, and a covered food market that seemed to sell mostly fish. Endless rows of metal tables were piled several feet high with fresh catches of glistening fish, from red bellied piranha to peacock bass, and from catfish to giant Jurassic pirarucu. In some places, long lines of linen aproned and white hatted workers stood wielding dangerous looking, long and pointed steel knives, which flashed as they gutted or prepared fish at lightning speed, with the expert skill and dexterity born of many years' experience.

"It stinks of fish!" exclaimed Tommy, pulling the neck of his shirt up, to cover his nose. "Yeah, let's get out of here," agreed some of the others. They started making their way out towards the harbour, into the open air.

"Stinks worse than that mushroom tea!" said Keith, and they laughed.

"You got your memory back!" said John, which delighted Keith.

"What's he on about?" Colin asked Mark, who explained to him about when they had taken the mushroom tea in the bar in the jungle, which story amused Colin immensely.

"Have you ever seen that bar?" John asked Colin.

"No, I don't think so," said Colin, without missing a beat, continuing to smile at the banter. "Sounds like a lot of fun, though."

By now they had reached the harbour.

*

A road ran along the top of the red harbour wall which was about 4 metres high. On the wide mud beach below, they could see workers carrying sacks of food, or large metal gas cylinders back and forth, to and from the numerous river boats moored to several piers. In front of them stretched the expanse of water, about two kilometres wide. They had emerged from the far bank in the riverboats from Leticia on the River Solimoes, Colin explained.

"I thought that was the Amazon," said Tommy.

"Most people refer to that as the Amazon, but technically it is called the Rio Solimoes," Colin continued. "Here in Manaus it joins the River Negro to become the River Amazon proper, and the largest body of moving water in the world."

"I think you will find that is the Nile," said Tommy. "I remember. We covered that at school. In geography," he added informatively.

"The Nile is the longest river. The Amazon moves the most water, more than the next seven rivers put together," Colin went on. "It's over ten kilometres wide in places. In the rainy season that can increase to almost fifty kilometres. The mouth at the estuary is two hundred and fifty kilometres wide."

"Whew! Over a hundred and fifty miles wide!" Keith whistled.

"Someone's been reading his guidebook," sneered John.

"Here in fact we are still on the River Negro," continued Colin. "You can see it's a completely different colour to the Solimoes."

It was true. They had seen the colour of the water change while they were on the riverboat earlier. From Leticia it had been the colour of caramel. As they exited the Solimoes and headed over to Manaus on the far bank, after half a kilometre or so it had suddenly changed from caramel to cherry cola. It was remarkable because the two colours did not mix but stayed quite separate, with a ragged but distinct edge, like the bite in a chocolate biscuit.

"For some reason," Colin explained further, "although no-one knows what it is, the two rivers never mix, but flow separately alongside each other for many miles."

"Isn't that your boat about to leave?" said John. Colin looked over, momentarily alarmed. Then looked at his watch. "Not yet," he said.

"We'll walk you down there," John led the way as they started strolling slowly down towards the relevant pier.

After they'd seen Colin off, John led them back into town for a beer or twenty.

Chapter 21

They slept on the boat that night because there was a breeze which kept the mosquito's away, and because the hammock deck was getting extremely full with other passengers and they wanted to make sure to keep their places as far as possible from the filthy toilets and noise of the engine.

The boat set off from the quay late the following morning. It was chock-a-block on the hammer deck, and they were glad they'd kept their places. It was a five day voyage, downstream to Belem. The two rivers ran side by side for hundreds of kilometres, the cherry cola eventually giving way to the caramel. In some places the river was indeed over ten kilometres wide, as Colin had promised.

There was little to do on the boat to fill the time, and they generally watched the river roll by in the day time and drank cans of lager in the evening. John seemed to be drinking non-stop twenty four hours a day, never sleeping.

One afternoon at a passenger stop somewhere, the four riders were alarmed to see up ahead fifteen or sixteen military policemen, standing on the pier, waiting for the boat to draw up. By the time the boat had moored it was evident they were planning to board. It was the only time on that boat that the noise level dropped to almost silence. The moment the ferocious looking submachine gun toting police began boarding the vessel, all the noisy chatter ceased instantly. Hundreds of Brazilian passengers fell into complete silence at once, and stood or sat almost motionless with glum expressions on their faces. 'Maybe everyone is smuggling cocaine,' thought Tommy.

The police walked sullenly around the boat in groups of two or three, barking questions, kicking people's feet out of the way, emptying the odd suitcase onto the deck to rummage through the contents.

John was thinking how weird it was that everyone appeared to immediately fall into discrete roles. The passengers fell into the role of victim, the police into the role of intimidating bully. Predetermined parts they were each compelled to act out, as though the boat was a big stage in a theatre on which a single crew strutted, or fretted; according. Not that John had ever been

120

to a theatre. But this, he imagined, was what it might be like. Was it two different people? he wondered. Or was it just one, kind of fluid person?

Mark and Keith pretended to be quietly absorbed in a game of black jack, they were playing on the deck, but they both felt a drill of alarm in their stomach.

A couple of police officers now stood in front of the four smugglers, hands on the nuzzles of their guns. John was standing, Tommy was in his hammock. One of them looked down at Keith and Mark playing cards on the deck. "Hey! No gambling," he barked.

They looked up at him, "We're not gambling. Just playing," said Mark.

"Don't argue!" bellowed the policeman.

"I'm not arguing, I'm just saying..."

"Shut up, Mark," hissed Keith.

"Passports!" said the other officer, holding out his hand.

Tommy jumped out of his hammock and fished the new passports out of his rucksack. He handed the top passport to the guard, with the police report procured in Lima folded inside it. The guard opened the report, read it, then tucked it back in the passport. Flipping through the passport's empty pages, he said, "Where did you come into Brazil?"

"Leticia, Tabatinga," said Tommy.

"From Colombia," said the officer.

Tommy nodded.

He looked at Tommy. "Drugs?" he barked suddenly.

Tommy looked at him blankly.

"Drugs!" he repeated. "Heroine? Cocaine?"

"No." Tommy shook his head, barely perceptibly. The officer glared at him while Tommy held what he hoped was an innocent expression as best he could.

Another police officer walked over to join the first two. He looked more senior, with a peaked hat and no machine gun. He looked at the red crash helmet lying on Tommy's hammock. The other three had latched their helmets to the bikes, but Tommy for some reason had brought his with him.

"You travel by motorbike?" the senior guard barked at Tommy.

Tommy nodded and put on a wide grin, "Yes, sir! All the way round South America. Let me tell you..."

"Show me the bike!" He shot a penetrating glare at Tommy which Tommy easily deflected with the speed and grace of a boxer.

"You have motorbikes?" the second officer looked at the remaining three. They nodded. "Follow!" he ordered.

The four riders followed the three police officers round to the back of the boat where there was a small hold containing three or four cars plus their motorbikes, in place on their stands. One of the officers was holding onto Tommy's passport, Tommy still held the other three.

"Which one yours?" the senior officer asked Tommy in broken English. Tommy pointed. The officer walked over to it and inspected it for a moment. Then leaning over he read the milometer.

He then tapped the petrol tank.

"Key!" he demanded, holding out his hand.

"It's in my rucksack." said Tommy. "One minute..." he rushed off.

One of the subordinate officers looked hard at Keith. Keith tried to ignore him for a moment, then looked at him and smiled politely. Inside he felt like jelly, and wasn't sure how long he could hold out before he started involuntarily shaking.

"Show me your motorbike!" he ordered. Keith pointed. To his alarm he noticed his finger quivering wildly at the end of his outstretched arm. Quickly he pulled his arm back to his side.

John was standing at the back swigging from a can of lager and belching loudly.

The senior officer walked over to the bike at the far end of the line, and started tapping the petrol tank lightly with a small truncheon, listening to the tone. Then he started tapping the seat. Then the mudguards. Finally he ran his truncheon round the spokes of the rear wheel.

Keith, who was standing to the side had started to notice how airless it was in the car hold despite the open sides. It was stifling, and suddenly he was sweating profusely. Images of himself incarcerated in a horrendous jungle prison swam through his mind and waves of guilt and self-pity swept through his stomach. Now feeling giddy, he realised he was swaying. Suddenly aware he was about to lose balance and fall over he quickly held out an arm to grab a metal post and managed just in time to steady himself.

The senior officer stood up straight and looked round at the three riders. "Whose?" he demanded.

John belched, longer and louder than ever.

Keith swigged at a plastic bottle of water with his free hand. Sweat was pouring down his face and his shirt was drenched. "Me," he said. "It's mine." The officer looked round, then catching sight of him began to glare suspiciously.

At that moment Tommy returned with the four sets of keys distracting the officer. He walked over to stand by his own bike and looked at the officer, who walked slowly back down the line of bikes.

"You ride this?" said the senior officer when he arrived at Tommy's bike. He then looked at Tommy, to size him up.

"Yes," Tommy laughed like it was a daft question.

"You have the key?"

"Yes," Tommy held out the four sets of keys."

The officer paused. "This one," he said after a moment, nodding his head towards Keith's bike. Keith felt a wave of dread.

They walked over, then the officer said, "Move it forward."

Tommy looked at him. "Unlock it?"

The officer nodded.

Tommy nodded at Keith. He wasn't sure he could let go of the metal post without losing his balance. The gentle sway of the boat seemed exaggerated to him and the boat stated swimming around him. "Keith!" Hearing Tommy's voice again, he managed to pull himself together and found that he didn't lose his balance. He walked over to join Tommy by his bike and and together they quickly undid the straps, then Keith, pouring with sweat and starting to look feverish, pushed the bike off its stand, and rolled it forward a couple of metres, away from the other bikes.

Walking over the senior officer nodded at Keith and as he caught sight of him suddenly he paused. "Are you worrying about something?" He said. Keith looked up at him and shook his head. "Bad stomach," he said rubbing his midriff and trying to look queasy. "Something I ate," he added, glancing at the ceiling as though making a joke of it. The officer held his gaze. "Ok," he said at last, nodding towards the bike. Surreptitiously swallowing, Keith pushed at the side stand with his foot, but his foot kept slipping. Finally he bent down and got the stand out with his hand, then backed away while the senior officer circled the bike. Suddenly the officer swung his leg over and sat his full weight heftily onto the bike straddling it, then lifted his feet on the pegs and maintained a balance for several seconds. The four riders tried not to react, looking at anything but the tyres.

Eventually it he jumped back down. Then kicking back the side stand, still straddling the bike the senior officer pulled in the clutch and the handbrake and once again jumped up with both feet onto the pegs. Maintaining balance as before he started to bounce the bike up and down. Little bounces at first. Then more and more vigorously, he bounced the bike, working the suspension, compressing the tyres. The harder he bounced, the more frenetic Keith's heartbeat. The four riders had not been privy to Colin's testing of the bikes in the workshop, and had no idea how rigorous they had been, or hadn't been.

The officer finally lost balance and put his left foot down. Then looked down at the back wheel. This gave Tommy a chance to overtly examine the wheel for a moment too. He could not so far see any leaking cocaine. How many more bounces it could take was anyone's guess and even Tommy's throat had a lump in it by now.

The officer depressed the clutch and handbrake and stood up on the pegs again, balancing the bike. Once again he started to bounce it, but this time putting weight onto the handlebars to heavily test the front wheel and suspension.

It seemed to all four riders by now that avoiding looking at the tyres was no longer an option. They all allowed themselves to look at the front wheel, as they watched. Keith was experiencing a sense of vertigo and felt he was watching it all happen in slow motion. The front tyre compressed, flattened, held for a second, an instant, an eternity, then... reformed as it sprang back. It seemed to the four that this bouncing went on interminably. They started to wonder if he would ever stop, or lose his balance before a tyre burst. Then 'bang!' The noise echoed round the hold. All eyes turned to look at the ground in front of John's feet. He had dropped his half empty can of lager on the metal floor of the boat. He hadn't noticed his fingers getting sweaty in the heat, and it had simply slipped from his grasp and landed hard at a forty five degree angle, making for maximum impact. Quickly he bent down and picked it up, before it all spilt and hurriedly put it to his mouth to capture the fountaining froth.

The officer swung his leg off the bike, kicked out the side stand, and strolled over towards Tommy's bike again. He glanced over his shoulder to see where Tommy was, who ran forward with the keys, and still also holding onto the three passports. "Move it forward," instructed the officer.

This time Mark ran forward to help Tommy undo the straps. Keith, having got the nod from one of the other officers, was shakily backing his bike into position to re-strap again.

Tommy rolled his bike forward. The officer took the handlebar and swung his leg over the seat.

"Start it up!" said the senior officer, now sitting on the bike.

"Start my engine?" said Tommy.

The officer nodded.

"In here?" Tommy glanced at the low ceiling above him.

"Yes!" bellowed the officer.

Tommy hurriedly put the key in the ignition and turned the ignition on, then pointed to the starter button. Depressing the clutch and handbrake levers, the officer thumbed the starter button. The bike burst into life, exhaust fumes started to full the car hold. The officer gunned the throttle a few times, then switched off the ignition. "Show me in the tank," the officer tapped the gas tank.

Removing the key from the ignition, Tommy inserted it into the gas tank cap and removed it. The officer peered inside, joggled the bike a little, then peered inside the gas tank again.

"Ok," he sat up straight, nodding at Tommy and suddenly smiling. Tommy locked the cap on the gas tank and removed the key. The senior officer nodded at the officer with Tommy's passport who fished a stamp out of his pocket and stamped it, before handing it back to Tommy. They were a patrol unit for the enormous stretches of unchecked borders. The senior officer remained seated on the bike, resting his hand on the throttle, admiring the machine beneath him.

"Would you mind?" Tommy held out the other three passports to the officer with the stamp. "Souvenir stamps," he explained.

The officer nodded, smiling and took the passports, giving them stamps each then handing them back.

Now the senior officer sitting on the bike started asking Tommy about their trip, where they had been, how long it had taken, but in a chatty way.

Tommy played along, pretending to be an enthusiast.

"I also ride a motorbike," announced the senior officer to Tommy, out of the blue.

"Oh, that's terrific!" said Tommy.

John sloped quietly away, and off back to his hammock while the other two officers casually asked Mark and Keith questions about the trip.

"May I have a ride?" The senior officer suddenly asked Tommy, putting both hands on the handlebars.

Tommy laughed.

"Do you mind if I have a ride?"

Tommy looked at him, perplexed. "What, ride my bike?"

The officer nodded, smiling.

The other officers thought this was a great idea and laughed out loud, calling out encouragement.

Tommy was stumped. "You mean, in here," he said, looking round the hold as though he hadn't understood the question.

The officer laughed. "On the road," he said, gesturing the lane that ran along the bank behind the pier. Tommy was now regretting that he had allowed himself to be drawn into conversation with the officer. He should have just taken the passports and gone with John.

Tommy looked at the officer. He smiled at Tommy. "I don't know," he said. "I mean, is there time?" He glanced at Keith and Mark.

The officer nodded smiling broadly. "Certainly. The boat will not leave within forty five minutes."

"Let's go!" He rested his hand lovingly on the handlebars, twisting the throttle. "You will help me wheel it onto the ramp?" He said swinging his leg back over and standing next to the bike. He nodded over towards where the ramp had been lowered from the boat onto the pier. They could easily wheel the bike out and over the ramp. "Give me the key."

Tommy hesitated for a few moments, then said, "I don't know... it's a very expensive bike... if something happened ... I wouldn't ... know what to do ..."

The officer looked at him sternly his hand still outstretched for the key. A moment's silence hung in the air, then suddenly the officer said, "I'm joking," he burst out laughing at Tommy. "Don't look so serious!"

The other officers burst into laughter. Tommy laughed weakly, "Good... joke... Nice one," he said as he reached forward to grab the bike, and roll it back into its position.

"Ok," announced the senior officer. Nodding at the other two he led them back towards the ramp onto the pier. Tommy exchanged casual glances with Keith and Mark. They waited a minute or so for their pulse rates to calm down, before checking over the bikes again and heading back to catch up with John. When they got there they saw he had already crashed out even though it was the middle of the day, and was snoring loudly, fast asleep in his hammock

The remaining police officers were also drifting off the boat by now. Some were pushing along in front of them two young Brazilian men with long hair and low quality clothing, who looked as though they could be druggies. They had each been handcuffed behind the back. The two men were made to stand, forlornly on the pier, facing toward the boat. However they kept their eyes fixed, staring blankly at the ground in front of them, until all the police had disembarked. Then they were marched off down the lane from the pier, into the trees.

"Look at John," laughed Tommy. "He'll sleep like a baby through anything." The other two looked at John fast asleep in his hammock and laughed loudly.

Chapter 22

The four smugglers continued the journey downstream for several days in the tropical heat, the sun often shining. For vast stretches they could see nothing but thick trees coming right up to the banks on either side. Occasionally they would pass a small town, or tiny village, or even individual forest lodgings made of wood. At these places there was always human life to observe: children swimming and splashing at the river edges, people paddling in small one or two man wooden skiffs. Sometimes people would paddle violently in the wooden skiffs towards the boat, stopping just before a collision at the bow, then skilfully throw a hook attached to a rope so that it caught onto a tyre fender on the riverboat. The skiff would suddenly be jolted forward and swept alongside the larger boat. The skiff would remain pinned to the river boat by the waves and wash, or sometimes the skiffs would half submerge at the back ends as they were dragged along. In the skiffs were people hawking shrimps or bananas to the passengers aboard the boat. Or small children who would clamber fearlessly over the side of the boat for fun.

Sometimes they would pass islands in the river or see other rivers almost as large joining the Amazon which grew wider and wider. At last they exited the mouth of the river. Although the mouth of the Amazon was hundreds of miles wide, it was full of islands, so there were few stretches of empty water actually more than about 10 miles wide. In the mouth of the river were three large islands, then the Atlantic Ocean. Navigating right around the headland a few hundred kilometres the boats turned right again into the river Para. In fact Para River was technically still the Amazon River, since the headland was Marajo Island: a fluvial island – formed by rivers. It was the largest such island in the world, with about 80% of the landmass of England for example, and around the same size as Switzerland. So really Marajo was another of the many islands that sit in the mouth of the river Amazon, which makes it then, about 300 km wide.

Eventually they drew into port at Belem about 150 km up the Para.

It was the end of the line so it took a little while for all the passengers and vehicles that the boat was transporting, to disembark. Foot passengers went first, so the four riders had to wait. The boat was still laden with industrial quantities of bananas and watermelons, which it had taken on board at Manaus and further down river, and which would be unloaded following the foot passengers and the vehicles.

They wheeled the bikes onto the quay, then rode them slowly off the quay and onto the road. They could see Colin waiting up head for them, on his motorbike. He waited for them all to catch up and then led the way at about 5mph inland from the port. It did not seem odd to drive at that speed as there were still other foot passengers milling around as well as cars collecting people, and so on. A little way up the road instead of following the other vehicles by turning left towards town where looming in the distance they could see several high rise office blocks, rather Colin led them straight onwards. Here the road surface was not maintained and was full of potholes, so it was appropriate to continue on at a very low speed. After a few metres the road broadened out with grass verges on each side, and piles of rubble and garbage strewn around. Beyond the verge to the left was empty wasteland and beyond that some large warehouses. On the right large shipping containers were piled tens of metres high stretching forward for perhaps a kilometre.

A few large trucks were parked here and there with drivers maybe sleeping. It was a very deserted road with nothing overlooking it, so they could carry on their business without fear of observation. Up ahead they could see two transit vans parked by the verge, the back doors open with two ramps leading up for the bikes. Juan Pablo and Federo each stood beside their rented van, waiting.

***

It was several days drive down to Rio. With Federo and Juan Pablo two passengers could go in each van, and one on Colin's motorbike following behind sometimes, or leading in front. They rotated taking turns on the bike except for John, who was always drinking and so sat in the vans. They were deep in the Amazon jungle as they crossed the equator. The jungle continued for about a hundred kilometres more then finally began to thin out. They drove past mountains, along palm lined roads, and took ferries over rivers. Eventually they reached the coast at Recife and then continued southwards through Salvador and finally down to Rio de Janeiro.

They had already missed the boat they were originally booked on and had no choice but to wait for it to come round again. The vans were put into storage in a multi storey carpark for a few weeks, the bikes still inside.

They booked into the Copacabana Beach Hotel and since they had no bikes to ride, hung out on the beach mostly.

To the four riders' surprise, when they arrived at the hotel, they found Brendan waiting to meet them in the lobby. He had come out for a holiday, he said. Colin had telephoned and told him they would be staying in Rio for a few weeks as they'd missed the boat.

The riders thought it a bit odd that Colin hadn't informed them of this news.

"It didn't occur to you to mention it?" John demanded to know when Colin arrived to join them in the hotel lobby.

"I wasn't sure he'd show up," said Colin.

"Did you tell him you were coming?" John turned to Brendan.

Brendan choked a bit. "I thought I did... I don't know ... perhaps I didn't ... " he said.

"We'll discuss it later," interrupted Colin. "Let's check in first," and he started hurrying them over to reception.

"Wait!" said John, loudly enough to stop everyone. "Why didn't you tell us he was coming?"

"Not now John!"

"Yes, now, you scheming two faced pillock!"

There was a silence. Colin glared at John for a moment, then ignoring him completely turned and began herding the others away.

"Oi Brendan!" John shouted loudly enough to cause people across the lobby to turn and look. Brendan turned round to look at John. "What?"

"Did he tell you he left me in prison all night?" John said, in a very loud voice.

People in the lobby suddenly carried on with their own business again.

"Alright, alright," said Colin, walking back towards John. "We will discuss it, but not here," he looked round him. "We will check into our rooms and then you will come to my room and we will discuss it alone, the second we get the keys. So we can talk in private."

John acquiesced. They checked in quickly booking a room each. John went into Colin's room and shut the door, while the others went to their rooms on the same floor to dump their bags then all met up in Tommy's room, which was next to Colin's, for a quiet discussion. Brendan assured them he didn't know what was going on. Soon they heard muffled shouting coming through the wall. John and Colin's voices were so raised they could hear them arguing, but they were unable to make out what was being said. Finally the voices ceased and they heard the door slam shut loudly. They waited in silence for a few moments. They heard Colin's door open and close again then they heard a knock on their door.

"Yes?" said Tommy.

The door opened and Colin came in.

Keith stood up to give him a seat and joined some of the others sitting on the bed, who shunted along to let him fit in.

Colin sat in the chair. "I've just fired John," he said calmly.

They looked at him in stunned silence.

"Brendan has told me that he didn't mind taking over at this point."

They looked over at Brendan, who shrugged.

He had initially declined Colin's offer to be involved in the four bike trip, however when he heard that John was going again in place of Dave, he had to his immense surprise felt a frustrating jolt of envy. He had begun to wonder if it was the right decision turning down such a lucrative opportunity, which was looking more and more fool proof and ingenious, the more times they did it.

The thought that John, whom he regarded as a mate now, would suddenly be twice as well off as him, had affected Brendan more than he expected. The notion actually gave him horrible feelings of a kind of flashing envy or jealousy or something. Sure, he had a quarter of a million sterling from the last trip. It was a decent sum, but it wouldn't buy everything he needed. It would either buy a house, or a lifetime of not working; but not both. After declining Colin's original invitation, he subsequently realised he wished have both; the house and the money to live on. He now regretted declining to take part again.

He had confided his doubts about his decision to Colin in London one evening in a pub in Camden over a few pints of ale, and suggested he might have come to regret it.

Colin had said that if he needed a back-up he would let him know. Brendan was very disappointed. Even though he already had a larger sum of money than most people would ever own, he became quite depressed about missing out on the current trip, which feeling he absolutely hated, but couldn't seem to shake off at all. Then when the boat crossing was delayed, and Colin knew they were going to have to wait for six weeks until the next round trip of the ship from Rio, he had suggested to Brendan that Brendan could join them in Rio for a holiday. He explained that there was every chance one rider was going to be withdrawn, and that Brendan could take the empty place.

Colin had become increasingly concerned about John's behaviour, his drinking and showing off, and felt there was a risk that he could jeopardise the entire operation. It would be irresponsible then to allow John to proceed any further. Colin felt bad about this decision on John's behalf, as he knew it would upset him. He paid John £50 000 for his work so far and determined to think of another way to further make it up to him in the future. John had been angry about it in Colin's room. The money made him feel better though, and as Colin said with some truth, John was really not in a good frame of mind for such a project right now. So John had finally conceded to this.

The following day in Colin's room, John signed the bike documents over to Brendan and booked a flight home a couple of days later. He didn't want to hang about on the beach doing nothing for weeks on end, he said.

Chapter 23

The evening before John's departure, the six of them were chilling out on the veranda beside the beach at the hotel, drinking beers. Some local girls were hanging around making friends with them. In their early twenties they were very attractive, scantily dressed and well made up. There was one each for the fellas. They weren't prostitutes they said, but the guys knew they were really. However they played a kind of game where they pretended to be a real girlfriend, and hung onto their fella, and had all kinds of sex very willingly on request, but then expected a generous cash tip at the end of each night, and a bonus tip when the guy had to leave at the end of his vacation. This would cover their rent for a month or college fees and such. They created a social situation where they would try to make the guy feel awkward if he tried to refuse to pay such 'tips'. If this social manipulation didn't work, things could get nasty very quickly and it would become quite apparent that there was nothing discretionary about the tips whatsoever.

This evening they each took their new 'girlfriends' up to their respective rooms for the night. The following morning, they each confessed to having a raucous time. John also confessed a little later on to Colin, in private, to not having had sex at all with his girl, Theresa, even though he was quite smitten with her.

Colin couldn't believe it. "Why not?" he wanted to know.

John explained that he felt guilty about cheating on his wife, and had just enjoyed talking to the woman all night.

That evening, after making sure all the paper work was straightened out, he flew back to the UK.

Over the next few days the four riders tried to focus on relaxing. Keith found it hardest, and kept feeling weightlessness or vertigo or something in his stomach every time he thought of the ensuing sea crossing. The date of departure inexorably drew closer.

One evening the remaining five were sitting on the beach veranda with the girls again. Theresa was there too, without a partner now John had left. Colin invited her to come and sit beside him, and told his own 'girlfriend' to push off. All evening he kept plying Theresa with prying questions about John. That evening he wanted to take her up to his room.

"I don't think so," she said.

"You want me to report you to the police is it? For solisssitation." Colin hissed into her ear, "and all your matessss."

"You wouldn't," she said.

"Oh yeah?" he sneered. He was drunk enough he just might for all she knew. She didn't believe he was physically dangerous to her, just a bit creepy that was all. He was unlikely to be violent, but with the potential to be spiteful. He only wanted her because he thought she'd slept with his mate, she reasoned. Nevertheless, perhaps it was sensible to go with him if he was the type to kick up a fuss. He was quite handsome after all.

These girls didn't have a lot of rights in their society. It wasn't protocol to row with paying customers whom the hotel management was good enough to let them hang out with. The clients had all the power of course. Who knew what could kick off? 'Maybe better not to turn him down,' she thought.

The next day at lunch, she joined Colin and the other four at Colin's insistence. Colin looked particularly worn out, and was making a bit of a deal of it. Theresa looked more sexy and attractive every time they met her. She was very sophisticated in her personal presentation, and totally gorgeous.

At one point over coffee, after they finished eating, when Theresa got up and went to the 'ladies'', Colin said to the others, "When she comes back, ask her who is a real man, me or John."

"Piss off," Brendan said.

"Go on," said Colin. "It'll be a good laugh."

"I'll ask her when she comes back," said Tommy.

"Excellent!" Colin grinned at Tommy. "Nice one, Tommy!" he said. "Listen to this fella's. This is gonna make you laugh."

When Theresa returned to sit down at the table with them, after a little while Tommy asked her, as promised. "Hey Theresa, you spent time with both my mates, John and Colin. In your opinion, as a young single woman. Who is the most of a man, Colin or John?"

"Que?" she said.

"Which is the biggest man out of John and 'th Captain'. Which is the most virile, you know, *manly.*"

"Oh, I see," said Theresa. "Oh well that's easy." Tommy grinned at Colin, who winked back. "Definitely, it is John," she said.

Colin coughed to clear his throat.

"But, I thought..." he started.

"You thought what?" said Theresa.

"Nothing, I mean, well it's just..."

"He asked me a question," she said, "now he has my answer."

Colin shifted uncomfortably in his seat while Tommy shuffled his feet. Catching sight of the waiter Colin put his hand up. "Check!" he said curtly to the waiter.

They spent their last few days enjoying the sun and surf on the beach. Colin was pleased to observe that the four riders were drinking less than they had been, however the mood amongst them had undeniably been on a downward slide ever since John was sent home.

The evening before departure, Colin called a meeting in his hotel room, excluding Brendan whom Colin had full confidence in.

The three riders arrived and they all sat down. Colin still sensed a low morale.

"Everyone looks so glum," he said.

"Maybe we're sad to be going home," said Keith.

"Are you not excited to see your kids?" Colin asked.

"If we do see them," said Mark.

"Come on now," cajoled Colin. "Don't lose sight of the infallibility of our method. They didn't even consider the tyres on the river, right?" They had previously told Colin about the search on the boat. His boat had also had a police search between Manaus and Belem, he had recalled.

"Look now, short of sticking a knife in the tyres, which they won't... and can't anyway, it's a fool proof plan. No one has thought of using inflated tyres yet, don't forget that fact."

Tommy's spirit began to pick up. "Colin's right," he said to the others. "Look lad's, we may as well try to enjoy it, right?"

Keith and Mark still looked doubtful.

Tommy explained, "It looks less suspicious if we're having fun. If we end up getting caught we may wish we had taken the opportunity to enjoy our last days of freedom. If we get away with it, there was nothing to be fed up about all along. Whichever way you look at it, we can afford to put on a brave face and enjoy ourselves. Innit."

Colin nodded. Keith and Mark kind of sensed Tommy was right. The psychological approach was an important facet, no doubt. They nodded. Their spirits weren't picking up, as much as Tommy's, but neither were they half broken like John's had been, Colin assessed.

"Whatever happens," said Colin, "if they are questioning you, searching you, searching the bikes, whatever; just never ever glance at the tyres. Not even for an instant. Not even a micro second. Do not look at the tyres. Find anything else, the clock on the wall, your fingernail, the petrol tank if you have to, but not, I repeat not..."

"Yeah, alright Colin," said Tommy. "We know all this."

"...the tyres."

"Yeah. Shut up Colin! You're starting to make me feel nervous again," said Tommy.

"Right, Ed will be waiting at Genoa with a truck to carry the four machines," explained Colin. "Ed knows a route into France on a small country lane. Of course you'll see no checkpoints going into France. Ed will drop you off when you arrive at Calais before you embark, and will travel separately. We don't want the same fiasco as before in Dover. But he will be on the same boat as you. Ignore him if you see him on the boat. Then he will wait for you after the first left turn out of the port at Dover. There's a carpark. So let him drive off the boat first and you can follow him but not directly behind. Do not disembark near the back or even riskier, near the front of the other traffic. Remember they'll be looking mainly for individuals smuggling booze or fags over the limit.

"Now, don't get excited and start cheering as soon as you clear customs at Dover," said Colin, engendering a little hollow laughter from Mark and Keith. Dover seemed like a long way off.

Chapter 24

It was the day of departure. The four riders had breakfast at the hotel, then packed their bags and walked with Colin towards the port. They met Juan Pablo and Federo a few hundred metres away from the entrance, around a corner where they unloaded the bikes and gave them a final check over. Juan Pablo had inspected all the tyres for damage and gave them the thumbs up.

Saying goodbye and wishing each other good luck and bon voyage, they rode the bikes at 5mph towards the dock.

At passport control, they dismounted and waited in a line with other vehicles.

Brendan was in front with all four passports, having been given leadership of the group by Colin, since he had experience.

Tommy hadn't minded this, but there had been a fracas the hotel this morning about his fishing tackle. Tommy had purchased some sea fishing rods and tackle, and now appeared in the hotel lobby carrying them with his other luggage.

"What the hell is all that?" Colin had said.

"Sea fishing," said Tommy, grinning.

"I thought I told you to keep a low profile," Colin had said.

"Colin, will you try to stop micro managing everything," Tommy replied. "Fishing is my hobby. How would I spend two weeks crossing the Atlantic without trying to catch something?"

Colin looked at him, a bit dumbfounded, even Tommy now seemed to be turning on him.

"Mate," continued Tommy, "it's called hiding in plain sight. Now, you've got to learn to delegate, which means... *delegate*."

Colin continued to stare at him.

"If you can't trust your staff to do the job you've assigned to them: well then, you've hired the wrong staff," Tommy concluded and then turned away. 'If Colin doesn't get this,' he thought, 'I might start to doubt his abilities.'

Colin suddenly snapped back to his senses. "Ok, Tommy," he conceded. "When you're right, you're right."

*

By now Brendan was at the passport check, ahead. He handed over the four passports and pointed to the line of bikes behind him, trying not to focus on the twenty kilos of cocaine hidden in each. Tommy inspected his new fishing tackle. Mark chewed a fingernail and Keith looked on, nervously. Keith's heart was pounding the most. He was the youngest. The inspector looked carefully down the line of bikes at each rider. Finally he stamped the passports and pointed Brendan over to the vehicle inspection area. A car was already parked there being turned inside out by four inspectors. They were checking every inch of the car; inside, outside, top and bottom. However not one of them was considering to investigate the tyres of the vehicle, Keith noticed.

The four riders wheeled the bikes and stood them in a line behind the car. After a little while a customs inspector approached Brendan, and asked to see the passports. Keeping these in his hand the inspector strolled down the line of bikes. Keith held his breath as the man walked past and tried to gaze at the middle distance. Keith heard him stop at Mark who was back of the line. He was asking Mark some questions. Then he walked back past Keith again to Brendan, and handed back the passports. Except one. He indicated Brendan to lead the first three bikes. Mark was to remain behind.

Without looking back, Keith followed Brendan and Tommy onto the quay and up the ramp into the vessel.

They lined the bikes up in the car hold, strapping them down without talking. They knew that if Mark got busted they would all come under immediate suspicion and their own bikes taken to pieces. They waited nervously in the car hold for ten minutes, then decided to go up to the cabins. Fifteen minutes later Tommy returned. The car hold was fuller but still no sign of Mark. He went back to the cabins. This was making them all feel uncomfortable, after they had seen the thoroughness of the search on the car.

After another agonising five minutes waiting in the hold, at last they saw Mark approaching the ramp on the quay. However he did not have his bike with him, and was being led by a uniformed official. The three riders exchanged alarmed glances. This was not what they had wanted to see. Mark followed the official up the ramp. At the top he paused. The official turned left, then Mark turned right, towards the car hold. He saw the others and started walking towards them. They could see he was grinning.

As he approached they looked at him with expectant faces. Mark grinned, shaking his head. "What's happening?" Brendan asked.

Still grinning, Mark said, "It's alright, I'm through. They're just putting the bike back together." The others continued to look at him.

"They dismantled the entire bike," Mark was smirking. "Every nut and bolt. Took the engine to pieces. But they never took off the wheels. Just left them on the bike on its stand. Now they've got to put it back together. It's gonna take them a while."

Eventually Mark was able to load his rebuilt bike and they left the port. The four rider's confidence soared.

They had a whole lot of fun on the crossing, often led by Tommy. He was ebullient and entertaining. The other passengers and even some of the crew took quite a shine to him as he spoke to anyone for hours on end, as though he had known them all his life. He made a big noise about his sea fishing, and everyone on board soon knew it was his favourite hobby. He even won special dispensation to fish through a purpose made hatch in the bottom of the boat. It is unclear from the accounts or official documentation whether he landed any catches on the voyage.

After a couple of weeks they rounded the coast of Morocco and headed into the Mediterranean Sea, docking in Genoa on December 15th 1995.

"Ten days before Christmas," remarked Tommy.

As they lined up to disembark, over riding their nervousness was confidence among the four in Colin's system. They were beginning to feel that it might genuinely be an entirely fool proof system as Colin had promised.

They filed through passports and customs checks at Genoa. The customs inspection area at Genoa harbour was partly in the open, and visible from an office block a few hundred metres away, where in a top floor office window binoculars glinted in the sunshine, trained on the four riders, while a disembodied hand wrote notes into a notepad, with a ball point pen.

The hand scribbled as the sight of Keith being stopped by an official was recorded.

Keith had been last in line as they filed through the inspection point at Genoa. The other three had all walked their bikes through and were on the other side, safely in Italy. Keith was last. He thought he had made it through, having received his passport back stamped and been waved on. His heart had just begun to soar with elation when he felt a tap on his shoulder. It was the tap he had been dreading. He looked around, a pained expression on his face. It was the customs inspector, pointing at Keith's back wheel. Keith looked down. His tyre had split. Cocaine was pouring out, making a pile on the ground.

"I'm sorry," Keith mouthed reflectively, grimacing at the inspector." He kicked out the side stand and stepped away from the bike, waiting for all hell to break loose.

But it didn't break loose. The guard continued to point. Keith looked again. Wait! He blinked. There was no split tyre, or visible cocaine. The tyre was intact. The inspector was pointing at the bungee strap holding his rucksack on the rack and rear seat. It had come undone and was dangling around the hub of his back wheel.

Keith was staggered. He must have hallucinated. Now was not the time to think about it however. Coming to his senses, he bent forward to tie up the strap, thanking the inspector. Then he wheeled the bike through the building and outside. He was through.

They gathered outside the building, exchanging glances but not saying anything. They were half way home. Brendan led the way riding slowly a couple of blocks to a carpark where they could see Ed waiting for them with a truck, on schedule.

The journey to Calais went without a hitch. There were five seats in two rows in the cab of the truck. They took a narrow lane over the open border into France.

The bikes were unloaded a little way from the port at Calais. The four smugglers mounted and rode towards customs at 5mph.

They were waved directly onto the ferry, where they parked the bikes and went straight upstairs to locate a restaurant and order four square meals. However when the food came, both Keith and Tommy found they had no appetite at all and left the food untouched. The other two realised they weren't as hungry as they thought either, but managed to pick at their food a bit.

It was about a one hour crossing. Soon they filed back into the car hold to prepare the bikes for disembarkation at Dover.

Chapter 25

As the ramp lowered at Dover, and the vehicles began to roll off, they could see a large number of customs inspectors waiting to pounce. Quickly vehicles were identified and taken to the side. Other vehicles were waved straight through after presenting passports. Amazingly the four riders were among the lucky ones, and were waved through. They each began to feel a sense of elation as they rode towards the steep concrete ramp of the road leading out of the port and into Dover.

Half a mile away, from a car parked on a particular cliff top, there was a clear view of the customs area at Dover. Inside the car through the wound down window a pair of binoculars was trained on the customs' exit.

It was almost dark and raining heavily. The ramp became wet as it extended out into the open air. It had a sharp incline. The four rider's road towards it in staggered file and drove out into the rain. Brendan was in front and immediately felt the weight of his front wheel on the incline. The others followed behind and noticed the same thing. It would require skill and experience to keep the bikes upright at 5mph on such an incline with 10kg extra in each wheel. All the bikes began to slide.

Tommy was struggling the most. His legs didn't properly reach the ground on such a large bike, with the incline the tips of his feet dangled six inches above tarmac. He needed to keep the speed down, and maintain balance. The road was wet and slippery, the wheels began sliding uncontrollably underneath him. Next concrete was coming towards him at an awkward angle. Tommy's engine roared terrifyingly as he lost grip of the throttle and lay sprawling on the ground.

Now customs officials began shouting from inside the customs area below. The other three riders heard the shouting and caught sight of the accident in their wing mirrors. Barely turning to look, they kept going slowly forwards into the pouring rain, following Brendan who had chosen not to stop.

As quick as he could, Tommy reached forward to hit the kill button on the bike. The engine stopped roaring. Raindrops sizzled angrily on the exhaust pipe. Officials were shouting and running up the slope towards him.

Clambering to his feet, Tommy tried to right the bike.

An official ran up the slope towards him. Tommy heard shouting. He was being shouted at. In the rain he struggled with the bike. The shouting grew closer; "Are you OK sir?"

Tommy looked round and nodded.

"Quickly sir. There's more traffic coming." The official reached down to help lift the bike up. Together they got it onto its wheels and pulled onto the stand.

Tommy stared at the official, dumbstruck.

"Fast as you can please sir," the official repeated. Tommy jumped on the bike and hit the start button. The official gave the rack a shove at the rear as Tommy twisted the throttle, and rolled forward off the stand. It was still a struggle with the incline and the weight in the tyres, but gunning the throttle and balancing the clutch, and with some help from one of Her Majesty's Customs officials, this time Tommy managed to keep the bike upright. As he pulled away he could see in his wing mirror that the official was disappearing back down the slope. At the top, he turned left and found the others waiting in the car park.

Exchanging electrified glances they still kept conversation to a minimum as they loaded the bikes on the truck.

No one had followed them out of the customs area. As they pulled out onto the motorway there was a palpable sense of elation. They were still not home yet however.

It was possible they were being followed but this too was looking less and less likely with each minute that went by unhindered. It was beginning to look like they had been successful. They were starting to look, and feel as good as four very wealthy individuals by this point.

It was a pitch dark starless evening less than three hours later as they unloaded the bikes and rolled them into Tim's lock up.

There was quite a gathering there that night. Colin of course and all the usual suspects.

Even John showed up to share in the divisions, relatively sober for once. He was carrying a stick wrapped in a blanket which he leaned against the wall next to the door.

"Who are you planning to shoot?" Tim asked.

"Anyone who gets in my way," said John.

"I should think everyone's gonna be in your way if you keep putting weight on at this rate," said Tim.

That evening huge quantities of cocaine changed hands, and vast quantities of cash supplied by those who had come to buy. Mark, Keith and Tommy took about £250 000 each. Brendan took £200k, and Colin took about a million pounds sterling. This gave each of them a warm glowing feeling. "Who's ready to go again?" said Colin jokingly. "Me!" said Tommy, "ready when you are Cap'n." After the weighing and exchanging was all completed there was something of a seasonal party atmosphere in that lock up.

It was not a very wise area to lurk around in after dark, especially alone; however if you were brave, foolish, or desperate enough to be scurrying down the quiet backstreets that ran beside those railway arches somewhere in Deptford in South East London at about ten pm on a rainy wintry evening; a week before Christmas in 1995: you may have heard what sounded like a drunken office party. You would have noticed at most only the faintest slithers of light that shone through the locked shutters of a mechanics garage in a lock up underneath one of the arches. You might have heard the tones of Bing Crosby, booming at some volume from a sound system inside, and sailing over the glistening black roof tiles of Deptford. Booming crooning that drowned out the chinking of champagne glasses and the sound of razor blades click clacking on pocket-sized mirrors, but not the noise of about half a dozen grown men. With more exuberance perhaps, than is ordinarily expected even during the holiday season, they sang along with each chorus: "Oh, I'm dreaming of a White Christmas..."

Chapter 26

Everyone had money, so it was beginning to seem. Colin and his crew were becoming quite well off. And not only them. A growing circle of close friends were soon taking advantage of the availability of copious amounts of top grade cocaine and were getting in on the game of distribution. Apart from Colin almost everyone involved was selling on occasions if not all the time.

This was because there was so much money to be made at the gram level. A 'gram' was always sold for £60. (US$100). It never varied. The variables were the weight of the 'gram' and the extent to which it was 'cut'. Each gram sold individually, was previously mixed with another similar looking substance to bulk it out. They used baby laxative which they purchased wholesale in large plastic tubs from a local cash and carry. Therefore for £60 the punters would receive usually less than a gram of between thirty percent and seventy percent cocaine, the rest being made up with baby laxative. The specific percentage amount depended on the nature of each punters relationship with the dealer. For those dealers purchasing it at £25 per gram directly from Colin, the mark-up was considerable. Each £25 investment returned about £120. Which equated to almost £100 ($160) profit per gram sold individually.

No one among this group was selling on the street. Which would have been way too risky, as well as entirely unnecessary. Rather they were selling from their homes, to adults whom they already knew. There was no need to 'push' the drug to create fresh customers because there were more than sufficient grown people among their existing friends who were requesting it without any solicitation.

As each day went by following the return of the four motorbikes, it looked increasingly certain they had got away with the escapade.

Things had seemed a little awkward between himself and John after the trip, and Colin hoped he could make it up to John by allowing John to take control of refurbishments of the run down snooker club they had bought at auction, which they planned to turn into a drinking club to act as a front for their cocaine money.

After a company meeting the three directors, John, Colin and Brendan agreed on this.

While John got on with club refurbishments, Colin disappeared 'up North' for a few months visiting acquaintances including Todd. It is unclear exactly where Colin went, or what he got up to.

Nobody heard from Colin for several months. When he re-appeared on the scene one of the first people he contacted was Tommy.

After a brief chat on the phone, Colin arrived at Tommy's house one evening in early summer 1996. Leaving his wife and two young children in the front room, Tommy led Colin down the hallway to his kitchen and opened a bottle of wine. They sat at the kitchen table sharing the wine, snorting up occasional small lines of cocaine and rolling cannabis spliffs while they arranged the next project.

None of the previous riders were interested in another trip. They all now had plenty of money and did not wish to take further risks. Tommy however was interested. Similarly to Brendan before, he found himself dissatisfied with his quarter million. He wanted more. Tommy also had a mate who was interested. Paul was someone Tommy knew well personally, and had known a long time.

Colin was happy to take Tommy's word about this.

"He's got a full bike license, obviously." Tommy explained.

"He won't need it," said Colin.

"Why not?" Tommy was baffled.

"You won't be riding bikes, you'll be driving a Land Rover."

"Both of us?"

"Two of you in one Land Rover."

"And the coke will go in the tyres," affirmed Tommy.

"No," said Colin.

Tommy looked at him. "Where then?"

After a moment Colin lent down and opened a briefcase he had placed at his feet. He took out a folder, then withdrew some documents and handed them to Tommy.

Bemused, Tommy took the documents and looked at them. They were technical drawings showing the exploded construction of a car wheel.

They didn't make a lot of sense to Tommy. Finally Colin explained.

"When I was up North, I designed a wheel with room for 30 kilos of coke to be hidden in the hub."

Tommy looked at him in amazement. "Go on," he said.

"Once these wheel shells are welded together, with the drugs inside, they will look like solid, normal Land Rover wheels. Short of actually literally destroying the wheels, they'll never know."

After a pause, Tommy said, "How convincing are the finished wheels?"

"Hundred percent," said Colin nonchalantly. It was a matter of fact.

"Thirty kilos per wheel," intoned Tommy.

Colin nodded.

"Four wheels on the Land Rover.... a hundred and forty kilos."

Colin nodded again. "Twenty," he said.

"Mm?"

"A hundred and twenty kilos."

The deal would be the same as before. Colin would get fifty percent, Tommy and Paul would split the remainder.

Colin would net £1.5 million, (about US$2.5m). Tommy and Paul would get half that each. The police and the press would ascribe a street value of nearly £20m (US$30m) to such an amount.

*

By October 1996, Tommy had purchased a Toyota Land Cruiser, which would accept Colin's wheels, and shipped it out to Rio de Janeiro. At this point it had its original wheels still fitted.

Some weeks prior to this, Colin had had his wheel parts made up in a discreet factory in the midlands and shipped the pieces to Juan Pablo's workshop in Colombia.

While Tommy and Paul drove through Argentina, Chile, Peru, Ecuador and into Colombia, Colin and Juan Pablo purchased 120 kilos of cocaine at 1000 bucks a kilo and welded it inside the specially designed wheels.

When the Land Cruiser arrived in Colombia, the new wheels were fitted one evening outside the workshop. Tommy took it for a little test drive down the track past the house, with Paul sitting beside him while Colin and Juan Pablo watched on from in front of the workshop.

Tommy, driving, was unable to detect any effect from the extra weight in the wheels. Pulling out onto the main road, he accelerated gradually. 10 mph, 20mph, 25mph. Still he could detect no effects. 30 mph, 31... suddenly the vehicle started swerving from side to side. Tommy took his foot off the gas pedal. They slowed down again to under 30mph, and he regained control.

They carried on a couple of miles keeping at 30mph, until they found a suitable place to do a U turn, and retraced the route back to the workshop.

"It looked good from where we were," said Colin as Tommy stepped out of the Land Cruiser.

"It was good up to 30mph," Tommy explained what had happened.

"That's good," said Colin. "That's more than enough. You two can go," he said to Tommy and Paul, who set off to stroll back to their hotel. Then Colin and Juan Pablo got on with exchanging the worn tyres from the original wheels onto the fabricated wheels containing the cocaine. With the worn tyres fitted, finally they threw a few handfuls of stones and dirt at the wheels to scuff up the metal a little.

*

The Land Cruiser was taken by lorry to Bogota, and flown cargo to Leticia.

At Leticia it was loaded onto a cargo boat for Belen. However this time they disembarked at Manaus, where Juan Pablo and Federo were waiting with a lorry to drive down to Rio.

Tommy and Paul travelled with the vehicle at all times. Colin caught up with them on his motorbike at various points along the route.

There was no police check on the road south from Manaus, as there had been on the river to Belen, and Colin realised with a rush that he had just discovered a fool proof route for smuggling industrial quantities of cocaine from Colombia to Brazil, for shipment on to the UK.

The car was unloaded at Rio, and driven into a hotel carpark. After a couple of weeks break, vacationing on the beach, Tommy drove the Land Cruiser, with Paul in the passenger seat, the short distance to the port, maintaining a low speed.

The car was loaded onto the boat after being searched inside and out with sniffer dogs. Tommy and Paul watched on, slightly bemused, slightly nervous. The longer the dogs didn't go near wheels, the more bemused they became.

Tommy had his fishing gear in the back of the Land Cruiser, together with their luggage, which was all thoroughly searched through. Panels were removed inside the vehicle and torches shone underneath. It was amazing for Tommy to observe as more time went on and still they did not even consider the wheels.

Eventually the Land Cruiser was put back together and they were waved on board, feeling a little smug.

"Phase one complete," Paul glanced at Tommy, grinning, as Tommy negotiated driving onto the ramp to board the vessel.

"Keep a straight face," advised Tommy.

Paul looked round at the officials watching from the side of the ramp.

They parked the car and went upstairs to the cabins to await departure.

A horn blast signalled the final ropes being cast from the shore and the ship started to glide slowly towards the harbour exit.

Tommy was less exuberant on the boat this time, but still enjoyed plenty of sea fishing through the special made hatch.

There were no other English people on board as usual, and the crew did not fraternise with the passengers, but they had a few drinks with some of the other passengers from time to time.

Tommy and Paul disembarked in Genoa on 24th March 1997. Unbeknown to them as they passed through customs check, they were being observed. In an office in a tower block a few hundred yards away, a pair of binoculars adjusted focus on the Land Cruiser, then on Tommy, and Paul as they stood beside it.

Tommy and Paul didn't talk but they both felt a flush of excitement. They had been at sea for nearly two weeks and now were at the half way mark. If everything kept on going according to plan they would both be sterling millionaires or near enough, within 48 hours.

The customs officer at Genoa waved them through without any check. They drove slowly out of the port and to the carpark where Ed was waiting as arranged with the lorry.

They drove the Land Cruiser up the ramps and into the lorry, where it was secured with straps and chains. Using Ed's route they drove into France and then Northwards to Calais. A short distance from the ferry port, Tommy and Paul unloaded the Land Cruiser and drove it the last half a mile to the port, and onto the ferry while Ed took the Lorry on board separately.

They all rolled off again at Dover without any checks for either of the vehicles. This was perhaps fortunate since Tommy and Paul were visibly quiet excited with the goal now will within sight. They met Ed in the carpark as before. Making sure they were not over looked, they loaded the Land Cruiser onto the lorry and drove it back to Tim's workshop in Deptford.

They were able to swing open a large a section in the front of the lock like a giant garage door and get the Land Cruiser inside.

John was there to help Ed with the wheels. Colin had wanted to include John at the top level, as he still felt a bit bad about his previous treatment of John, even though having already given him complete control of the club refurbishments which John had much requested.

The wheels were removed inside the closed lockup, and John and Ed attempted to open them up while Colin, Tommy, Paul and Tim looked on. It soon became evident that this was not going to be an easy job.

The two smugglers had arrived back at Tim's lock up by about seven pm. Pat and Todd were due to arrive at ten pm to take delivery. (John was also taking delivery of some merchandise.)

By nine pm it became evident that John and Ed were unlikely to open even one wheel that evening let alone all four. The wheel halves designed by Colin were made of steel and welded solid. After nearly two hours of attacking a wheel with sledge hammers, they had barely even dented it.

Chapter 27

Phone calls were made to delay Todd and Pat. Neither Tommy and Paul, or Colin were prepared to leave without finishing the deal. Tim wasn't so bothered, and left the five of them to work through the night.

Eventually after huge efforts and an all-night session the four wheels were finally broken into pieces using welding torches as well as the sledge hammers.

Pat and Todd showed up as soon as they were called the following morning. Ten percent of the merchandise was water damaged. Apparently the seal had split in the plastic and water had got in somehow. Todd took this portion to give to Dr Bill, to be cleaned. That left about one hundred and ten good kilos. The lock up was seemingly filled with millions of pounds and hundreds of kilos of cocaine as they worked out their deals. Tommy and Paul were the first to leave around noon, each proudly carrying three quarters of a million pounds in unmarked cash wrapped in white plastic carrier bags.

Colin had to wait a couple of weeks for Dr Bill to clean the tainted coke to get all of his money. Pat John and Todd took the produce in bulk to shift.

There was now so much cash floating around Colin didn't know where to begin using it.

He and John started visiting foreign exchange booths in the west end of London. There they could exchange up to quarter of a million pounds at a time into US dollars for example without being asked for ID. This was largely to provide cash to purchase more cocaine in Colombia.

Colin also began making regular trips to the Caymans, ostensibly to holiday with Ana and the kids – they had had another baby a few months previously - but in fact to bank millions of dollars in cash over several trips, which he secretly carried with him, hidden in his clothing or luggage.

While Colin holidayed in the Caymans, back in the UK, John continued to shift more of the cash through the club refurbishments. In fact John was now successfully shifting so much of the green stuff through refurbishments to the club, and progress on the work was so slow, that as Colin swung in a hammock one evening, admiring the tropical sunset and holding some paper documents, he began to seriously wonder what John had done with all that money.

As soon as he got back from his current trip he would, he determined, go straight to the club office, and demand John provide some explanations. In fact the more he thought about it, the more worked up Colin became. Finally he jumped out of his hammock and stormed up to the reception area of his resort, to make a phone call right now. He rang the club office to no avail. He then tried John's home number. The phone rang a dozen times before a sleepy voice answered: "It's nearly midnight!" It was John's wife.

"Oh, I am sorry," said Colin, in his fury he had completely forgotten about the time difference. "I'm trying to reach John."

"Well he's not here. Try the club office tomorrow."

That night Colin was unable to appreciate the serenity of his environment as he fumed. He worked himself into such a frenzy that he stayed up all night, waiting for office hours in the UK. In any case he didn't expect anyone to show up before about midday, which was about 8am in the Caymans.

Yet Colin was by now furious. It was the culmination of months of arguments as he had become increasingly suspicious John was fiddling the refurbishment costs. He now had in his hands accounts for £750 000 of expenditure on building work. Colin honestly couldn't see where even a third of that had gone.

The work John had over seen had been shoddily made, or quite unnecessary, from the beginning. He had constructed a cellar at great expense, which Colin had never seen the need for. Then the brand new roof had entirely collapsed and had to be built again from scratch. Costs on kitchen equipment had been astronomical. When Colin had started to investigate, he quickly discovered that every single worker on site was a member of John's immediate family. To get to the bottom of it he had brought all the paper work with him to go over slowly and carefully.

Now he had the total accounts and they stood at three quarters of a million that he had paid out. It started to dawn on Colin what had been going on. Whichever way he looked at it, someone was pulling a fast one. He was being swindled. As the penny dropped, Colin began to seethe with rage. He was scarcely able to comprehend it, but the evidence was clear. "They're ripping me off! They're ripping me off!" he repeated out loud, through gritted teeth. The thought of John's dad – who Colin secretly considered to be a 'pikey', and even more so John's brother and brother in law all laughing at him behind his back while they pocketed hundreds of thousands of his money was enough to drive Colin to distraction.

After almost no sleep, he was up again at dawn, phoning the office. It was about midday in the UK. Kenny answered.

Kenny had been hired as the club manager a few weeks before when they had finally opened for business.

Tim later described Kenny very succinctly.

"He was born in Jamaica and came to the UK as a kid. He was about 55 at the time (late '90's). He had been a good pro boxer and was a bit of a local hero in the sixties and early seventies. For a while he had a women's dress shop, ran by his wife in the (Deptford) high street. For some years he then ran a small 'shebeen' in a cellar just around the corner from the high street under a mini-cab office. He only sold Red Stripe, rum and ganga (quite openly).... Kenny was a typical Jamaican in skin colour not light skinned or mixed race but not black like an African. He was about 5ft 8in and had been a light or welter weight boxer."

Kenny's cellar bar was very popular. Due to this Colin and John had figured he would make a good manager for their club. Also the fact that Kenny tolerated the open smoking of ganja in his bar in contravention of current drug laws, suggested to Colin and John that Kenny could be relied upon to turn a blind eye should he ever happen across an old cocaine wrapper for personal use that one of them (most likely John) accidentally left on the office desk or something.

Now Kenny answered the phone to a fuming Colin.

"Hello?"

"Kenny. Is John there yet?"

"Alright Colin? He is yeah, hang on."

Then muffled voices, Kenny calling to John who was cleaning up the bar area.

"John! Colin's asking for you on the phone."

"What does he want?"

"I dunno. He wants to speak to you."

"I thought he was abroad," Colin could hear John's muffled voice growing louder and footsteps on the wooden floor.

"Nah. He's on the phone."

Eventually Colin heard the receiver changing hands the other end of the line, then just as he was ready to let rip down the receiver, John's voice again, still muffled. "Kenny," Colin heard John say. "Give us a minute will you?" Kenny's footsteps faded. "Shut the door for me. Ta."

He heard the sound of the door closing, still muffled to Colin, as John held a hand over the receiver.

Colin breathed in, focussing on the blast of fury he would send down the phone. Then John spoke first and completely took the blast from Colin's furnace. "Dr Todd and Bill've been busted," John said, simply.

There was a frozen pause, while John allowed Colin time for it to sink in.

Todd and Dr Bill. Busted! Colin ran over the notion in his mind which was beginning to reel. "Todd and Dr Bill, you mean," he said while he tried to gather his thoughts. "What, er... What with?"

"Twenty keys." There was another pause. Colin's mind was still spinning. This was potentially sufficient to unravel his whole network. His mind raced: the police could be onto them already. Would he be able to go home?

"What... What's the..." In his confusion Colin was struggling to think of a way to ask the extent of the damage without incriminating himself on the phone.

"What?" said John.

Colin spluttered. How could John not know what he was trying to get at? "Have they ..."

"What?"

"... given anything up?"

"They've not provided any information according to the news reports. Said they found it... Thought it had fallen from an airplane...."

Colin snorted a laugh of relief. He had known Todd was a good 'un

From what Colin could gather it looked as though Todd and Dr Bill were going to remain quiet.

"Anyway, what are you calling for?" said John.

The news of the bust had taken enough momentum from Colin's fury presently, that he decided to tackle the finance issue when he returned to the UK. He had the figures in print, the showdown could wait until he got back to the UK. Which would be as soon as possible in the light of the news about Todd and Dr Bill. Having ascertained it was safe for him to return to the UK, Colin now needed to find out the details of the bust and assess the situation, as a matter of urgency.

Leaving Ana and the kids in the Caymans Colin took the first available flight back to the UK. A few days after his phone call, he caught up with John one afternoon in the club office. They sat across the big office desk from each other while John filled Colin in with the details of the bust.

Dr Bill, Todd's friend had a tenured position at Edinburgh University as a research chemist. With a specialist interest in recreational pharmaceuticals, Dr Bill had built his own secret chemistry laboratory at his home in Edinburgh. It was completely hidden in the back of his house and very few people knew of its existence.

Dr Bill was able to obtain any chemical he desired by virtue of his position at the university. Increasingly he began to take home ever larger quantities of certain chemicals for his 'research,' thinking no-one would be any the wiser.

This went on for some time until Dr Bill was not only cleaning large amounts of tainted cocaine for Colin, but was also turning cocaine into crack and producing MDMA for example. The MDMA was not for sale but for personal consumption as Dr Bill strove to find the most effective formula for himself.

It was well known to Dr Bill that the customs authorities maintained a list of proscribed chemicals. Indeed the manufacturers of the chemicals on this list are under a statutory obligation to inform the authorities of where they are being dispensed to. Such chemicals could be used to create MDMA or 'ecstasy' for example.

For a researcher in the Chemistry Faculty of a major university however, there could be a legitimate use for such chemicals in small quantities. Or so Dr Bill had assumed.

For a while he did get away with it, but eventually someone in a police office somewhere had become curious as to the continuing dispensing of suspect chemicals at Edinburgh University and eventually Dr Bill was put under surveillance.

Then one evening as he and Todd were driving over the border south into England they were stopped by a police check, under suspicion of possessing MDMA, and were found in possession of 2 kilos of crack cocaine. They both got sentenced to 14 years each after pleading not guilty. A guilty plea might have led to a reduced sentence but they were possibly penalised by the judge for their refusal to reveal any names. Crucially for John and Colin now sitting in the new club office, it was evident through various sources that both Todd and Dr Bill were going to do the honourable thing and keep their mouths shut about where the cocaine was coming from. Even at the cost of potentially reduced sentences. Nevertheless, as Colin pointed out to John, they had got themselves busted going about their own business. It would be untoward to drag everyone else in just to save themselves a few years. In any case, it seemed they were not going to do that. John and Colin and company had been left in the clear.

Discussing the bust created sufficient rapport between Colin and John that afternoon that once again Colin opted not to broach the topic of money. However driving home to his new house in Fulham a short while later, inside he was seething. He wasn't' a big drinker but as soon as he got home he poured himself a large whisky he was so wound up. Sipping it on the terrace in the June evening sunshine helped calm him a little. A terrace like that was one of the benefits of being a millionaire. He and Ana had moved some months before, now that Colin was doing so well. It wasn't an ostentatiously luxurious house but it was very well to do. Colin still drove a standard saloon car, not wishing to draw too much attention with a flashy motor.

The club had been open a few weeks and Kenny was getting into the swing of things as manager. He sensed some tensions between the two main owners, John and Colin, from the beginning. However after Colin returned suddenly from the Cayman's the relationship seemed to be going from bad to worse.

Almost every day now Colin would walk into the office in the afternoon to discuss issues with John. Through the closed door he would hear their voices raising until Colin stormed out slamming the door behind him. Each day the arguments were more acrimonious than the previous.

Eventually amid one particularly explosive row when Kenny was beginning to wonder if the world was about to end, he heard Colin screaming an ultimatum, then stomping out declaring the relationship between him and John was over for good.

Colin turned out to be serious about it, and over the next few days paper work was completed and cheques signed and that was it, Colin was gone. John was sole Director, Brendan still Secretary, Tim was Treasurer.

On his way out of the club, Colin stopped in the bar where Kenny was pretending to clean, and asked him to come outside for a moment. Out in the street, Colin invited him to be manager of a new club nearby, on double his current wages. Kenny didn't have to think twice about this and shook hands with Colin on the spot.

Colin had had his eye on a successful club with an existing clientele somewhere in London for some time. He was now convinced John was ripping him off financially and sharing the gains with his family, and had reached the end of his tether. Deciding once and for all to part ways with John he allowed John to buy out his share of the first club and used the proceeds to purchase the new club. Kenny was duly installed as manager.

Sometime before the split with John, Colin had been visiting Tim one afternoon, and revealed his plans for another trip to Colombia.

Tim was amazed. "What on earth do you want to do another trip for Colin?" he asked. "You've got more money than you know what to do with already. You must have over a million under the mattress that you can't launder as it is."

Colin thought for a moment. "It's not just about the money," he said at last. "It's the game... it's about winning, about pulling the wool over the eyes of the authorities. It's about the kick."

Chapter 28

It is not clear how Colin spent his time previously when he was visiting up North. It seems he probably made friends with some business people who ran a kitchen fitting company. He had presumably grown to trust them a great deal and eventually revealed the source of his great wealth to some of them. They had been very interested and offered to take a role should he plan another trip.

The Land Cruiser trip with Tommy had gone very smoothly, and the method seemed as fool proof as he had hoped. It had occurred to Colin that this was the system to really scale up. He had noted that the Land Cruiser could not travel over 30mph without problems emerging with vehicle handling, when laden with 120kg cocaine in the wheels. With a view to engineering a reason to drive slowly he had hit upon the notion of hooking up a trailer. Towing a trailer would also provide two extra wheels' space for 50% extra contraband.

Now, it occurred to Colin that if he were to send two such vehicles with trailers, he would be able to load 180 kg per vehicle including the trailer, or three hundred and sixty kilos altogether. At a wholesale price of £25 per kilo that would net, tax free nine million pounds sterling, about US$15m. The police or media would ascribe a street value of about £60m or US$100m to such a quantity. Colin would split his proceeds 50 – 50 with the drivers, as before and pocket £4.5m himself.

The first task was for Colin to recruit a new gang of smugglers. The previous crews were all relatively well off by now and not interested in any more trips with Colin.

So Colin turned to his contacts in Yorkshire. Greg Baker was the proprietor of the kitchen fitting business in Drewsbury where Colin had spent time in his stay in the North.

Greg brought with him three other Yorkshiremen who had volunteered for the job. Danny Grigsby was the grown son of a head mistress at a secondary school. Both Greg and Danny, in their early forties were married with children. Jack Goode, the youngest at about 23 was unmarried, and Ronnie Smith, a big built shaven headed fellow of about 38, also had a young family.

Two would go in each Land Rover taking turns to drive. Once the four recruits were identified and Greg had finally convinced Colin that they could all be completely trusted, all four made a trip to London, where they could stay for a few days in an empty flat in Lewisham that belonged to one of Colin's companies. Colin had set up two or three business ventures largely to launder cash but ostensibly they were legitimate businesses and included a furniture importer and a butcher's shop.

The London trip was to allow the new recruits to get to know Colin and to gel as a team. They did a bit of cultural sight-seeing in central London, the Houses of Parliament and Big Ben, Buckingham Palace, Madam Thausaud's and the like. And they went clubbing one night in Covent Garden where despite numerous efforts no one managed to pick up a one night stand and get laid.

On another evening Colin had them over to dinner cooked by the lovely Ana at his big house in Fulham. Also he invited them to see his new club one weekend, and to discuss some details of the trip. It was around mid-June 1997 and Colin had bought the club just a few weeks before. As it turned out the refurbishments were not going to be complete by the time they arrived and a couple of weeks before. Somehow word got through to John who graciously offered used of what was now his club before doors-open in the evening. It was now a themed gay club. John has suggested it to Kenny late one night as they sat at the bar after everyone had gone. He thought there could be a burgeoning market. Kenny thought it was a good idea.

The theme rather bemused the four burly mid-nineties Yorkshire men when they arrived, to be shown into the club office at the back, by Kenny. Receiving them in his office Colin explained to their appalled faces that it was just business. They knew he was a family man so they conceded at length that it needn't automatically be considered a deal breaking issue on this one occasion, bearing in mind the amount of money they were going to earn.

"They're not going to be coming in while we're here are they," asked Ronnie, the burly 38 year old, looking round anxiously, to see if there were any concealed potential assailants in the office.

"We're not open yet," Colin chucked. "Kenny!" he called through the open door to Kenny in the club area. "Shut the office door please." Kenny walked over and shut them in the room.

They talked a little about general principles and basic routes. At this point Colin and not told them about his wheel design, and told the four instead that the cocaine would be packed into the inner tubes as had been done on the bikes, which method they already knew about. He figured they did not need to know every detail at this point, and the fewer who knew about his new method, the better. He then gave them a pep talk, and they asked a few questions. Before he finished, Colin stressed the need for sealed lips.

"Remember," he said, "there ain't no-one anywhere gonna find the goods where we hide them. But don't forget there are other potential weak spots in a venture such as this. The main one being your own gobs. Geddit?"

They looked at him.

"Therefore whatever you do, not a word to anyone, particularly when you're sitting in the pub having a chat over a few beers. You can forget where you are if you're not careful, but you never know who might be over hearing. Trust me, I know."

They nodded.

"'Loose lips sink ships!'" Colin affirmed.

The four men nodded again. They knew he had a point. There was a temptation to get excited about the amounts of money involved, and start shooting off at the mouth. Colin was right about that.

It was about five pm and they were not yet in danger of any punters arriving. So Colin offered them a free beer from the bar each.

This cast the men into something of a quandary. An offer of free beer was not something a Yorkshireman could realistically turn down and still maintain his sense of self-respect. On the other hand, if anyone ever found out they had been drinking beer in a gay club, their reputations would surely be in tatters. After much discussion, it was decided they would take the risk. "Well it may be gay beer, but it's still beer," said Smith as they clinked the pint glasses round the table.

Nevertheless, the four Yorkshiremen opted to consume their beers in the office rather than risk the bar, just in case there were any early arrivals.

Colin actually had to run some errands, but the club didn't open until 8pm, so they could safely have a few beers, he said.

Kenny had brought them the beers then left them to it. He had some cleaning to do.

The beer gave them a buzz and the idea of joining Colin's private hall of fame of his previous crews, as rich men, added to the intoxication. They talked about the various experiences of their stay in London and before long they had called Kenny in to supply a fresh round of beverages.

The four were getting along swimmingly and enjoying the beers, as Colin had hoped.

"He's dead right," of course, said one.

"Who is?"

"About what?"

"About keeping our gobs shut."

The others nodded.

"It's easy to get carried away," said another.

"When you're talking this kind a money, ya gobshite!" They looked at each other laughing, amazed at the notion of becoming instantly rich.

Colin had warned them against it, and that they knew they could not indulge in discussion at all. No if's no but's. Sitting in Colin's private club office, this seemed a good opportunity to savour their imminent wealth vocally before they went back into the world outside, and zipped their lips for real. No matter the temptations to brag, from this moment on, they would have to resist them. Even when they were drunk and in a bar chatting up a pretty lass. From now on if they had understood Colin correctly, it was their number one job to keep their mouths shut. To help get it out of their system, since they were still safely in Colin's private office, and because it was before any else had arrived in the club, they indulged themselves in a final self-congratulatory discussion of what they were now involved in, all the fabulous places they would visit, and how ridiculously much they would earn.

Jack Goode first noticed the office door had not shut fully the last time Kenny had departed after bringing more beers. The others were still talking loudly. Gently, Goode shushed them and nodded towards the door which had been left ajar.

Conversation lulled. The others started to follow

Could someone be right outside? Could someone be listening?

Tiptoeing, Goode crept towards the door, the others now in silence. When he reached it he suddenly flung it open.

Standing right there was Kenny. He was just outside the door and had to step back sharply to avoid being struck by it as it was flung open. One of his hands was still raised as if to knock, and he had a look of complete surprise on his face.

Nevertheless the four men, their criminal instincts coming into play, were immediately suspicious and alert. Had he been standing there all along? Or had he really just approached at that moment to knock? The four stared at him, trying to read the situation.

"Hey guys," Kenny broke into a smile, looking a bit perplexed at the sudden scrutiny. "You gave me a fright. Bloody 'ell. What happened? Everything alright? I was just coming to warn you, punters may be arriving in a little while." He grinned. "In case you want to … if you wanted to…"

Kenny's manner was so straight forward that the four men guessed all was ok. Only a highly skilled actor could appear so sincere in his innocence, if he had overheard and made sense of their discussion. They sensed it was fine.

Relaxing again, the four looked at each other and agreed to push off to another pub.

Outside in the street, they questioned each other once more about the issue with Kenny and the door. Did anyone think Kenny had heard anything? Was there any risk?

They assured each other eventually that it was not possible. It was nothing but paranoia. Kenny couldn't possibly have made sense of anything he had heard in any case, through the almost closed door, all talking over each other in thick Yorkshire accents. It was most unlikely indeed.

"It was only Kenny anyway, wasn't it?" said Greg, finally. "He works for Colin, doesn't he? I mean he's hardly going to grass on his boss, is he? And Colin wouldn't have hired a grass, would he?"

Baker was right. He was the smartest and they always listened to what he said. It was a good warning lesson for them. They all agreed that that is exactly what it was.

Shrugging the episode off, they headed in to the next pub for more beers and a game of pool.

Kenny waited behind on his own at the club after they had left until the evening bar staff arrived at about seven thirty pm. Explaining that he had to run some errands and would be back in a couple of hours, he took his jacket from the clothes' peg in the office, and headed out into the street and walked down to where his car was parked.

There was still some traffic at this time of the evening. As he sat in a jam, Kenny recalled his late night chat with John at the bar in the club some weeks previously. In their drunken state, the conversation had somehow twisted into a discussion of the best methods to exact retribution, in the unlikely event that it should ever be considered necessary. Kenny had mentioned to John that if he was in fact, ever in such a situation, Kenny might indeed be able to help.

John, naturally had begun to pry. Hadn't John ever wondered how Kenny got away with openly selling drugs in his own club? Kenny asked.

Once the traffic started to move, Kenny drove for about ten more minutes before turning left, then left again and pausing at the entrance to a carpark. There was never any suggestion that John had at any time prior to this particular evening, told Kenny about the nature of the meeting that had taken place at his club, earlier the same afternoon. Kenny waited for the electric barrier to raise, then drove his car into the carpark of a particular local police station.

Walking round and into the front entrance, he nodded at the sergeant behind the glass window, who immediately buzzed the door without question, letting Kenny in.

Kenny walked down the corridor to the third door on the left and knocked.

"Come!" said a voice. Kenny opened the door and walked in. Kenny was a police informant, a professional 'grass', and he had just overheard every detail of a rather ambitious smuggling plot.

No one seems to have questioned how Kenny was able to permit open smoking of ganja at his cellar club. Apparently everyone had simply assumed that this was a good indication of his laid back attitude towards illegal drugs. No-one had suspected it was because of a special relationship he might have with the local girls and boys in blue.

A couple of weeks after this, Greg Baker and Danny Grigsby who were to be nominal owners of the vehicles came down to purchase the Land Rover Discoveries, and trailers, with money provided by Colin.

The two Land Rovers were driven from London to Southampton in July 1997 by Baker and Grigsby, and put on a ship from there to Rio.

Shortly afterwards, in August 1997, Smith and Goode joined Baker and Grigsby again at the flat in London, for one more overnight stay before they all headed off on the train to Manchester Airport, to board their flight to Rio.

They weren't expecting any problems at all at Manchester. Four mates flying out to Rio for a vacation. What could be more innocent than that? Therefore Baker was surprised when he got so thoroughly turned over at the customs check at Manchester on the way out.

It wasn't just the thoroughness of the search, it was the way it happened, he explained to the others in the hotel bar later in Rio.

"They were looking for me, I know it," Baker was saying.

"Nah. You're just paranoid," said Grigsby.

The others laughed. "Paranoid!" they passed the word back and forth.

"Well they kept the map and guide books. Why would they do that," Baker continued to complain.

The others looked at him. Yes, there was the confiscations to consider. Baker had mentioned that when they were on the plane. In fact it had been a dummy map anyway showing a fake route, so it wouldn't get the customs very far if they were onto them.

Was it possible? Silence fell on the group as they pondered the idea.

"Well they didn't find anything incriminating did they," said Smith at last.

"We'll tell Colin about it when we see him," said Goode.

"No," said Baker, "wait. We don't want to unsettle him right? In case he pulls the plug on the mission." The others nodded their agreement. "I'll think about it, tell him if I decide it was important." concluded Baker.

Chapter 29

Over the next two weeks they enjoyed the beach vacation in Rio. During this time they retrieved the Land Rovers and trailers from the ship in the docks. Also Colin dropped in for a few days to check everything was going ok. Baker decided it wasn't the right time yet to tell him about the search. Maybe it was nothing anyway, he was thinking. Smugglers are gonna have to put up with some searches, he reasoned with himself. It's what the search is able to uncover, which was nothing, he decided.

In early September they set off on the drive up to Colombia. The trailers slowed down their progress as Colin had foreseen, therefore he allowed three months to make the trip, which would be plenty of time even driving slowly. They could go at an easy pace, take some scenic routes and really enjoy the experience. They went across Argentina, then parallel to the coast Northwards through Chile, Peru, Ecuador and so on, following the same route as the previous drivers and riders had.

They had enormous fun. Colin caught up with them at various points to ensure everything was going ok. Baker kept quiet about the search and confiscations.

They arrived in Colombia at the beginning of December '97. Colin and Juan Pablo had already obtained the three hundred and sixty kilos of cocaine, a couple of weeks earlier. There had been some issues with the whole sale purchase this time however.

One afternoon, two and a half weeks previously, Colin was sunbathing on a deck chair in Juan Pablo's and Ana's parents' garden alone, after a morning's riding. He was waiting for Juan Pablo to appear in his van with the goods in the back. He heard a vehicle pull up and the door slam shut, but assuming it was a delivery or a neighbour or something didn't bother to open his eyes. Then suddenly he heard a commotion by the garden path. Juan Pablo was struggling with the gate which stuck sometimes. He had left the van parked on the lane, instead of driving it up to the workshop. Something was up, thought Colin. Juan Pablo finally got the gate open and rushed up the garden towards him looking furious. Colin had begun to sit up when Juan Pablo sat on the deck chair next to his and leaning forward, whispered, "There's been a problem."

Colin lifted up his sunglasses and looked at Juan Pablo. "What sort of a problem?"

"A problem with the blow man what do you think?"

"What problem?"

"They want more money."

"How much more?"

Juan Pablo looked around the garden then back to Colin. "Two thousand a key."

"Two thousand ... what? ... US Dollars?"

Juan Pablo nodded.

"They've doubled it!"

"Yeah."

"Jeez." Colin inhaled deeply. That was a lot more than he had expected. Now he was buying more and the price was going up. It didn't make sense. More importantly, how much more! At the quantity they were purchasing that was an extra three hundred and sixty thousand dollars. Colin didn't have that sort of cash available. Colin quickly started to recognise that this could lead to a crisis, unless he was able to manage it with some skill.

Having determined this much, Colin's feelings began to give way to a simmering fury.

"How could they do this to us?" he said through gritted teeth to Juan Pablo. Juan Pablo shook his head in dismay.

"Where's the money?" said Colin.

"In the van." It was in a small briefcase on the passenger seat.

"Right, you need to set up a meeting for me with your supplier," said Colin.

Juan Pablo looked at him then shook his head. "Wait a minute. I don't know if that's a good ide...."

"Just do it!" said Colin intensely. "He wants me to come up with a third of a million dollars, then he can at least stand to meet me, right? So just arrange it." Colin stormed off inside to get his clothes and ride his bike back to his hotel to try to cool his temper. Leaving Juan Pablo sitting alone on the deck chair, wondering how he would arrange the meeting. His supplier was a well-connected cartel member. 'This might not be easy,' he thought.

*

It turned out not to be as difficult to arrange a meeting as Juan Pablo had anticipated. Colin still had all the original payment intact, three hundred and sixty thousand dollars, in cash. He didn't have the newly demanded money though, neither had he made any attempts to begin to gather it.

The meeting would not be with Juan Pablo's usual contact, but someone else. "A negotiator I suspect," Colin said to Juan Pablo as he arrived to collect Colin in the lobby of Colin's hotel, and drive him into town. The meeting was to be in a large corporate office block near the town centre. Not what Colin had expected at all after Juan Pablo had warned him to be careful. He was kind of expecting army guerrilla types, but when they parked up, true to his word Juan Pablo led Colin towards a posh office building containing various corporate presences. They walked through the glass doors into the plush lobby and travelled in a high speed elevator to the 11th floor. There they waited in a well presented reception, Colin balancing the briefcase on his knees, until a glamourous receptionist ushered them along a corridor towards an office.

As they approached the door Colin turned to Juan Pablo and instructed him to go back down the corridor and wait at reception. Then he knocked and walked through the door into the office alone. Inside a very well dressed and carefully groomed man in a suit, with a well-educated English accent, smiled politely as he stood up from behind his large oak desk to introduce himself. He was more than happy to discuss Colin's situation he said, waving Colin to take a seat.

As he sat down Colin noticed behind the gentleman suspended high on the wall was a decorative Japanese samurai sword.

The man followed Colin's gaze. "Ah, the Japanese always make the best swords," he said.

"I hope you're not planning to use it on me!" Colin joked.

"Not unless we have to," laughed the gentleman.

After a few moments polite and smiling small talk, Colin tackled the issue head on.

"Why have you doubled the cost to me?" he asked.

"Ah, well. Let me explain the situation..."

But Colin had started to work himself up, and allowed his feelings getting the better of him, "I mean, in any business I have ever heard of, if you buy more quantity the price goes down right?"

"I see. If you'd just let me expl..."

"So I buy triple the amount and you double the price? I don't get it. It should be half the price."

The suited man laughed politely, holding his hands up, encouraging Colin to calm down a little.

"Colin, please. Slow down."

Colin paused for breath, getting a hold of himself at last.

"We have been following your career with much interest, I can say." The man started again, courteously. "Certain powerful people are very impressed with the progress you have made so far."

"Mm?" Colin looked at him quizzically, slightly caught off guard.

"You have done very well, and we can assist you to grow your business much bigger, much faster."

Colin looked at him for a moment. Then he exploded again. "What is this? A joke? "Grow my business? And you plan to do that by taking twice as much money? I can understand how that grows your business, but how does it help mine? Exactly?"

"You misunderstand, this is just a preliminary measure to ensure..."

"No, you misunderstand." Colin seemed to have lost his temper. "You can't just expect me to hand over double the money like that. Not when that amounts to nearly a million dollars, for fuck sake," he said with gritted teeth.

"Please, no swearing,"

"Yes, I'm sorry. It's just... I don't have that kind of money available." His eyes darted from side to side and he ground his teeth in anger.

"Surely it's not such a big deal to a man such as yourself. You have become very wealthy since you began your relationship with ... Colombia."

"I can't just conjure up a quarter of a million pounds this afternoon for fuck sake."

"Please, no swearing."

"Whatever I've got left is tied up in properties and investments around the world. It would take me weeks or months to get hold of that amount of money, even if I had it. Not least arousing suspicions."

"We are happy to wait as long as you need," the man offered.

There was a pause, then Colin shook his head. "Forget it, I'm not interested in that case. Just cancel the lot. I'll go elsewhere. I'd sooner quit the business right now than pay double the money... I'll just cut my losses."

"We wish to help you Colin."

Colin snorted derisively.

"You require protection at Genoa."

This really caught Colin off guard. "Do what?"

"You plan to put the merchandise in the tyres right? You will need protection."

Colin tried not to look startled, but how could he know about his previous system of using the tyres? "No. Actually, you're wrong. So I think I don't need your protection," he said adopting his best poker face.

"The extra money, the added thousand dollars per kilo, is the amount required to ... grease the palms ... as it were, in Genoa. For protection. You see, we don't want a media spotlight shone on Genoa if you happen to get busted trying to import just a few hundred kilos in tyres.

"So if you insist on using Genoa, you must take our protection. We are obliged for our own reasons to cover you, by paying the usual service costs to various insiders who can pull the strings at Customs in Genoa. We are simply asking you to cover our costs."

"I think I invented the Genoa route," muttered Colin.

"Then perhaps you are a naïve young man," said the gentleman.

"And you're a greedy twat," Colin muttered, under his breath.

The man bristled in his chair. "We can't afford for you to get apprehended at Genoa this month. We have an extensive operation underway."

"Don't worry, I won't get 'apprehended'."

"There are unavoidable added costs required if we are to supply you with this amount of cocaine to be transported via Genoa. We do not want any spotlight shone on Genoa. So if you will insist on using Genoa, you must take our protection. We have to cover your operation, the least you can do is cover our costs. Or choose another route."

Colin wasn't prepared to tolerate it. He was an intelligent man obviously. Hence his wealth, if anyone felt they needed to ask. Now he was rich, these people wanted to take a piece of him. They knew full well he couldn't possibly begin to work out another route from scratch now. It is not certain that Colin was thinking clearly at this juncture, although it is not evident why that was. Of course, things that are fully apparent in retrospect are not always immediately obvious in real time. It is not clear to anyone why he chose to quibble so inflexibly over what was indeed to him at that time a relatively small sum of money. Perhaps it was pride, or arrogance, or a kind of psychotic greed. Or maybe he simply overlooked to sit down for a couple of moments and actually think about what he was doing, and the actual value of the sums in question. It could be that he had a kind of mental blind spot for the financial proportions concerned. For whatever reason he had begun to stand on some unknown principle that appears to have existed only in his own mind. He was not willing to pay the extra money whatever, even though it was just a tiny fraction of his potential profits.

"Well as I said, I simply don't have access to the kind of money you are now demanding." Colin explained. "I do have the three hundred and sixty thousand as originally arranged here on my lap. Now if you don't want to take this money, perhaps I will have to look for a new supplier."

"Of course we appreciate the sum of money is relatively large here in Colombia...

"That's right. I've been making you very rich…

"And we you. Also I think it is not quite so large a sum for a man such as yourself from London…" the gentleman interjected. "But! We concede it may take even you a little while to accumulate such this amount of cash for us. Therefore my superior has very generously given me permission to offer you interest free credit terms until you can offload the shipment in London. So I think you can see we are very understanding people. We would expect to be paid first of all creditors including yourself and any couriers. All standard conditions apply of course."

Colin thought for a moment and suddenly perceived an opportunity. He said, "So I can pay the extra money after arriving in the UK?"

"The very first three hundred and sixty thousand you recoup must be paid immediately to us."

Colin liked this idea, because he was certain he could not be held to honour his side of such a deal, and he would be able to evade them and escape having to make any further payment. They wouldn't know his address in the UK. Not even Juan Pablo had the Fulham address so these guys couldn't possibly know it. It was all ex-directory of course, so there would not be much chance of them tracking him down. For whatever reason his mind was almost made up that he wouldn't give them the rest of the money. This offer would also buy him some time to think about it, just in case he wanted to do more business, in which case it may be wise to pay up, he thought. But he really intended this would be his last trip and he would have no need to maintain a relationship any further now with these people. Even if he was to end up paying up, he liked that he was not being asked for the extra up front any more. He could portray that to Juan Pablo as an immediate victory. "OK," he said at length.

Juan Pablo was still sitting in reception on his way out. He stood up and joined Colin as he entered the elevator.

"How'd it go?" said Juan Pablo as soon as the doors slid shut. They were alone.

"I'll tell you when we get outside," said Colin.

"I don't know why you wouldn't let me come in," complained Juan Pablo.

"All you need to know is that you were not involved in any agreement. That was made only by the people in the room, see?"

Just then the doors opened at ground level. Juan Pablo said nothing. They exited the elevator and walked out through the lobby and onto the street.

*

By the time the four drivers had showed up in the two Land Rover Discovery's with attached trailers, the cocaine was purchased for the originally agreed sum and already stored discretely out of sight, ready and waiting in Juan Pablo's father's workshop.

Soon after they had arrived in Colombia, Greg decided to tell Colin about the search at Manchester airport, and the confiscation of maps and guide books. Colin was furious. Why hadn't he said anything until now?

"You think it's significant?"

"Yes! Of course it's significant." Colin paused for a moment. "It might be significant. I will have to think about it."

After a couple days' thinking, Colin had decided that although the search was no doubt just a co-incidence, it was nevertheless worth taking some emergency crisis precautions.

A fifth driver had previously been identified also from Drewsbury and part of Baker's close network. Phil Jones was well known to the four riders. Colin now decided that Smith was to fly home to the UK, meet up with Jones and purchase a third decoy Land Rover. They should drive this over to France using a cross channel Ferry and wait for instructions from Colin.

This was a dramatic shift of events, and would have alarmed the four drivers perhaps. However the intensity of Colin's approach to resolve potential problems before they arose also filled them with confidence in him and encouraged in them a tendency to follow his instructions perhaps without much thought sometimes.

Smith was despatched to the UK in early December. There were now just three drivers, one would be alone in one vehicle, and two together in the other.

The cocaine was loaded into the twelve wheels which parts were welded together, enclosing thirty kilos of cocaine in each. The wheels were refitted to the two Land Rovers and trailers, all the work taking place in Juan Pablo's father's workshop.

The vehicles were transported to Colombia in three lorries, and flown cargo to Latecia, as before. They drove slowly the short distance from the airport into Latecia, then the Land Rovers were loaded onto cargo river boats and shipped down river to Manaus. At Manaus they disembarked then loaded the vehicles and trailers once more into three lorries which were then driven to Rio.

The lorries were stopped by a police check on the road south out of Manaus.

The lorry drivers and Land Rover drivers stood at the side of the road smoking roll ups while military police armed with machine guns swarmed all over the vehicles. The arrangement was that the lorry drivers could deny all knowledge of the drugs. The Land Rovers were owned in the name of Baker and Grigsby. It would probably be impossible for Goode, the remaining co-driver to get away with denying all knowledge. As they stood by the side of the road they pretended to engage in small talk, and to be enjoying the chance to stretch their legs. However there are probably very few smugglers on the planet who actually derive any pleasure from such moments. The three drivers logically understood the brilliance of Colin's wheel design, and the infinitesimal likelihood that it would be uncovered, particularly by a mobile unit in the jungle. Nevertheless occasions such as these were not much fun. You never quite knew what might happen.

After an hour or so, the heavily armed police had satisfied themselves that no drugs were concealed anywhere in or under the lorries or the transported vehicles. The drivers breathed surreptitious sighs of relief and at last set free, were permitted on their way again.

In as much as each smuggler underwent an experience of dread during any routine search, they also enjoyed a sense of elation on release. This smugglers buzz, could reputedly become as addictive for some, as the drugs they were transporting. It was dark by the time they started off down the road again and as they picked up speed the four Land Rover drivers looked out of the truck windows in silence at the hot black starry night, touching the thrill of their first successful scrummage with customs.

Chapter 30

On December 22nd at about 11.30am Greg Baker manoeuvred the first Land Rover slowly down the slope towards the customs checkpoint at the docks in Rio. He was startled to notice up ahead an unusually large number of customs officials buzzing around, some holding clipboards, some in uniform, others in suits. Greg's first sense, although he conceded it may just be paranoia, was that they were looking for particular vehicles.

Then Jack Goode in the seat next to him said, "Are they looking for someone?"

Greg said nothing. He had hoped Jack would say something else. Or shut up.

They had driven down from Manaus in a few days without further trouble after the roadside check, and after a few days break in Rio were finally ready to board the ship. Juan Pablo and Federo had unloaded the Land Rovers and trailers a few blocks from the port, allowing them to drive slowly the last few hundred metres and join the queue of traffic at customs.

Slowly they moved forward, watching as the officials ahead seemed to identify each vehicle and mark it off on various clipboards.

Greg turned round to look over his shoulder and see if he could make out Danny Grigsby's expression at the wheel in the Land Rover behind. With the reflections on the glass he couldn't quite see him.

Eventually it was Greg and Jack's turn. The car in front was waved through the checkpoint and several officials turned their attention to the Land Rover. One stood in front surveyed it, then looked up to see Greg behind the wheel through the glass. The official looked down again to read the number plate, 'N761 DWW'. Greg was pretending not to pay attention but was watching out of the corner of his eye. He was certain the official looked startled for a fraction of a moment in some way, as he checked the registration against his clipboard. Or was he just being paranoid again? The official strolled slowly towards Greg's open driver door window. He smiled at Greg, but just with his mouth, not his eyes. Greg smiled back. 'Stop thinking so much,' he told himself.

"Documents!" The official held out his hand, and Greg passed over the passports and paper work. Taking the documents the official strolled to the back of the Land Rover then round behind the trailer. In the wing mirror, Greg saw him begin to take an interest in the identical Land Rover behind, when another official appeared at the driver window, then another at Jack's window. They both began to ask questions. What was the purpose of the trip? Where had they been? How long had they been travelling? Were they hiding any illegal drugs? Had they travelled on this ship before? And so on. Greg scarcely had time to think. Fortunately he could provide honest answers to all the questions, except the one about drugs of course. In the quick fire succession of questions he almost missed a beat before denying carrying any drugs, but somehow managed to maintain sufficient rhythm with his one dishonest answer.

By the time they had retrieved the documents and finally been waved through both Greg and Jack's faces were dripping with perspiration. However it was a hot day so this didn't arouse suspicion in itself.

"Whew," Greg sighed, as soon as they were out of earshot, as they trundled towards the loading ramp on the ship.

"Put's some stress on the old ticker, eh!" mumbled Jack. He was the youngest and probably had the most to lose if they got caught.

"Yeah. Somewhat," agreed Greg. "That just put about ten years on me I would think. I can see why people don't want to do it too often." He drove the Land Rover up the ramp and into the car hold of the ship.

Danny drove up the ramp a few minutes after them, and both vehicles were strapped down in the hold.

*

Fifteen days after they had left port at Rio, on January 7th 1998 the three men once again took their seats in the Land Rovers, ready to disembark as soon as the ship docked. They were now approaching the port at Genoa.

No doubt there were many people standing and waiting on land watching for the ship's arrival that morning. Certainly there were several in particular that are of direct concern to this narrative.

On a top floor of an office block several hundred metres from the port, with a clear line view of the customs inspection area, a pair of field binoculars was made use of to observe the boat as it approached the dock. A finger jostled with the focus knob in an attempt to identify either of the Land Rovers on board. It was not possible to see them yet. The bearer of the binoculars removed them from his face to reveal... it was Colin. He stood in the window of the rented office watching the boat glide towards the port. While his couriers were essentially unaware of it, he seldom let his merchandise out of his site, at any point for even a moment.

However there were other interested parties on this particular morning who were also looking out for the two Land Rovers. For example, in a hotel window, some few hundred yards from the dock, a Colombian individual trained another pair of binoculars on the boat. Two other men sat in the same room, and he relayed progress of the vessel to them in Spanish.

Yet there was still one other keen observer. This one stood actually on the dock out in the open, beyond the customs checkpoint, looking out to sea at the ship as it approached.

At this moment, Greg and Jack were standing at the handrail of the deck having come up to watch as the harbour approached. Danny was still sitting in his Land Rover downstairs, waiting in the car hold. As Greg and Jack looked ahead Greg spotted the man standing out on the dock, legs akimbo, hands on hips, eyes fixed on the ship. Greg couldn't believe his eyes. His blood ran cold.

Not only because the man was dressed in a UK customs official uniform. What really rocked Greg was the fact that he knew who the man was. It was the same official that had identified Greg at Manchester and who had led the thorough search, confiscating the maps and guidebooks.

"He's waiting for us!" Greg spluttered involuntarily under his breath as he tried to contain a surge of emotion.

Over the noise of the engines, the wind and waves Jack did not manage to catch what he said, and thought maybe Greg was having a coughing fit. "You alright," he said, patting Greg on the back.

Greg looked at him, his eyes bulging. Should he tell Jack? He wasn't sure. Tell him what exactly? 'Jack, I hate to break it to you, but we're about to get busted.'?

Greg shook his head. To himself, quietly he said, 'Pull yourself together, man. Now then, find yourself a way out! Got it?' He let this notion sink in, then answered his own question deliberately, in the affirmative, 'Yes!' He struggled with himself for a moment as with determination he chased round for a sense of conviction. Finally he looked back to Jack. "Yeah, I'm fine, Sunshine," he said. "Come on then," and he started leading the way down to the car deck. No point in unsettling young Jack now, he had decided.

About twenty minutes or so later, Greg carefully drove his Land Rover onto the ramp. Jack was in the passenger seat next to him, Danny driving the second vehicle behind, alone. Greg had said nothing to either two about the UK customs official. Now he could see ahead there were a number of officials in UK uniform milling around amongst the Italian customs officials.

As he drove onto the dock and towards customs he saw the suited official from Manchester twenty or thirty yards in front of him, watching him approach. A shiver ran down Greg's back, still he mentioned nothing to Jack.

The official started indicating to Greg to pull the Land Rover over to the side. He was clearly referring to both vehicles. A couple of uniformed UK officials joined the suited man.

"Are they English?" Jack noticed the UK uniforms for the first time.

Several hundred yards away from his rented office window, Colin, fascinated, watched proceedings through his field binoculars. From their room in the Nova hotel, unknown to Colin the Colombian representatives also using binoculars, observed events carefully and with interest.

Greg had moved the Land Rover to the side as instructed. Now he pulled on the handbrake and switched off the ignition. The suited official, followed by two UK uniformed customs officials, at least one of whom was carrying a clipboard, started walking towards the parked Land Rovers.

"What the heck's going on?" said Jack.

Greg said nothing. Then just as they were approaching there was a loud shout, in Italian. It was aimed at the suited official. He and his followers stopped in their tracks and started turning round. Behind them running towards them was a uniformed Italian customs officer. Behind him also running were other Italian officials, some uniformed, one or two suited. They caught up with the English officials and some kind of discussion appeared to ensue.

Greg and Jack sat in their Land Rover watching through the windscreen. Danny didn't have such a good view behind and could not see what was going on.

As Greg and Jack watched, what had started as a discussion between the Italian and UK officials appeared now to descend into some sort of argument. Quite a heated argument indeed. Voices were being raised on both sides, the suited UK official from Manchester apparently remonstrating without reserve now with his Italian counterpart, as his English face convulsed through increasingly alarming shades of purple.

Finally when the Manchester official's apoplexy reached its zenith, the Genoan he had been rowing with dramatically moved him and the uniformed UK officials to the side, then waved Greg on.

Greg was staggered at this turn of events, but he didn't pause to question the order. He switched on the ignition, threw the gearstick forward, and started easing the car towards the exit, Danny in the other Land Rover close behind.

As they drove past the Italian and UK officials the suited Englishman continued to remonstrate with his counterpart, who was still insisting on holding him back out of the vehicles path. The UK official probably didn't shake his fist at the drivers as they disappeared without a single check through the barrier and out the other side of customs, but if this had been all happening in a cartoon, perhaps he would have.

In the window at the top of the office block, Colin put down his binoculars and allowed a huge wave of relief to wash over him. He had a lot of money invested in those vehicles apart from anything... everything else.

The three Colombians in the Nova hotel had already lost interest and were now rolling dice on the hotel room floor and gambling fistfuls of hundred dollar bills.

As they drove out into the street, Greg couldn't quite believe it, or understand how they still had their liberty. Jack and Danny had both been a bit more relaxed, neither having recognised the Manchester official.

Now in the street, in the January sunshine, Greg's spirits lifted. He led the small convoy of two Land Rovers and small trailers, six wheels each packed with cocaine, driving slowly to a pre-arranged meeting point on the autostrade, the Italian freeway.

Before they reached it, they heard police sirens behind them. Greg looked in his mirror. He saw flashing lights approaching. It was one of those faith testing incidents people in his line of work must from time to time endure. The police or sometimes even ambulances, happen to be innocently racing up behind as people are transporting some contraband from point A to point B. It is simply a case of waiting for the screaming flashing posse to overtake and pull ahead, to continue their pursuit of whichever criminal they happen to have identified. During that moment however, which can last a seeming eternity, trying to invade the intellect is always the horror striking notion that it is the smugglers themselves that have in fact been identified as the recalcitrant element. This is of course simply paranoia. It has to be endured, but will be over the moment the flashing vehicles race on ahead.

Greg, Danny and Jack each held their breath and waited for them to pass.

Then there is the moment they are actually overtaking. This can really seem to last for ever. Then, if it starts to last too long, for all but the truly faithful, those pesky invading thoughts might begin to gain the upper hand, and begin to insist: this is not overtaking, but catching up. The flashing police vehicles were now hovering for too long on the shoulder of Greg and Jack's vehicle. They pulled alongside, beside Jack's passenger window on the outside lane and hung there. Why didn't they pull ahead yet? Why hadn't they overtaken already?

With a slow dawning of recognition it began to register on Jack and Greg, and Danny that they three were after all the quarry that was being hunted down. It was no longer rationally possible to deny it, they had been busted.

Italian uniformed police officers in marked police cars were waving them to the side of the road. The air was filled with sirens and flashing blue lights.

"Tell me this isn't happening," said Greg in disbelief.

"Oh shit!" said Jack. The three couriers each consciously struggled momentarily to prevent any involuntary loss of bowel control.

Both vehicles drew over to the side of the road. They had been pursued by three police cars. Now coming up the road behind were even more flashing lights and sirens, and an approaching police van with room for a dozen armed officers.

One of the police cars pulled in front of the parked Land Rovers to prevent onward escape, although at no point had they yet been seen to drive at more than about 25mph.

Italian uniformed armed officers appeared at the Land Rover windows and in broken English instructed the occupants to remain seated in the vehicles. Various policemen began to swarm around outside the two parked vehicles and trailers. By now the van had pulled up. From the rear emerged half a dozen UK uniformed customs officers and the suited official who Greg had recognised. There were apparently no Italian customs officers, only local police.

Chapter 31

The three Land Rover occupants waited, each feeling devastated. Jack was sweating so much his shirt was soaked, and he was shivering despite the heat. Greg had gone white in the face and was completely perplexed. This wasn't what he had intended for himself and his companions at all. This wasn't supposed to occur. Of course, they haven't actually found the drugs yet, he reminded himself, finally finding space to breathe again.

"Stumm, mate," Greg muttered under his breath, telling Jack to keep quiet.

Jack nodded barely perceptibly.

"Quiet!" shouted one of the armed officers at the window. "No talking!"

Danny sat alone in the Land Rover behind, looking dazed and puzzled.

The suited UK official had emerged from the van with several UK customs officials and was now engaged in discussion with a small group of senior Italian policemen. Eventually some agreement appeared to be made. People started returning to their vehicles. A police officer approached the guards at Greg's window and spoke in Italian. He then left, and the guard turned to Greg. "Follow the car in front," he commanded. On the other side of the Land Rover, another guard opened the passenger door and instructed Jack to get out. Jack looked round at Greg in the driving seat.

Greg looked at his plaintive expression and experienced an emotional tug. He had taken on young Jack as an apprentice in his kitchen fitting business as a favour to Jack's mum, who Greg had known for some years. He had promised her always to look out for Jack, and felt a sense of paternal responsibility to the boy. He wouldn't have brought him on the trip if he had thought Jack would get into trouble. He wasn't about to break any promises now, even if he had no idea how he would engineer that yet.

"You'll be alright, Jack," Greg assured him. He winked at Jack, and there was a twinkle in his eye. Jack had faith in that twinkle in Greg's eye. If Greg said he'd be alright, then that was good enough for Jack.

Jack allowed himself to be hoisted by the arm out of the Land Rover and was then led to one of the police cars and put in a back seat.

They drove in a slow convoy, lights flashing, for about ten minutes to a local police station.

At the police station the Land Rovers and trailers were driven onto long raised ramps allowing police inspectors to examine the undersides with torches and prodding-sticks. They continued inspecting the vehicles inside and out for half an hour or so.

The three drivers stood to the side, with policemen standing by each. They were separated so they couldn't converse, but were not handcuffed. They hadn't been found guilty of anything yet. In any case the police had the keys, and they wouldn't get far especially on foot if they tried to escape.

At one point the suited UK official strolled over towards where Greg was standing as he watched the searching.

"Hey Greg!" the official was smiling broadly in recognition, as he approached.

Greg nodded.

"Remember me?"

"Yes! Can I have my map back now please."

"You're a smart guy Greg. What did you do it for?"

"I've done nothing wrong," said Greg sullenly.

"Ah. So our intelligence is wrong is it?"

Greg shrugged.

"You're suggesting that the thirty officers I've assigned to your case are all wasting their time are you?"

Greg looked straight ahead. "I'd just like to get on my way please."

By now the search had more or less ceased. An Italian official approached the UK officer who was talking to Greg.

"We have found nothing," he explained in English. "We have looked everywhere."

An image of imminent release flashed across Greg's mind and he felt a glimmer of hope in his stomach, and it drew his attention from that which was outside to that which was inside.

The English official rubbed his trendily goateed chin. "We haven't quite looked everywhere yet, have we?" he addressed the question at Greg, who seemed oblivious.

"Where haven't we looked Greg?"

Greg ignored him and concentrated on investigating a golden glow he had glimpsed somewhere inside his stomach. It had felt so good for a moment that it drew his attention as he sought to locate it again and recapture the sensation.

"We haven't checked the wheels yet, have we Greg?"

Greg continued to ignore him, and glanced casually around at the scenery, and tried to his mind on the sense of positivity that glimmered in his belly. The officer's question however directed his thoughts back to reality. At the moment he had relocated the inward glimmer which was the only thing that stopped him feeling like his world was falling apart around him, he suddenly lost sight of it once more and it vanished back into darkness as the officer dragged his attention back to the wheels. Greg knew very well what they hid. Now his head began to go into a spin. Everything was going pear shaped. They had figured out it was in the wheels, soon they'd break into the hubs... While trying to look completely relaxed and at ease, he struggled vainly to drag his mind back to his own preferred version of events, where they all went free.

"Will you let tyres down please," the UK official now instructed the Italian officer.

Very faintly Greg sensed his inner buzz again. They would find nothing in the tyres. He concentrated to avoid revealing any of his thoughts at all and did his best not to think about the cocaine in the wheel hubs, and to maintain a blank expression. But the more he tried not to think about the wheel hubs, the more he found himself doing so. Now he started to glance around surreptitiously and check that no-one else had started considering them. Recognising the folly of this he fought the urge to look at the vehicles at all and he struggled to contain his growing sense of panic. Catching hold of himself he suddenly realised that the best way not to reveal any thoughts was in fact to not have any. The situation was beyond him, he could responsibly give up trying to do anything about it. Which notion calmed his mind and he allowed all his thoughts to blank out.

When his mind stopped leaping from one possibility to another, and calmed down, Greg began again to pick up again on the warming inner feeling that they might just get away with it. That was the feeling that interested him he remembered. It gave him a cosy glowing sensation deep in his belly. His sense of the events happening around him began to fade. He now became detached, somehow indifferent to the threat of imminent arrest. It was less painful to focus his own sense of inner satisfaction, which held up all the time he kept thinking about their release, and this made him feel better. As he completely withdrew his attention and allowed it to dwell on his own inner feelings, the sensation of comfort grew, until it became quite as pleasurable and just as powerful as the very best high he had ever had from a line of cocaine.

"The tyres?" In the background of his daze, Greg vaguely registered the Italian officer confirming that he understood the UK official's order. Greg dragged his attention back to his inner senses, they were such a wonderful pleasure.

The Italian official went over to relay the instruction to other officials. Now another discussion ensued about letting the air out of the tyres. Eventually some people went into the station and then re-emerged some minutes later with an even more senior Italian official. More discussions followed then finally the first officer walked back over to the UK official who had been watching on, next to Greg. The sound of approaching footsteps brought Greg back out of his daze, but his warm glow of inner satisfaction remained with him while his eyes tried to regain focus on reality.

As the official approached, Greg saw that he was shaking his head. Greg had given up trying to resist events now. It was beyond his control. A sense of confidence persisted within him however. He still felt strangely certain, that they were all about to walk away free. Even though rationally he knew such an outcome was almost impossible. He preferred the feeling he derived from it so much that he tried to cling onto it. As though to sleep, just when the alarm starts to ring.

"What does he want this time," muttered the UK official under his breath.

The Italian official drew up in front of him and announced, "Unfortunately we are not able to deflate the tyres... because we do not have the correct air pump to reflate them."

The UK official stared at him, momentarily dumbstruck. Greg sensed another surge of elation, but managed to keep it hidden.

"Say what now?" spluttered the UK official.

"We are unable to reflate the tourists' tyres. Therefore because there has been found no evidence of criminal activity, the chief is unwilling to subject our tourists in Genoa to such damage which we cannot repair. For this reason he has not permitted the deflating of the tyres."

This incensed the UK official, and pleased Greg by an approximately equivalent measure. As the UK official once again transcended through his various shades of purple, Greg, Jack and Danny were given back their keys and invited to continue their holiday without further interference.

The three men were very gracious about having their time wasted, nevertheless they got on their way again pretty sharpish.

Soon they were back on the road, in a small undisturbed convoy of two Land Rovers and trailers. They were driving at twenty miles an hour because of the cocaine in the wheels. Some of the police had stood watching them drive down the road for a considerable time after they left. Such was the slow progress they made. Eventually the sounds of the UK official's furious remonstrations faded into the breeze and they were once more heading towards their rendezvous point on the autostrade.

As soon as they were out of sight of the police station, Greg and Jack relaxed.

"Oh my god!" yelled Jack.

Greg looked at him, grinning, eyes twinkling. "That's the way to do it, my son," he said.

"Whoo ooo!" Jack whooped with delight through the open window, his eyes alight. Greg honked on the horn. Behind them Danny joined in with the honking.

"Yee ha!" whooped Greg.

A short while later they drew into the service stop on the autostrade where they had arranged the meeting. There was an enormous coach park and carpark behind the buildings that made up the petrol stations and café areas, with sections separated by trees and hedges where they could find a relatively secluded place to park the Land Rovers. The three then traipsed back over to the café to get a good plate of food each, and wait for Colin to show up.

"Do they do English breakfast?" Danny asked the other two as they walked.

"Ahh! I could go for a full English. What d'you think Jack?"

"Oh yeah!" said Jack, enthusiastically. "Two eggs!"

"Chips and beans."

"Mug of tea."

"Oh yes. A mug of tea!"

At around the same time, Colin was leaving the office block near the port, carrying his crash helmet in one hand. His bike was in the carpark nearby. At this moment the phone rang in the hotel room at the Nova hotel interrupting a noisy argument about the dice game. One of the three picked up the receiver and listened. He then hung up and nodded at one of the others who picked up his own crash helmet and left the room immediately. A few moments later, the other two followed him out. One of them having picked up a set of car keys from the counter top.

Before long Colin pulled into the service station carpark on the autostrade and started looking for somewhere discreet to park his bike. He couldn't see the Land Rovers from where he was. They were presumably somewhere else in the extended parking area. There were very few cars or other vehicles and plenty of empty spaces. He found a secluded spot behind a large hedge and had just stood the bike on its stand and was undoing his crash helmet strap, when he heard another bike behind him. Something made him look round, and he saw the bike slowly heading straight towards him. As it approached it veered slightly and pulled up a few metres from his own bike. The rider took off his crash helmet as he sat on his bike and looked directly at Colin.

"Do I know you?" Colin asked. He guessed the man was Colombian now he had removed his helmet.

"You know my boss," the man replied in a Colombian accent.

At that moment a car drew into the same area of the car park and also drove slowly towards them, parking close by. There were two male occupants, Colin noted. Also both apparently Colombian. Colin's pulse rate began to increase slightly, and his hair tingled on his scalp. The occupants of the car remained inside it, and just sat there even after they had switched off the engine.

Ignoring the three men Colin began to walk towards the café. The bike rider stepped off his bike, and picking up his pace walked in front of Colin to block his path.

"What?" Demanded Colin.

"My boss has asked me to talk to you."

"I don't even know who your boss is!" shouted Colin at the man, feeling a bit upset.

"You visited him in his office, in Colombia. He has provided you some protection. He would like to offer you the opportunity to replay his money now. I think three hundred and sixty thousand dollars? Will you be paying in cash?"

His way ahead blocked by the man, Colin turned and walked back towards his bike. The man followed him over and they stood each side of it facing one another.

"What protection?" muttered Colin. "There wasn't any protection."

"There was protection," the man corrected him.

"Can you prove it?"

The man looked at him and said nothing.

"I think your boss is full of shit," said Colin. "We did not require any so called protection because they would never have found it."

The man continued to look at him in silence.

"I don't believe you," Colin went on. "I don't buy your bosses story that he has any influence whatsoever on Italian customs."

"My boss has told me to say that you can make the repayment immediately. It is a generous suggestion, you will be wise to accept. How will you be paying?"

"The generous offer is to pay the money now?" Colin was incredulous. Was the man joking? He could not see a hint of irony in his eyes.

"How is that generous to me? You're just mugging me," wailed Colin. He was feeling very frustrated by all this. He suspected he was being tricked. The Colombians had no more insiders in Genoa's customs than he did. These guys were small time coke dealers, who had got lucky and rich through Colin's ingenuity, and had now become plain greedy, was how it looked to Colin. Now this fellow thought he was doing Colin some kind of a favour by requesting immediate payment. Was he stupid? Or was he deliberately trying to wind Colin up.

Colin looked at him. 'He can't be very smart,' he thought. It wouldn't be difficult to lose them on the bike now he knew they were tailing him. He was irritated by the nonsense suggestion that they were somehow providing him protection and also he didn't have the cash yet anyway. He was also irritated with himself that he had not recognised that he was being followed from the office. He was usually very sharp about such things. It was particularly galling for him to have been caught out by people he now considered to be half-wit clowns, goons at best.

"Ok, let me talk to my partners and see what the situation is, Colin said at length. " But I won't have the money anyway. Not until at least 24 hours after we get into the UK," he looked at the Colombian, who seemed to understand. "Your funeral," Colin thought he heard him say. Then realised it was too idiomatic an expression for a non-native speaker, he must have misheard. "Look, just wait here for a few minutes while I go and talk to the fellas. Ok?"

The man nodded, and stood aside to indicate he would not block Colin's way this time.

Colin strode towards the café, smiling to himself. 'This is interesting!' he thought. 'They probably don't know my address in the UK, or they wouldn't be following me here in Genoa. And what's more, they followed me and not the Land Rovers. (I can't believe they managed to follow me and I didn't notice it. Still, it's a good lesson for me. I must be more alert.) Let's see. Maybe I can lose them in the UK, and save the money.' He considered the idea for a moment. 'Stop fantasising,' he admonished himself. 'You have to just pay it. You did agree to it. You're good for your word.' Then a dagger of frustration in his gut, 'But, blow it. The bastards are just ripping me off. They doubled the rate overnight and concocted some nonsense about protection at customs. They're being dishonest. What a joke!' He was still not certain he would pay the extra money despite his previous agreement. It was less than a tenth of the extraordinary profit he expected to reap, yet still it filled his stomach with agonies of frustration to have to give it away to these guys. They had contributed nothing extra, and had already earned a fortune from him. Now they had got above themselves and were trying to con him. Except now he had thought about it, Colin wasn't sure whether he would be able to tolerate that. As he turned the corner to join the walkway which led to the café area entranceway, Colin glanced over his shoulder quickly to check on his bike, which was by now some distance away. The man was still standing next to it, and still watching after him.

Greg, Jack and Danny had just finished eating when Colin burst in through the door of the café. It had a large mostly empty seating area and the three of them had found a table by the window where they could talk out of earshot of other customers if they kept their voices down.

The café did do English breakfasts, which was excellent and hit the mark superbly. While they were waiting for the food to arrive, they had had an intense and quiet conference, and come to a group agreement. As they filled their stomachs they became more certain in their decision, and steeled themselves to reveal it to Colin when he arrived, and to stick by their guns in face of the anticipated objections.

The last one had literally just put down his fork and they were gazing in contentment out of the window at the bright winter sunshine when they heard the door fly open and suspected it might be Colin. Indeed it was. He stood in the doorway for a moment, crash helmet in hand and surveyed the large room until he spotted the three drivers. A waitress appeared to lead him to a table, but he pointed at the other three and strode right over to join them.

He sat down at the table as they smiled and greeted each other. "Everything alright?" he asked.

"Yep." Yes, everything was alright.

"Where are the vehicles?"

"Parked at the back, a ways." Greg explained how to locate them, driving from the service station entrance.

"Great! Well, you're doing very well fellas."

The three looked at him, in silence. Then Greg spoke, "Colin, we think there's a problem with customs."

Colin looked at him for a moment, then laughed. "Eh? I imagine you sailed right through at customs, didn't you? I told you I'd sort customs, didn't I?"

"Yes ... you what?"

"Guys," Colin said conspiratorially, "I told you I would arrange protection for you guys at Genoa."

"What? Who said anything about protection?" Greg asked. "When did you... Did he?" He looked at the others confused. They were equally lost. But they were drifting from the point. "Colin!" insisted Greg in a low voice. "We were arrested."

"What? At the port? I don't think..." Now Colin was suddenly confused, he remembered having seen some UK officials in uniform milling round at Genoa. It had concerned him momentarily, then he reasoned that it was just co-incidence – to think otherwise would have been paranoia.

When the Land Rovers had driven almost straight through, it appeared to confirm this assumption.

But now Greg was suggesting an arrest? There had been no arrest. Colin had been watching everything. Was Greg going to lie to him? Colin wondered. 'This will be interesting,' he thought.

"After we left the port area, we were followed by Italian police and arrested."

Colin looked at him, stunned. He looked at the other two for confirmation. They nodded.

"They were being directed by UK customs."

"What?" said Colin, incredulous.

"Colin," said Greg leaning forward, "It was the same inspector who confiscated the maps at Manchester."

Colin looked at Greg and his eyes grew wider.

"Are you sure?"

A waitress appeared at the side of the table, to take Colin's order. He wasn't hungry and they simply ordered a round of double espressos. The waitress cleared the table and then went off to fetch the coffees.

"After we left the port," Greg explained once she was out of earshot again, the police caught up with us, and arrested us. They put poor Jack in the back of a police car."

Jack nodded confirmation.

"They took us to a local police station and searched the vehicles thoroughly."

Colin looked at Greg intently, nodding as he spoke, hanging on his every word. Colin liked the sound of this very much. He always liked it when they searched his vehicles and didn't find anything, when he had pulled the wool over the customs eyes, and won another round. He loved it. It was in part what he lived for. He also loved the idea that they might already be in the middle of a game that was playing. Something to properly test himself against. "Go on," he encouraged Greg. Just then the waitress appeared with little cups of espresso and a glass of still water each, on small metallic platters, causing a pause in proceedings.

Chapter 32

When the waitress had disappeared once more, Greg explained how the UK customs official from Manchester had really seemed to know something. He then explained how he had finally instructed the deflation of the tyres.

"The tyres!" confirmed Colin.

"Yes, but then the other one said..."

"He was interested in the tyres, but not the wheels!"

"Yes, he wanted to deflate the tyres, but then the other one..."

"You see? He was going for the tyres. But they will never think to look inside the actual wheel structure."

"I know, that's what I keep saying. He wanted to let down the tyres. But I want to tell you what happened next."

"Oh yeah, sorry, go on."

"So then the other Italian bloke says he can't deflate the tyres because they haven't got the equipment to reflate them again afterwards. So they had to let us go."

Colin looked at him, "Was that true? That they didn't have the equipment?"

"Was it true that they ...." Greg spluttered. "I really don't know! The point is UK customs are onto us. Colin, are you following me? They know about us."

Colin thought for a moment. "But they still couldn't find the blow."

Greg looked at him stunned. Did he not realise the game was up? "It's just a matter of time, mate. My guess is the next time you go through a port they will find it."

Colin stared at Greg. "What are you suggesting?"

"I'm suggesting ..." he looked at the other two for moral support. Colin bristled and glared at him. "I'm suggesting... we shift the gear here in Italy."

Colin was bemused by this suggestion. "What, here in Genoa?"

Greg shook his head. "I'm thinking Rome, we could drive to Rome."

Colin nodded then said sarcastically. "You know anyone in Rome?"

Greg said nothing.

"Do you know the going rate for a third of a ton, in Rome?"

Greg didn't have an answer.

"Have you got anywhere to stay in Rome? ... Look, that's just a nonsense idea. Anyway, I am not sure that it is such a big deal. We've known about this for a while right? So, I've been working on a backup plan haven't I?" The other three had been looking sullenly at the table top, their idea having been so quickly dismissed. Now they began to look at Colin again.

"Do you want to hear it then?" Yes, they wanted to hear it they said, visibly perking up a bit.

"Now, Ronnie remember, went back to the UK and bought a third vehicle. So he is waiting for us already, in France. I suggest that in the first instance, we transport the Land Rovers and trailers to France where I've got a place we can stay while we properly assess the situation. My idea is to switch the wheels onto the new clean Land Rover, and use that. Once we have one load home at least I can cover my costs. Then we simply purchase two more vehicles to switch the remaining wheels on to, and which you three can then bring into the UK. But the crucial thing is to get it into the UK where it has a sensible value. Otherwise we're just wasting our time."

It was finally agreed to go with Colin's plan and move the Land Rover's to France to begin with. Ed would be arriving with the lorry in the next few minutes to transport the Land Rovers and trailers over an unchecked border crossing into France and then to Colin's safe house. He would take one set of Land Rover and trailer at a time on the four hour trip. The other vehicle and trailer would wait with drivers here in the carpark until Ed returned about ten hours later to collect it.

"We've got a chalet in a ski resort. In a place near Grenoble," explained Colin.

"Grenoble?" said Jack, looking alarmed. "We can't go near there!"

"Why not?" the others looked at him.

"Because it's a nuclear disaster zone, that's why," said Jack impatiently.

"That's Chernobyl. You twat!"

Jack shuffled his feet feeling sheepish.

"Cheer up Jack," said Danny. "They've got the best prisons in the world in France you know."

"France?" said Jack. "I thought it was supposed to be Sweden or something."

"Well, Swedish prisons are very good in many respects of course. But the French prisons serve the best food. You know, really top rate cuisine." He winked at Jack who grinned back saying, "Piss off Danny."

"I'm telling the truth," wailed Danny looking to the others for support.

"Us three will not be going to prison." Greg growled at the other two. "Because I am not going to let it happen. So shut up about it, alright?" By this time Colin had already left them to sit and wait for Ed, and had disappeared outside again, to direct the lorry when Ed arrived.

Turning right round the corner of the walkway back into the carpark, Colin looked ahead to check his bike was still there. It was, but his heart sank when he saw the Colombian man still there. He was sitting sideways on his own bike, watching Colin's bike. The car had disappeared. But as he walked across to his bike, the car showed up once more, pulling back into the section of the carpark and driving into its former position again. 'Hmm,' thought Colin, 'What have they been doing?' He had instructed Greg and the others to check on the Land Rovers once every 15 minutes. He hoped one of them was there checking on them already.

As he drew near his bike the Colombian man stood up off his bike, and strolled over for another chat.

"You still here?" said Colin.

"I've been taking care of your bike for you."

"Thanks."

"There are a lot of thieves round here. Plenty of crooks. Dangerous people. You need to keep your wits about you, at all times."

"Thanks for the advice. I'm sure I can manage."

They were now standing looking at each other across Colin's bike again.

"So did your friends tell you about the protection my boss has provided you so far?"

"No!" said Colin. "In fact they told me there had been a search, but they didn't find anything, because they could only think of looking in the tyres, so that's why they had to let them go. Therefore I do not think there was any such thing as protection."

"They didn't find anything because the search was stopped."

"Bollocks!" said Colin.

"So they investigated the tyres?"

"What would it matter? They could check the tyres all they liked. So even if you were providing some protection, which I simply don't believe, but even if you were, I wouldn't have needed it."

Just then Colin was distracted by a commotion coming from the car. The two occupants appeared to be engaging in some sort of horse play in the two front seats to such an extent that it was rocking the car from side to side. There was shouting and yelling emerging. As he watched Colin suddenly saw something flash. One of the occupants appeared to be holding what looked like an unsheathed samurai sword, similar to the one he'd seen adorning the wall of the office in Colombia. Colin's first thought was that he was threatening the other occupant in a play fight, but judging from the reaction of the other, the sword was not an ornamental replica, but was very real. Colin was stunned, and a bit startled. He shivered. 'Is this a set up for *my* benefit?' Colin thought, 'was I supposed to see the sword?'

"You have agreed to pay, nevertheless."

Colin looked back at the bike rider, trying not to express any sense of alarm or convey that he'd noticed the sword, and now beginning to wonder if in fact it was a real sword. Of course it would have been an ornamental replica. Or perhaps even he had imagined it from a reflection on the glass window. "I agreed to pay on arrival in the UK, not before."

"Well my boss would prefer you to pay now."

"No! We've been over it. He'll have to wait." Why were they suddenly demanding the money now? Was it really a sword? What's going on? Questions flooded Colin's but couldn't he couldn't see any answers. Instead he pushed the questions to the side and held the other man's gaze.

The other man looked back at Colin for a moment. Then nodded. "Ok," he said at last, and walked back to his own bike. Colin watched as he got ready, then drove slowly out of the carpark, followed by the car.

From where Colin was parked he could see glimpses through the hedge of the entrance from the road to the service station, therefore he would be able to see Ed arrive hopefully. Now he looked through the hedges towards the entrance to watch the bike and car exit, and see where they went. But they can't have gone to the exit he realised, when after a few moments they did not become visible through the hedge. They must have gone the other way, further into the parking zones. From where he was he could not see in that direction.

He wandered towards the entrance to his section to try to get a better look. At the same time he fished out his mobile from his pocket, to see where Ed was. He dialled Ed's number but couldn't get a signal on Ed's end. He'd have to wait. He strolled out of his zone to get a clear view of the entrance. He didn't have to wait too long, after a few minutes, he saw a large lorry approaching. Colin waved to catch Ed's attention behind the wheel, then ran back to jump on his bike and lead Ed and the lorry to where the Land Rovers were parked.

As they drove slowly through the parking complex to find the Land Rovers, Colin kept his eyes peeled for the bike and car with the Colombian gangsters, but couldn't see them anywhere. 'They've disappeared into the woodwork, like worms,' he thought. "They are nothing but parasites," he muttered to himself.

It took some minutes to find the Land Rovers, it was such a large carpark, with so many different sections separated by high hedges. Once they'd located them, Colin waved to Ed to park up, then zoomed off back towards the café area to collect the others. It took a minute or so to get there. Parking up his bike in the same place as before, he walked quickly over to the café, then collected the other three and walked with them back to the Land Rovers to help with the loading. By the time they'd arrived Ed had already set the ramps up on the lorry.

Danny's Land Rover and its trailer were loaded into the lorry using the ramps and they were ready to go. Colin would go ahead on his bike while Ed drove Danny and his Land Rover and trailer on the four hour trip to Grenoble. He would unload Danny and return to collect Greg and Jack and the other Land Rover. It was now early afternoon, so it would be nearly midnight by the time he returned. Jack and Greg could hang out at the service station for the afternoon, and would keep a regular check on the second vehicle and trailer, which wasn't visible from the café area. Colin did not anticipate there would be any issues for them to contend with. It was a secure built up modern carpark and service station and would be well lit at night. It was only for a few hours anyway.

While Colin walked back to his bike, the other's helped load the Land Rover. Once it was securely strapped down inside the truck, Danny jumped up into the cab to join Ed. Colin was waiting for them at the exit on his bike, and led them onto the main road. As soon as they were on the right road, he tooted his horn and shot off ahead towards Grenoble, as they had arranged, to get things ready. Meanwhile Greg and Jack had walked back to the café area to spend the afternoon drinking beer and chatting up waitresses.

Ed and Danny watched Colin zoom ahead on his bike from the lorry window. Soon they saw him disappear round a bend in the road ahead. What they didn't see, was that as soon as he was round the bend he slammed on his brakes and turned the bike into a small side lane leading into some woods behind a stone wall. Quickly he killed the engine and rolled it out of site of the main road. Then he waited. After a few moments he heard the lorry approaching, then he saw it drive past, taking care to keep out of site from the road. He waited. Sure enough, several seconds after that, as he had feared, he heard another vehicle approaching. A motorbike. He watched through a gap in the wall. Yes! It was the Colombian man, he observed him clearly as he drove by. Then a few moments after him, the other two goons in the car. "Shit!" said Colin out loud. "They are following me. The bastards!" he spluttered. This really would him up.

He was beginning to hate them with a searing vengeance for trying to outwit him. No one ever got the better of him when it came to tailing. Colin was the tailing master. So now it was Colin who was following them. He had watched for some time, to see if there were any other worms or parasites on his tail, but there were none. Then it had not taken him long to catch up with his own pursuers, as the lorry ahead of them was nowhere near as fast as his bike of course. He was able to nip ahead at times taking alternate routes, then again taking cover, observe them repeatedly as they all filed by. It turned out the car and bike drivers were actually quite skilled at the following game themselves: always keeping a sufficient distance, alternating between the car and bike if there was a chance of being spotted, using the bike to zip ahead where there was some question about route, otherwise always hanging way back. Colin was impressed. They were good. Not as good as him, of course. But good none the less.

Ted drove northwards out of Genoa on the A26, then turned left at Alessandria after about one hour, onto the A21. They continued past Turin, onto the A55 then the A32 and into the foothills of the Alps. These were all toll roads, dual carriageways with several lanes allowing for high speed motor travel.

Somewhere around Oulx instead of following the main road as it curved to the right towards Modane on the other side of the border, in France, Ed turned onto a smaller road leading the convoy to a border crossing route through the mountain lanes that he knew and had used before.

They were now above the snow line. Ed stopped the lorry at some point to put snow chains on the wheels and the proceeded again. Colin had set up a position in the woods, to spy from as Ed put the chains on. As the bike and car following realised what was happening, they had some discussion it appeared, then the bike headed back to the main road, while the two men in the car took out some snow chains from the trunk and fitted them to their wheels. "Damn! They've got snow chains," muttered Colin to himself.

It was dark and starting to snow by the time they drove over the border in the lorry followed by the car, always just out of their sight. There were no customs checkpoints anymore. They were able to join the main road again somewhere near Modane after less than an hour on the small mountain roads across the border. Colin followed the other road back to the main road to cross the border on the gritted toll road and wait for them to catch up.

Once he had seen them back on the main road in France, realising they would not be able to shake the tail, Colin shot ahead to Grenoble to wait for them at the Chalet. Ronnie and Phil had been there for a week or more already, enjoying the ski season and snowboarding daily. The third Land Rover was parked underneath the chalet in a large garage, which had sufficient space for all three Land Rovers plus the two trailers.

Danny's Land Rover and trailer were unloaded a little way out of town in a quiet mountain lane, fitted with snow chains, and driven the last kilometre or so by Danny at about 20mph. Ed set off immediately, back towards the main road, and straight back to Genoa to collect the other vehicle and trailer. Colin had come out to meet Danny on the way to the Chalet, after Ed had called him on his mobile to let him know they were there. Colin knew the Land Rover would be followed to the chalet by the Colombian gangsters, but there was nothing he could do about it.

Anyway he was going to pay them back the money so it wasn't a big deal he decided.

Glimpsing the imagined sword in the carpark, even though it was nothing but a reflection in the glass window, nevertheless left him with a sense of unease about the gangsters. It made him feel uncomfortable enough that he decided it may be best just to pay them off as soon as they arrived in the UK. Then he would at least see the last of them very quickly. In that case he concluded it didn't matter if they followed him all the way to Tim's lock up, which he was suspecting they would. In fact he would just invite them in and give them the first money he got as soon as it reached three hundred and sixty thousand dollars. Which would be no more than a few hours after they arrived in Deptford. Although it would infuriate him, perhaps it was better to bight the bullet on this occasion. He would just stuff it into their sticky little fists, give them a good kick up the rear, and send them back to Colombia. 'The horrible little creeps...' he thought.

Ed had collected Greg and Jack and delivered them to Grenoble without any issues. They had both been a bit drunk by the time Ed got back to the service station and then slept most of the way to Grenoble in the lorry cab. Before sunrise at around 7am the next morning both Land Rovers with trailers had joined the new Land Rover in the garage under the chalet, and Colin, Jack, Greg, Danny, Ed, Ronnie and Phil were all fast asleep in its various luxuriously presented bedrooms. The three Colombian men had also booked into a nearby hotel.

They were woken up a few hours later around 11am, by Colin. He had already been up a couple of hours. He had popped out at about half past nine to buy some milk and been accosted by the three Colombian men.

Something about this situation had started to give Colin the heebie-jeebies. He had come to the conclusion that the best course of action was to pay them off and be done with them as soon as he could. They now surrounded him on a snowy street corner, his back against a wall, demanding to know when he would have their money.

On the spur of the moment, to get them out of his hair, "Tomorrow," he blurted out.

"Tomorrow?"

"Tonight we will go to Calais, and take the first boat in the morning."

Colin thought for a moment, but could see no reason at this point not to tell them everything. He was going to pay them as soon as he could, he had decided that already.

He suddenly recalled a vivid and unpleasant dream from the previous night. In it he was dancing to music in a crowd. Dancing right next to him were the three Colombian men. At first it was fun and friendly, but then they began jostling him and forcing him to go in a direction he didn't want to. Suddenly he realised in the dream that he couldn't walk properly. Looking down he saw that his ankles were tethered, to a chain surreally made of Samurai swords. The chain lead over a clifftop. To his horror the chain yanked his feet from under him and started pulling him through the dancing legs of the people in the crowd and towards the cliff edge. Then the dancers were gone, it was too close to the precipice. He scrabbled in the dirt with his fingers but couldn't stop himself sliding inexorably towards the edge. Then he had woken, soaked in sweat.

Coming back to his senses now, standing in the street in the cold wind, he knew, he had had enough of these people. So Colin explained exactly where he would be on the cliff tops in Dover the following day at around 8am. There was a lane. They could also park there. It was discrete. He would be there watching through his binoculars as the Land Rover emerged from customs, then they could follow him to Tim's lockup in Deptford. That afternoon people would be there to make bulk purchases and he would pay them off first, in cash tomorrow afternoon. Colin momentarily winced inwardly at the thought of giving away so much of his first shipment's profits, then managed to steel himself again. "So you will get your money tomorrow afternoon." He had made up his mind.

At 11am back in the chalet he rudely woke everybody who was still in bed by loudly announcing a group meeting in the main room. 'NOW!'.

"What's all this shouting?" complained Greg as they began to stagger sleepily out of their rooms and down stairs.

Chapter 33

They gathered on the couches and armchairs in the front room. A large wood fire roared under a wide brick chimney breast. Colin was standing with his back to the fire watching people arrive. One or two of them mentioned later that Colin looked a little peculiar that morning; his eyes were a bit poppy, and his face looked puffy.

As soon as everyone was there Colin started.

"Right, if everyone's listening?" Colin was lisping slightly, as if a bit of food was stuck awkwardly between his teeth. Once he had their attention, he continued. "We'll make the first shipment tonight." All eyes were on Colin now. "Today we will switch four wheels to Ronnie's Land Rover. This evening Ed will drive Ronnie and Phil overnight to Calais. Tomorrow morning they will take the channel tunnel train to Dover. Ed will pick them up and Dover and drive them to Deptford. By tomorrow afternoon we will have shifted the entire first shipment. Ronnie and Phil will go home to their wives tomorrow as rich men."

The others looked at Ronnie and Phil, who nodded and grinned widely to show they understood. They had already been brought up to date about the arrest in Genoa, however Ronnie felt fully confident that the new Land Rover would not be marked in any way, and he and Phil were happy to make the first run.

Greg on the other hand was happy not to be making the first run. Fortunately it wasn't being asked of him yet. He, Jack and Danny would wait with the other Land Rover and the two trailers for news from Colin about how to proceed. In the meantime they could spend a few days snowboarding, and relaxing at the Chalet.

Details of tasks for the day were hammered out and tasks delegated. The main preparation would be switching the wheels, which Ed and a couple of the others would be able to manage that afternoon in the garage underneath the chalet. The others had the afternoon off. Ronnie and Phil should be ready to leave by 9pm.

Arrangements having been made, Colin and Ed went out to the shops, leaving the others to get breakfast.

At 9pm they left on schedule in Ed's lorry. The wheels had been switched to Ronnie's vehicle. So now there were four wheels with cocaine in them. A total of 120kg. Eight wheels remained in the garage of the chalet, under the charge of Greg, Jack and Danny. Four of the wheels were still on the other Land Rover and two each on the trailers; totalling 240kg.

Colin had left on his bike earlier in the afternoon, and would be waiting for them in Dover. He would telephone Greg at the Chalet tomorrow evening to arrange the next step. Therefore Greg should stay at the Chalet by the phone tomorrow evening. Otherwise the remaining three had a chance to relax and have some fun.

The Land Rover was unloaded from the lorry at about 6am the following morning, a few blocks from the station. Ronnie and Phil then drove it slowly the last few hundred yards, to load it on the channel tunnel train.

Everything went perfectly smoothly. By 7.30am, they had arrived in Dover and were waiting to drive off the train.

Colin was in position on the lane that ran close to the clifftop exactly where he had described it to the three Colombians. He sat on his bike holding his binoculars, with a clear view of the exit below, waiting for the first vehicles to emerge. It was cold and drizzling, but he had his biker leathers on and was quite comfortable. To keep his head dry he still had on his white open face crash helmet. Goggles on an elastic strap had been shifted upwards so he could use the binoculars. Only a small slice of neck above his tight fitting collar line, was left exposed to the elements. He turned his head, scanning for his Colombian friends, but they were nowhere to be seen. "Hmm. Suits me," Colin murmured to himself.

Before long at around 8am, he noticed the first vehicles starting to emerge below. He put the binoculars to his eyes. The Land Rover was not amongst the first vehicles. 'Good boy, Ronnie!' thought Colin. He always advised them not to be at the front or back of the queue.

More cars emerged, Colin watched patiently. Still no Land Rover. More cars. Nope, no Land Rover. 'Oh no!' thought Colin. 'Patience,' he counselled himself. More vehicles. Yet no Land Rover. 'Oh no! Thought Colin. And then the vehicles stopped emerging. 'Is that it?' he thought. Wait, another vehicle. But still not a Land Rover. 'Is he at the back of the queue?' thought Colin, his temper rising. 'Don't tell me he's at the back of the queue. How many times must I say something, for crying out-loud. I've had it this time. I've had enough. If that's what he's done, I'll chop his stupid head off!' he thought in his mounting desperation and fury, and his now boundless arrogance because momentarily, he meant it.

However Ronnie was not at the back of the queue either. Colin's fury could no longer be aimed at Ronnie's queue management skills, and would now need to find somewhere else to land. After the last car had left, Colin waited a further ten minutes, watching, hoping... praying and venting fury. Still nothing. Colin continued to stare at the exit below. As he watched, whether it had dawned on him yet or not, his reality had already changed before his eyes. For the Land Rover never did emerge.

As far as Colin was concerned, this was not yet a disaster however. Colin suspected they had been delayed by a customs search. This shouldn't be a problem anyway. His vehicles had been searched countless times. While the customs apparently had begun to catch up with the notion that tyres might be worth an investigation, the odds of them thinking of breaking the wheel hubs apart, was so close to zero, as to not be worth considering. Therefore Colin began preparing himself to wait for however long it took, which could be a few hours. So it was not the prospect of a bust that had caused his temper to flare. Rather he was secretly hoping the Land Rover would have emerged quickly through customs, and they could have been on their way before the mafia party showed up. That could have saved him a quarter of a million pounds ($360k). This is what he found really upsetting.

The prospect of waiting another hour or two wasn't a big deal in itself. Although the drizzle had turned to a steady rain, and one or two freezing riverlets were beginning to find their way past his collar and down his neck. Before settling in to wait though, there was one more thing he needed to check. Taking off his glove, he unzipped a jacket pocket. Squeezing his hand in past the metal zip, he fumbled around and eventually managed to retrieve his mobile. He checked his signal, then quick dialled Ed. Ed had brought the lorry back from Calais to Dover by ferry. He should by now have just about arrived to collect Ronnie and Phil and the Land Rover, in the carpark as arranged. Ed would be able to confirm whether they had boarded the train. After unloading the Land Rover early that morning, it had been part of Ed's job to make sure that the vehicle was loaded onto the train correctly.

Ed answered the phone after a few rings.

"Where are you?" said Colin.

"I've just docked at Dover, I'm still on the ferry. I'll be out in 20 – 30 minutes..."

"Ed, did you see them onto the train ok and everything?"

"Um, yes I did."

"They definitely got on the train!?"

"Yes, why? What happened?"

"Nothing. I'm just checking. Alright, no problem." Colin hung up and rested the corner of the phone against his lips, fixing his eyes on the gun metal grey clouds on the horizon, way out on the brooding sea, as he tried to think. In the worst case scenario, he stood to lose a third of his stock. Two thirds remained in France. There was nothing to connect him to the present Land Rover. The agreement was to pay the money on successful shipment and conversion to cash in Deptford. But they could not expect him to pay for confiscated drugs. He knew there was an understanding among the criminal fraternity that when someone got busted, outstanding debts were written off, as a gesture of commiseration. The mafia would therefore be prepared to forego their share of the money in the event of a bust; just as he would have to forego his. He had encouraged his three mafia friends to assume all the coke was loaded into the one vehicle, and that there was none left in France. 'So if there was a bust, at least it will get the pesky bastards off my back,' he thought: and it was *not* the first time that the idea had occurred to him.

That was a worst case scenario however. For the moment, he just had to sit and wait and assume the best. For the moment the only logical outcome was that they would get through any searches in the end. Anything else was logically impossible as far as Colin could see, and from a financial perspective it was too distressing a thought for him to wish to dwell on very long. Thinking like that could send a man crazy, he concluded.

Colin shifted on the black vinyl covered foam rubber seat of his bike. Streams of water were running over it, and under his legs but his bike leathers were still keeping him mostly dry. Except for a couple more riverlets which were now seeping past his collar, and now down his arms towards his elbows. He looked around, scanning up and down the lane. The good news was there was still no sign of the mafia. The bad news was the steady rain was turning into something of a downpour.

Ronnie and Phil had loaded onto the train successfully at shortly after seven am as Ed had confirmed. As they drove slowly down the boarding lane towards the customs checkpoint, suddenly they both felt like they'd been locked into a roller coaster ride. They moved inexorably forward, they were past the point of no return. Anything could happen, but the most likely outcome by far was that within the hour they would be converted into millionaires. The moment they were on British soil, their job was done. Colin and his crew had previously negotiated dozens and dozens of customs checkpoints, and never fallen foul of one yet. The odds of Ronnie and Phil being the unlucky pair, were close to zero. Practically zero. They had as much chance of *not* becoming millionaires that morning, as they had of buying a jackpot winning ticket on the national lottery. After Colin had explained the statistics, this was the way they saw it.

Nor were they wrong, it seemed. They cleared customs at Calais without a single look or question. Ed was able to ascertain that there had been no problems and went back to his lorry, while Ronnie and Phil continued down the boarding lane towards the train. As they went they grinned with delight. It was just like swooping over a high bit on the roller coaster. Now they wooshed down the other side, arms in the air. Metaphorically that is. They were careful to contain their excitement, sitting in the Land Rover. Trying not to grin to widely even, Ronnie muttered to Phil, "This is the easiest job I ever had. We just made half a million pounds each!"

Phil snorted with laughter, excitement, and glee through his nose, trying to maintain his composure.

They stayed seated in the Land Rover on the train. As they sat waiting for the train to start moving, Ronnie and Phil felt like astronauts ready to be launched in a rocket to the moon. Soon they felt the first tug of the train as it began to move forwards. Another tug, another tug. Slowly it picked up speed. Thrills of excitement ran through them both as they sat in silence and savoured the moment. Now they were on the rollercoaster proper.

The train sped through the channel tunnel and 35 minutes later they arrived in Dover. There was a short delay, then Ronnie turned the engine on and they followed the vehicle in front as they filed off the train. There were so many things to look out for, and work out what to do driving the vehicle that Phil and Ronnie were now absorbed in the task at hand. Essentially the job was done. Just another few minutes through customs and that would be it. They just needed to focus on being normal, eager to get on the open road again.

Ronnie focussed on following the vehicle in front. Out of the corner of his eye he noticed a customs officer pointing at his number plate, and another officer standing next to him checking a clipboard. Looking out the window on his side Phil was looking absent-mindedly at three or four sniffer dogs that were being kept by handlers at the side.

Quickly it became evident that their vehicle was being singled out. It was all very calm and business like. One officer walked over to the window on Ronnie's side. Ronnie opened it and looked innocently at the man.

"Can I have your passports please sir?"

Phil had the passports ready, and handed them over to Ronnie who handed them through the window. The officer did not look at them but instructed Ronnie, "Move the vehicle to the side please sir."

This sent a shiver through the two in the Land Rover. That was just part of the job though. These were the motions one always had to tend with. They had to deal with these situations, and their emotional and physical impacts. Ronnie pulled the Land Rover over to the side and switched off the ignition.

Quickly two customs officials opened the door on each side and asked them to step outside. They were led to a wooden bench and seated, in sight of the Land Rover, chaperoned by the two officials. This was at about eight thirty am.

As the pair sat and watched, two 'sniffer' dogs were set about searching all over the vehicle, inside and out. The two dogs scurried around, tails wagging, desperately trying to find even just a hint of their favourite olfactory treat, and made a fuss of by their masters. The dogs found nothing and were led away. Now a complete strip down of the vehicle was instructed. Ronnie and Phil continued to look on as panels were removed inside and out of the vehicle, and every nook and cranny was investigated. Up to six mechanics worked on the Land Rover together with screw drivers and spanners. Removed items were stacked carefully in neat rows on the floor. The chairs, inside and outside panels, the headlights. You name it, it was stripped out added to one of the growing rows.

By about 10am the Land Rover was a sorry sight. It looked more like a skeleton than a vehicle. Almost everything had been removed except the windscreen, the engine, and the wheels. There were no sign of any drugs anywhere. Customs inspectors scratched their heads and looked puzzled. Ronnie and Phil were feeling quite confident by now, and very proud of Colin's genius. If anyone can outwit the UK customs, they thought smugly to themselves, it's Colin.

Soon after 10 am the chief inspector called off the search, and instructed the vehicle be put back together. He walked over to the bench where they were seated to explain, and apologise to Ronnie and Phil. Of course, they surely understood, customs could not afford to be too careful in this day and age. Oh yes, they graciously understood.

'That Colin is brilliant,' thought Ronnie.

Ronnie and Phil waited patiently for an hour or so while the car was pieced back together.

Finally, both feeling slightly punch drunk they were able to clamber back in. Ronnie started the ignition and pulled the car slowly back into lane. Ahead, across the lane was a red and white bar, manned by a couple of customs officials from a kiosk. Beyond it, ten metres ahead was freedom, and instant millionaire hood for Ronnie and Phil. The guard was watching for the ok signal. He got it, and pulled the lever. The red and white bar rose electronically. Ronnie did not even need to touch the brake. They rolled forwards under the raised bar, the guard smiled and touched his cap. Ronnie and Phil nodded and smiled. Ronnie touched the gas pedal just a touch, then.... "Stop!"

A cry came out of nowhere from behind. Ronnie wasn't stopping now, he kept his foot touching the gas. The Land Rover rolled forward. But it was too late, the red and white bar came down quickly, right above the engine hood and stopped bouncing and quivering just in front of the windscreen causing Ronnie to slam the brake pedal.

Ronnie and Phil jolted forward in their seats.

Looking round they saw a suited customs official running towards them. The two in the Land Rover did not recognise him, however it was the same customs official that had searched Greg at Manchester, and met the other Land Rovers at the port in Genoa, and was present at the search in Genoa.

The guard at the gate asked Ronnie to back the Land Rover up so he could shut the bar properly. Ronnie obliged. The suited official approached the guard, then some of the officials who had been involved in the previous search arrived.

"Thank god for that," muttered Ronnie to Phil as the other official approached to join the suited official. "They can tell him about the search and we will be on our way."

A heated discussion ensued outside the Land Rover. Ronnie and Phil felt quite confident it would be over quickly, and they would be on their way. The vehicle had already been searched after all. Then they heard a phrase which jolted them into the present moment.

"I want you to check the tyres."

Ronnie's eyes widened slightly. Phil glanced at him, but Ronnie shook his head. It was still ok, they could handle a search of the tyres.

They were rolled back to the search bay.

Once again Ronnie and Phil climbed out of the vehicles. The suited man stood by supervising while a couple of mechanics let down the tyres on the front right wheel.

It hissed and slowly flattened under the weight of the vehicle. Then mechanic looked up questioningly at the suited man.

This did not please him. He pursed his lips and his eyes flared in barely contained fury. "It's in there somewhere!" he said with an angry growl. "Take the damn wheel off, will you? I want to see inside the tyre."

Ronnie and Phil standing watching from a few metres away shifted on their feet a little uncomfortably.

The mechanics jacked up the front of the Land Rover, undid the wheel nuts, and pulled off the wheel. He rolled it carefully hand over hand on the flattened tyre two or three metres to the side, where there was a tool box and air pump. Standing the wheel up the mechanic pulled the tyre rim back using a couple of tyre irons, not to remove it but to expose the inner tube and inside of the rim. Leaning forward the suited official put his hand underneath the tyre as the mechanic held it back. He flattened the inner tube, then felt around inside the tyre and on the rim.

Standing upright again, he looked if anything even more furious. Turning to where Ronnie and Phil were stood, "Where is it?" he demanded. They stared at him shaking their heads. "I've no idea what you are talking about," said Ronnie.

"Ok, next wheel," said the man, walking towards the back of the Land Rover. Once mechanic began pumping air into the removed wheels tyre, while the other fetched another jack and raised the back end to remove the back wheel.

By the time he was unscrewing the nuts, the first mechanic had inflated the tyre of the first wheel. He aimed it towards the front of the Land Rover two or three metres from where he was standing. He had rolled the wheel over hand over hand, but with a pumped tyre, it would be just as easy, and a little more fun, to roll it, he thought. He gave it a slight push towards the Land Rover. Strangely though, it did not roll forwards, rather toppled over almost immediately onto its side. 'Hmm,' thought the mechanic, 'that's odd.'

The noise of the wheel falling over on the concrete caught Ronnie and Phil's attention. The mechanic stood the wheel upright again, and gave it another push. Again it fell over almost immediately. Phil began to shuffle his feet apprehensively.

"Sir?" the mechanic called out. The suited official span round and marched straight over to him. He explained about the wheel, then the suited man span round to stare at Ronnie and Phil, a look of triumph on his face. "Is that it?" he said gleefully.

Ronnie and Phil shrugged and shook their heads innocently.

Now the suited man ordered the removal of all four wheels and the opening up of the wheel hubs. Ronnie and Phil's hearts sank at this at first. However over the next four hours, their spirits gradually rose again. The mechanics were having some tough time opening up the welded steel wheel hubs. In fact they had almost given up entirely once or twice and now it looked as they were going to throw in the towel.

They had brought in angle grinders, blow torches, welding torches, you name it. But they couldn't seem to make any headway breaking open the wheels. Ronnie thought, "That Colin is a genius."

Chapter 34

It was now about 3pm. Colin had been standing on the lane above the cliff overlooking the channel tunnel station exit for about seven hours. The rain eased up about eleven am, but it was nevertheless a thankless task, he felt. Every thirty minutes a new cohort of vehicles would exit, which he'd have to watch, and also keep an eye out in between. He had spoken again to Ed and told him to call him straight back on the mobile the instant they showed up in the carpark, in case Colin missed them filing out of the port exit. He kept telling himself to be patient. That it was just part of the process. They'd be out any moment, as always. But today, they were taking longer than ever before. It would start getting dark soon, the short winter day would be over. What would he do then? Colin was beginning to wonder.

Back inside the customs area on the other hand, Ronnie and Phil's spirits were now definitely on the up. After a long and hard effort, the inspection had still got nowhere. Eventually there was a suggestion that if nothing turned up by half past three, the search would probably be called off. So when the call rang out at just before 3.30pm, they almost jumped for joy.

"Sir!"

Immediately they knew what was happening by the tone of the voice; and they slumped back down on the bench in horror.

The suited man appeared from an office where he had been solemnly drinking tea, and rushed over with renewed enthusiasm to where the mechanics were pointing. He crouched down and inspected the wheel. Finally the mechanic had broken through the steel, now they saw black plastic inside, stuck together with sticky tape. He turned and smiled excitedly at Ronnie and Phil. They looked at him in dread at the thought of the inevitable long prison stretches they now suddenly faced.

"Well whadya know, boys!" said the main in the suit.

And that was it. Game over.

Not just for Phil and Ronnie. Colin had been wrong when he thought there was no way to trace the other members, as long as Phil and Ronnie kept quiet.

Over the next few days the Manchester official, leading the investigation established that the ship he had watched arrive at Genoa with the other two Land Rovers was the only ship Colin's

186

gang had ever used. Not only that, it turned out that no other UK nationals had ever boarded that particular ship, unless they were smuggling cocaine. The only people with UK passports ever to have bought tickets on the ship were Colin, Tommy, John, Brendan, Greg, Danny, Jack, and Dave and Ronnie, who had booked tickets but never boarded. Therefore it was easy to trace all the couriers. (Colin's initial pushbike trip was never uncovered.) Starting some months after the seizure at Folkestone, just when they were beginning to think they had got away with it, the other couriers began to get arrested at home. The police would arrive usually early in the morning, read them their rights and take them to the station, their wives and children watching on aghast. Most of the accused pleaded innocent in jury trials. One or two members turned Queen's evidence in return for reduced prison terms. Sentences were passed largely according to the number of tickets purchased on the ship from Rio to Genoa as follows.

Brendan, whose flat Colin went to after his first trip: 20 years imprisonment.

Tommy, who liked fishing: 20 years imprisonment.

Ronnie, driving the final load: 14 years imprisonment.

Phil, passenger with Ronnie: 10 years imprisonment.

Paul, accompanied Tommy in the Land Cruiser: 10 years imprisonment.

Keith, one of the members on the four bike trip: 15 years imprisonment.

Mark, one of the members on the four bike trip: 15 years imprisonment.

Tim, who introduced Colin to many of the ring members: 14 years imprisonment.

Dave, whose wife forbade him to complete the trip: 10 years imprisonment.

But what happened to the others? Officially, no one knew. That is, what happened to Colin, John, Greg, Jack and Danny? Well, it turns out that this is where things began to get interesting.

Firstly, what became of John? People were very cagey about this. Eventually I was able to find out the following. Around the time people started getting arrested, he was known to have contacted the police by phone from Southampton during which conversation he promised to turn himself in at a local police station. However he never did turn himself in, and this phone call may have been a deliberate red herring. It is suspected he boarded a ship as a foot passenger from South Hampton to South America using a false passport. He is reputed to have had at least a million, possibly several million in sterling in cash to take with him.

Then what happened to Colin? It turns out I had stumbled upon a bone fide mystery. Nobody knew what had happened to Colin. Even the police were at a loss to explain events. The court documents concluded that the facts surrounding the case were "inexplicable."

Further, to my dismay not one of the actors in the events, who I had managed to meet and interview, was prepared to shed any new light on the issue. It was beginning to look as though the story would end here. This would not be satisfactory however, to my purposes. It would be necessary to try to dig deeper.

Unable to find any helpful information at all in press reports, police and court records, or in any of the accounts of the people involved, in desperation finally I fished out the business card of the legal professional from that Victorian era pub in the court district of the city of London. He was the man that had put me onto this story, surely it was not going to turn out to be just a wild goose chase! So one afternoon I went back to the pub where we had first met which I knew was a short walking distance from his place of work.

Ordering a drink, I stood at the bar and called him using my mobile phone, to voice my concerns. I was furious, I told him, and brought it to his attention that if he had been on any sort of payroll for the information he had given me, I would have fired him by now. I commanded him to present himself at once in the pub, and defend himself in person. Moreover he'd better come armed with some pretty good explanations I told him. I advised him to expect a good dressing down as soon as he got there, and that if he didn't show up, he could be sure of a visit at his place of work forthwith and he would get it in front of the reception desk and right in front of whoever happened to be there to enjoy the spectacle. I still had his business card, I reminded him knowingly.

He politely but firmly declined my invitation, in the end forcing me to scream at him, and to shout abuse and ever escalating threats down the phone until I was hoarse and was asked to tone it down by the bar staff and a rather stroppy member of the public, and some side-kick who was tagging along behind him. Fortunately at that moment the legal gentleman conceded on the phone. He could indeed make room in his afternoon schedule, and immediately rush to meet me. I had thought as much.

I stood drinking at the bar in the pub and waited, furious yet terrified that he wouldn't show up despite his promise. Suspended high on the wall at the back, a large flat screen TV was showing an old Peter Jackson movie called the Hobbit or something. I tried to watch it across the largely empty pub to keep my mind off things. There were wizards and dwarves and 'hobbits'. Eventually, thank God, the door opened and my legal friend appeared in it.

Rushing over and snatching him by the elbow I steered him forcefully back to the bar where I vehemently expressed my stern disapproval and let him know it was my intention to get to the bottom of this story whether he was prepared to help or not. He parried that he would have been completely happy to help me out and give me the lead I required. However my belligerent manner on the phone had given him cause to reconsider. He was not now inclined to assist me any further and had come down to meet me with the express purpose of 'putting me in the picture'. To my increasing astonishment, he then muttered something about having had enough of me and stormed out of the pub before he'd even bought himself a drink.

Forced to leave my own drink unfinished, I hurtled out of the door after him. As urgently as possible I scuttled along in the gutter of the sidewalk, trying to keep up as he strode purposefully ahead, ignoring all my remonstrations. I pleaded and pleaded. I told him I'd under estimated him. I could see now he was a gentleman. I fawned and begged him for forgiveness or at least, understanding. - Anyone would quite reasonably expect more than he had provided. Didn't he even feel any sense of responsibility? It just wasn't right. He wasn't just to leave me holding the can! – This could *embarrass* me I hissed, glancing over my shoulder.

In the event, I am sorry to say it was all to no avail. Honestly, I tried everything. - I had mishandled myself. It was only because I cared too much, goddammit! I was sorry. Oh, *please*. - I tried harder, with even more desperate, heart felt apologies and excuses. - Tiredness had made me upset. No one could be more appreciative of all his help so far than me. I'd been working way too hard. I had become stretched too thin, like not enough butter scraped on too much bread. Had I not demonstrated my dedication sufficiently yet? The threat to visit his place of work and cause utter carnage just that. An idle threat. It had simply been intended to motivate him. It was nothing but a joke! Surely, even a fool would have recognised that! -

Eventually, after much insistence I could see I was getting through to him. He stopped his striding and turned sharply towards me. Wagging a long, perfectly manicured finger in my face, he advised me on no uncertain terms that if I should ever attempt to make contact with him again he would report me to the police and have me arrested for intimidation. I watched him turn away again and walk off down the sidewalk. My mouth still gaping with surprise. Did this mean the story was through? I had to give up? How could he do that to me? There was however still one last idea to try out.

Running with a bit more self-awareness and grace this time, I caught up with him quickly, and implemented my final last ditch strategy. It was a desperate and fingernail clinging all or nothing attempt to cajole his cooperation. After some pretty intense name calling and rather nasty cursing, he was still bent over staring at the ground, with his head firmly locked in the vice like grip of my arm. Choking and struggling he eventually coughed out the name: "Tim Peach.

"... and don't you dare ask for my help with anything, ever again." Those were his final spluttering words to me as I gave him a rude shove and pushed him out of my way.

As it happened Tim was one of the gang members I had never met. In fact the descriptions of him: a huge ex con with a big commanding voice, his previous high standing in the civil service, and his involvements with the criminal fraternity led me to feel somewhat apprehensive at the prospect of visiting him. There was something that scared me about this one, even in advance.

Nevertheless I steeled myself, and made direct contact with Tim by email first and then by phone. I explained the project and that my good legal-gentleman friend had urged be most insistently to get in touch.

Tim did not seem at all keen especially at first, however he did at last invite me round for a cup of tea one afternoon.

I was full of trepidations that day lurking outside his house. It was the same house I had heard described. I hesitated on the sidewalk, looking at the imposing stone gateways and the semi-circular double gravel drive. There was one car parked, an expensive looking Jaguar, and two seven-fifty cc Honda motorbikes. Eventually summoning the nerve to crunch over the gravel, I climbed the two or three steps and rang the bell. After a few moments the door opened and there was Tim. He was as huge in height, girth and voice, as everyone had said. But he was jovial and welcoming. "My friends call me 'Peachy'," he said.

He led me into his flat, past the kitchen where he introduced me to Melanie who was preparing food. She was gracious and charming. Then we went through the dining area to the armchair section of his front room and sat down admiring the view of his garden through the French-door windows. Melanie brought us a cup of tea and a piece of cake, but declined to join us. Tim showed me a picture of himself and Melanie together with Colin in the garden. To look at, Melanie and Tim had hardly changed in the twenty years since it was taken. Colin, Tim told me, was about 5 foot seven. I could see he had a mop of dark brown hair almost hiding two dark, coal hard eyes.

Putting the photograph back on the cabinet, Tim explained that in the mid-nineties he and Melanie had been fortunate enough to meet with the opportunity of purchasing the two flats above his. This was a little while before he went to prison, when the housing market was still very low. They had made the purchase at a very reasonable rate. The subsequent property boom in the late nineties and early noughties turned it into a very sound investment. They now rented the flats out to city workers for a small fortune each month. It provided a very comfortable retirement for him and Melanie since he had been released. Tim had been sentenced to 14 years for Intent to Supply and Conspiracy to Import cocaine. He had pleaded not guilty on both counts but had been convicted by a jury with a 10 – 2 majority verdict, as had all those that had pleaded not guilty. His defence council had explained that it was usual for a couple of jury members to vote to acquit in drugs related cases such as his. This was because a percentage of people were naturally opposed to the contemporary fashion for legal prohibition of recreational drugs. The two bikes on the driveway belonged to the city workers currently living upstairs.

"They don't use them to smuggle cocaine hidden in the tyres or anything, do they?" I joked.

Tim laughed. "No, I don't think so," he said. Then he became thoughtful. "Still, you never know," he added as he pondered the notion.

After what I considered to be a suitable amount of time on small talk, I brought up the topic of my project, and that I had got so far and was now investigating what on earth had happened to Colin.

Suddenly Tim's attitude changed. He stiffened and prickled visibly.

"I can't help you there," he said. "I know nothing about any of it."

"Are you sure you can't tell me anything at all?" I gasped in frustration, then explained that my good legal friend had insisted I come and question him about it.

"I don't care what he insisted. I only know what was in the police and press reports," he said sullenly.

"But they were so inconclusive, and baffling" I complained. "They tell us nothing. They do not even seem to make any sense."

"I said, I can't help you. Sorry."

He hurried the rest of his cup of tea and announced that he was very busy and had a lot of things to get on with. He then showed me the way out.

"Peachy!" I implored as he shut the door in my face.

I can certainly document that I was left feeling extremely frustrated at the end of it all. I was truly stuck for ideas on how to proceed. As soon as I got home, I went over and over my previous research notes and gathered documents, with a growing sense of exasperation, but could find no further leads. I felt I had pushed my relationship with my legal contact as far as I could without risking our friendship. He had sent me to Tim once already, and I suspected it was indeed Tim who had the answers I required, but there just didn't seem to be a credible reason to invite myself back round there again. And even if I did manage to get back in to his flat, unlike my gentleman legal friend, Tim was a large man.

Prevented from moving forward by this conundrum, thinking about it again and again, perhaps deluding myself, I decided I had noticed something in Tim's demeanour during my visit. There was something, a longing in his expression perhaps, even desperation in his eyes. If he did harbour some secret, he must have been gestating the story for a long time all alone. The very story itself was ready to be born I was sure of it. I became certain that he did know something and he or it wanted me to drag it back out of him. I had no other ideas. Yet still I could not think of a single excuse to go back round. Or how I would I make him squeal if I got in there again. I just didn't know. It seemed the story was starting to slip inexorably through my fingers right at the last hurdle while I stood by watching, helpless. 'How can this be happening?' I would often think, during that long dark afternoon. 'Why me?!'

By the time it was it was getting dark outside, I had realised that there was nothing else for it but to throw the towel in, and see if I could dream up another new project idea somehow, and start all over again. Such is life sometimes. What can be done? I was just trying to work out how to put all this into writing, when the phone rang. It was Tim himself. He had after all remembered something, he said. He did have something to tell me in fact. He *could* help regarding completion of my narrative. I was stunned. It wasn't over yet. I was stymied no longer. The story was presenting itself at last, and of its own accord.

Delighted with this turn of events, my enthusiasm returned immediately. I promised to rush back over to Tim's house at his earliest convenience, which was the following afternoon.

When I arrived I learned that Tim was prepared to tell me everything that happened following the seizure at Folkestone, which had never been made public before. However he also said he would have to commandeer a veto on whether we could go ahead and publish the final write up, or not. As we sat in his front room, looking out of the French windows at his pretty spring garden in March 2015, I agreed to his terms, and Tim finally set free something he had kept hidden for many years even it seemed, even from himself. He supplied the following account of the horrifying events which took place on the night after the cocaine seizure.

My intention at the beginning of this research had surely been to uncover the truth. However a funny thing happens during an attempt to do so, when dealing with a narrative such as this. Firstly we must wonder if people who lived through the events are themselves telling us the truth. If they are the type that has made a career from criminality and for example would maintain a plea of innocence under oath in the face of damning evidence, they are clearly not prone to telling the truth in most situations. Indeed they may show a marked tendency to do the very opposite, almost as a matter of course, perhaps by sheer force of habit.

And even if people are telling us what they believe is the truth, how can we know for sure that it is what really happened? At some point one finds oneself contending with the concept of truth itself. What is it exactly? Whose version is correct? Because everyone has their own unique perspective on events. What I'm trying to explain in part, is that the police have a different version of the events surrounding Colin on that night, which we shall consider shortly. The intention here is not to challenge the official version. However there is another hitherto untold version of events which seems more credible in all respects. The following account then is a narrative interpretation of Tim's version of what happened on the night following the seizure of Colin's cocaine at Folkestone Channel Tunnel terminal. It can be stated for the record that Tim has no financial stake or claim in this project, and has nothing to gain from reporting what he says he knows. According to Tim, events unfolded in the following way, on that dreadful winters' night.

Chapter 35

From his clifftop position Colin was fairly certain the game was up by the time he saw police cars and a police van arrive. This was around 4pm. At 4.30pm he witnessed Ronnie and Phil being led away in handcuffs, and he could deny his new reality, no longer.

Momentarily Colin's face crumpled. This whole operation had been his baby. He had nurtured it over many years. How dare the customs people try to kill it like that? That's what they were, murderers! What was Colin? A grownup or a child? Whose life was it anyway? His or theirs?

But Colin didn't have too much time to indulge in such self-absorption. As soon as he could pull himself back together and start thinking creatively again, he turned to face the implications as they began to hit him in the stomach like 4 inch cannonballs one after the other.

He had just lost £3million.

He would have to start again and dream up a whole new smuggling method to shift the final two thirds that was still in France.

He'd have to get to France before Greg and the others discovered the news on the internet or radio. It could be disastrous if they heard the news without him being there to explain everything. They might begin to lose confidence in him, and then take it upon themselves to disappear. With the rest of his merchandise! This thought alone was enough to veer Colin towards panic.

Also, he was now dependent on Ronnie and Phil keeping their mouths shut. He felt sure they would but there was always the worry. However as long as they kept quiet there was nothing to connect any of this to Colin so he was not expecting that the police would start looking for him.

Feeling quite winded, Colin now began to turn to practical considerations and quickly began to formulate a plan.

He would need to tell all the buyers waiting at Tim's house in London that he had let them down.

He would have to tell Ed to take the lorry home empty.

He would leave for France tonight and be back in Grenoble by tomorrow morning, before any news reached the three in France in charge of the remaining 240kg of his cocaine.

Sitting on his bike Colin fished out his phone and dialled Tim's number. He had to remove his crash helmet to use the mobile.

Tim answered jovially. This would be the news of the delivery of the good quality narcotics everyone in his front room was excitedly waiting for. "Yuhallo?"

"Tim."

"Colin! The main man! We thought you'd emigrated. Where are you? Are you nearly at the lockup?"

"Tim, something's come up." Despite his best efforts Colin was unable to prevent a slight quiver to his voice. Tim picked up that something had gone wrong.

"What's happening? ... Colin? You still there?"

"Tim... I've got a small problem."

"But everything's ok right? For today I mean."

"Not for today. No."

"Eh?"

"Not for today. I've got something I need to discuss with you. Tim, meet me in Fulham at my house in ninety."

"Oh. Ok. What everyone?"

"No! Just you. Alone."

"Oh no! You're joking... you mean... ok gottya." Tim hung up. It would be a huge disappointment to everyone waiting, however Tim was flattered to be on the in group so to speak, invited to a secret meeting with Colin, to be party to whatever drugs were available. Whatever amount of cocaine had got through, Tim would at least get some of it. That was the main thing from his perspective. Colin always had the purest stuff. Tim was very eager to get some of it. Having been waiting on tenterhooks for several days for this, he now wasn't quite sure how he'd get through the evening without it.

Explaining that the deal was not going off today for the others dampened the party spirit considerably. Not only were huge profits at stake but most of them were very much looking forward to sampling the fresh import of drugs too. Stock had run low. The thought of not only missing out on the massive profits, but also having to go without their own personal cocaine especially after all the build-up of expectations depressed them enormously.

At least, Tim indulged himself again with the thought as he delivered the bad news, he would be able to sample whatever Colin had managed to get through, as soon as he met him in Fulham shortly. It was unthinkable to Tim that nothing had got through. Colin had sounded disappointed but did not sound like he had just lost the whole three hundred and forty kilos. Tim simply assumed that one Land Rover must have got through with perhaps half the stock, and Colin wanted to discuss how to divide up whatever there was, amongst the waiting dealers.

So the other dealers all traipsed off into the evening rather forlornly but with the promise from Tim that they would be first to hear once everything was set up again. Tim then prepared to go to Colin's house in Fulham. He would take his nice Jaguar.

After calling Tim, Colin dialled Ed's number on the mobile and told him to go home for the day. Ed understood without need for explanation. Colin put the mobile in his pocket and started pulling his crash helmet on. Glancing in his mirror he noticed a car had appeared behind him. It now pulled up next to him and the window wound down. It was the two Colombian men in the same car from Genoa. Colin's heart sank. He had gradually convinced himself over the course of waiting all day, that they must have given up on him. 'What do they want now?' he thought with indignation. They could hardly still be expecting him to pay for the cocaine now. They presumably knew that he had just been busted!

Stopping the car beside Colin as he sat on his bike at the side of the road, the man called his name. "Colin. It is time to give us our money."

Colin looked at him gobsmacked. "Are you kidding?" he said.

The men in the car looked slightly confused.

"I've been busted!" Colin announced, with rising intonation.

"You still owe us the money."

"No!" Colin asserted. "I don't think so. It's a failed shipment. I agreed to pay on arrival in the UK. Well it didn't' arrive, did it. We all gotta just cut our losses. Sorry."

The man in the car looked concerned. "All of it?"

Colin nodded. The men in the car started to confer. Colin took advantage of the moment, and kicking his bike of the stand started to drive forward, quite slowly, and proceed down the lane. Watching in his wing mirror he noticed the car start following him, but not racing, just following. At the bottom of the slope there was a road running left up the hill perpendicular to the cliff face, with terraced Victorian houses on each side. Colin turned into the street and started driving up the hill. The car turned and followed.

Towards the top, Colin knew an alleyway that ran between the houses. Without warning he turned right into it and twisted the throttle, now flying along between the houses. The car pulled up behind him. It was two wide for the alleyway. Then he heard wheels screech as it shot forward, to round the block. But now Colin slammed on his brakes. Half way along the alleyway was a gap in the wall with a dustbin area. In the dark it was not visible from the street. Cutting his engine Colin rolled the bike as quickly as he could into the area, out of the alleyway and disappeared into the shadows.

Then he heard the car pull up at the other end of the alleyway. It paused presumably checking in case he'd doubled back, then he heard it accelerate away, in the opposite direction, chasing where they thought he had gone. Colin smiled at himself and shook his head at the simpletons. He waited a few minutes then poked his head out from the area. They coast was clear, the car had disappeared.

Colin wheeled the bike back out of the dustbin area and down the alleyway retracing his steps. Out on the street again he jumped on the bike, started the engine and drove back down the hill. All the while keeping his eyes peeled for signs of anyone else looking for him. He didn't feel comfortable now driving though the lanes as he wasn't sure where the other car was and kept thinking it might appear out of nowhere and catch him again. However he had no such problems and was soon on the A2 headed back to London at top speed. He was careful to keep scanning his mirrors, but he was certain there was no-one tailing him.

At about nine pm, Colin was already at home in Fulham, his bike parked in the street in front, when he heard Tim's knock on the front door. Colin's wife and kids were abroad as usual during any such project, so he trotted down the hallway and answered it himself.

Tim came bounding in full of bonhomie.

"Alright Colin? So how much did you get through?" Tim was smiling expectantly. Colin shook his head solemnly and Tim's face fell.

Colin led the way and they walked down the wide hallway past the doors on the left and the staircase on the right, through the door at the end. Straight ahead was a sitting room with French windows leading to the garden. To the right was a kitchen area. A heavy wooden door led to a concrete patio, the other side of which was the tall wooden fence of the neighbouring house. Above the concrete a corrugated plastic roof had been erected on wooden posts, covering the space between the wall of the house and the fence. Colin unlocked the door and opened it to show Tim as he was explaining about the bust. Tim was following after Colin, listening with increasing shock. Beyond the kitchen area sitting on the covered patio was a new 1100cc motorbike Colin wanted to show Tim. On the wing mirror was an open faced crash helmet. The bike was on its stand, facing the garden. A footpath led from the patio to the gate at the rear of the garden.

"It's my getaway bike," Colin said proudly. "Shame I never got a chance to use it," he said wistfully.

A couple of narrow shelves had been screwed onto the wall of the house. There were half a dozen small flower pots growing herbs, and a couple of small pots of paint and such. Colin picked up one of the pots. Underneath was the key to the bike. He showed Tim. In an emergency, he explained, he would have jumped on the bike and been off through the garden gate in an instant. The gate was not firmly secured from the inside and would have opened easily when the bike hit it. At the back there were half a dozen or so garages in a line for use by some of the neighbours. From here a back street led round the corner, onto the front street again, about 200 yards from his house. It was a very good secret escape route. Tim was impressed.

Now they went back inside, Colin locked the back door leaving the key in the lock. Now Colin continued to talk, telling Tim his plans while he led him into one of the doors off the main hallway. He would leave the UK tonight by channel train from Folkestone, and go straight from Calais to Grenoble. He would be there by tomorrow morning. He should get out of the country as soon as possible just in case Ronnie or Phil talked. He led Tim into a small oblong room. Inside there was a large oval table that almost filled the entire room. Six straight back wooded chairs were spaced around it. However it would be impossible to squeeze in at the sides between the table and the wall if you wanted to sit down. Especially for a large man such as Tim. He wondered if he'd even squeeze in at the corners. As soon as he'd packed his backpack, he'd be off on the getaway bike, Colin explained.

In the far corner was a desktop computer on a small compact specially designed unit.

"Why d'you put the biggest table in the smallest room?" Tim complained.

"So that no one comes in here," explained Colin.

Tim stood squeezed against the wall near the doorway. Colin was much slimmer and had sidled round to where the computer was. He switched on the computer and indicated Tim to come over and have a look, but Tim didn't want to squeeze past the table. He could see from where he was, he said. On the table at the far end, where Colin was now standing where piles of cash bundles, check books, a passport, bank cards and such. Also a backpack. As the computer warmed up Colin started sorting through the bits and pieces and loading them into the backpack. He picked up a cash bundle and as he held it in his hand he was momentarily transported back to the English language classroom he had been sitting in 1992. What would that Colin on virtually minimum wage think, if he could see the new Colin now? Casually tossing ten twenty five thousand pound bundles into his back pack, as though they were nothing. Colin had become so rich, a quarter of a million pounds was like small change to him. It was almost nothing.

Now Colin started telling the story of the Colombian guys in the car and bike. This was just for entertainment, some comic relief now that he had brought Tim up to speed sufficiently. Colin seemed to think it was all a bit of a laugh.

"Wait a minute," Tim interrupted Colin, and asked him to repeat a couple of details.

"What?" Colin laughed.

Tim paused for a moment. "I thought you knew about South American criminal culture," he said. Colin looked at him blankly. "In the underworld," Tim continued, "they'll tell you that in England, when there's a drugs bust, all debts are written off." Colin nodded. Obviously, he thought. "I think in Colombia, that isn't the case," Tim explained.

"What?" Colin looked amused. "They expect you to pay the money back? Even after a bust?" He laughed out loud at the notion. It was ridiculous.

"Colin," Tim said patiently, "they expect the debts to be paid. In money or blood. You don't know about this?" He was amazed at Colin's ignorance. Colin frowned.

"But you've got the money there haven't you?" Tim indicated Colin's backpack. He had seen him load at least a quarter of a million sterling in cash.

"No chance," said Colin. "They're not getting that. Anyway it's academic now. I'm about to leave. Look, they don't even know where I live!"

Tim was looking concerned. He looked at his watch. "Well it's probably time I be getting on my way," he said, moving towards the door.

"No, wait just a minute," said Colin. He was doing something on the computer. "I want to show you this." He turned to look at Tim and saw he had started to leave. Colin laughed. "Don't worry Tim, I think we're safe for the moment."

Tim paused and looked at the computer. Colin showed him the CCTV images of the front door and porch area. What's he showing me this for? Thought Tim. He's just wasting valuable time. Also there were views of the back porch and the escape bike. Tim nodded impatiently. "Come on Colin, let's go." At last Colin switched off the computer, and picking up his backpack squeezed his way towards the door. Tim walked into the hallway and towards the big front door. The house was tastefully presented with clean white walls, bookshelves, pine floor boards, moulding on the ceiling. All very nicely done, thought Tim. As Colin was exiting the room the strap of his backpack caught on the back of a chair and tipped it upside down. A wad of money and a couple of bank cards spilled onto the floor. "Damn it," said Colin as he crouched to scoop the items back into the bag.

Tim had now opened the front door to exit, but instead stood inside the doorway like a rabbit caught in headlights, as he had the fright of his life.

Just beyond the porch, outside the pool of light visible to the security camera, lurked a shadow. A human shape. As the door opened, it sensed its opportunity and lunged forward. For a brief micro second Tim saw other shadows rushing forwards from the garden, out of the darkness towards the front door. His heart suddenly pounding he moved back as fast as he could to shut the front door again. He swung it shut as hard as he could, but the figure who had been waiting had managed to leap forward and get a foot into the doorway at the bottom, lodging the door open. At least Tim was behind the door now. Terrified he threw his considerable bulk against the door, but the foot at the bottom remained in place. Now Tim was aware of other figures adding their weight to heave against the door. Colin had become aware of the commotion and came out into the hallway, a look of alarm on his face.

"What the fuck do you want?" Tim bellowed through the door as he struggled to keep it closed.

"Colin! Give us our money!" A voice came through the door.

Tim looked round over his shoulder to see what Colin would do. In that instant he lost his advantage on the door and it began to heave open. Tim put his shoulder back to the task of closing it. He at least stopped it opening further but to his astonishment, instead of helping him, he heard Colin's footsteps leading away. Turning again to look he saw Colin disappearing through the door to the kitchen. Tim was gobsmacked. 'He's run away and left me?' he thought incredulously. Now the three men outside gained the upper hand and forced the front door open. Tim moved quickly to stand out of the way and avoid getting slammed against the wall by the door. He stood with his back against the wall as the three men raced passed him and through the house down the hallway towards the kitchen in pursuit of Colin.

With his backpack in his hand, as soon as he was through the kitchen door, Colin slammed it shut and flipped the bolt. It wouldn't hold for a moment though, turning to the right, he raced to the door that led to the patio. He fiddled with the key. Why had he so stupidly locked it earlier? He could hear the footsteps approaching down the hallway. He managed to undo the bolt and pulled the door open. He heard the sound of his pursuers in the hurling themselves into the bolted door. As he pulled the door shut again he saw them burst through from the hallway. They started towards him. Colin was now really scared, panicking. He pulled the door shut. Holding the door knob with one hand to keep it shut, he fiddled the key into the lock. He tried to turn it but it wouldn't budge. Now he felt the door knob jolt as it was grabbed from the other side. He turned the key and the lock bolt slid.

An enormous bang came from the door as someone kicked it hard. Then another. It wouldn't last many kicks, but how long until they spotted the French windows. He hurriedly picked up the pot and scrabbled for the key. He felt it in his hands, but then a huge bang on the door made him jump and he fumbled it. Colin could now hear the lock working on the French windows. He stepped on the bike pulling the helmet on his head with one hand. Somehow the key flew up out of his other hand into the air. He grabbed on thin air as it jumped between his hands evading his grasp. Then the sound of the French windows rattling and shaking. Another enormous bang on the door, it was now beginning to splinter. One more bang would open it. He heard the sound of the French windows, finally unlocked, being slid open with force. His backpack over one shoulder, his open faced crash helmet still unstrapped, the goggles perched on top, Colin hit the start button. The bike shot forward as two figures emerged round the wall from the side, out of the garden having got through the French windows. They darted forwards towards Colin on his bike, reaching their hands out as they approached him. As Colin shot by their fingers grazed his shoulders but didn't quite get a hold on him.

Now he was flying through the fence and into the parking and garage area behind, the back wheel spinning out sideways as he tried to turn too sharply, and he lost control of the bike. One of the men darted forwards through the still open gate. Then Colin regained balance and accelerated away. Turning round, the three men – the third having now joined them in the garden via the French windows, raced back through the garden and out through the house again.

They raced back down the hallway, past Tim, who was still standing flat against the wall, and along the front garden path, jumping clean over the garden gate in single bounds. Tim heard the roar of Colin's bike as he exited from the back road a couple of hundred yards away. His pursuers heard it too. It spurred them on even faster. Two raced to a car, the third to a motorbike. Moments later they had all sped off in pursuit of Colin and the well-to-do suburban street descended once more to its customary night time silence.

Tim stood in the doorway, trying to avoid a complete panic attack and nervous breakdown. After he saw the car and bike had gone, quickly gathering his senses, he raced down the hallway. Rushing in through the door to the kitchen and sitting area. Walking to the right and inspecting the damage he saw that the door was still in one piece, just. He rushed back into the living area and pulled the French windows shut and turned the lock. Then switching off the lights as he went, out of habit, he hurried back towards the front door. He wanted to get out before the thugs returned, perhaps expecting him to know where Colin had gone. As he passed the door of the small oblong room with the oval table, he opened it to switch off the light, which Colin had left on. As he did so he noticed something on the floor. He reached down and picked it up. He looked at it for a moment, staring in disbelief.

It was Colin's passport. It must have fallen out of his backpack. This was disastrous. Colin would not be able to leave the country. He would be stuck at Folkestone.

Not sure what to do at the moment, Tim slipped the passport into his pocket then switching off all the lights as he left, he quickly exited the house, pulling the front door shut behind him. He hurried down the garden path and along to his parked car. He glanced up and down the road. There was no sign of anything, so he jumped in the car and drove back to his house in South East London. He arrived forty minutes later, and checked the answer phone. There were no new messages.

Melanie was staying at a friend's house for a few days so Tim had the house to himself. He was tempted to pour himself a whisky to calm his jangled nerves, but something stopped him. Instead he turned all the lights out and sat down in his armchair in the dark, and waited Twenty minutes later Tim almost jumped out of his skin, as the phone rang.

Admonishing his nerves Tim sat still, unsure whether to answer the phone or not. He listed to it ring. It continued ten, fifteen rings. At last Tim jumped up and picked up the reliever. To his immense relief it was Colin, who was already in Folkestone, and in a complete state of panic. The news that Tim had his passport much calmed him down however. After taking a few moments to regulate his breathing, Colin wanted to know if Tim had been followed. Tim said he didn't think so. Colin explained that he had led the pursuers away from the house for ten minutes to give Tim a chance to slip away, and then managed to lose them. Was he sure? Tim wanted to know. Colin was sure.

Colin now suggested that Tim bring the passport to a meeting point half way between Folkestone and London. This would enable him to get the passport quickest and still board a train to the continent tonight. Night trains ran about every two hours. Tim was happy to do anything he could to help and felt eager to get out of his house for a while. It was about eleven pm, and thankfully Tim had not had anything to drink so he was happy about the driving.

"There's a bridge where the M20 crosses the A20 at an oblique angle. Just past Brands Hatch, near Kingsdown. Do you know where I mean?"

"Yes. I know it."

"OK, meet me there in forty minutes. Underneath the bridge is a lay by. Part of this will be unlit. Pull into the unlit part under the bridge, and switch off your lights. I will be keeping out of sight somewhere nearby. As soon as I am certain you were not followed, I will come over to your car, and you can give me the passport."

"Ok," said Tim.

Making sure he had the passport Tim went outside, climbed into his Jaguar and set off for the arranged meeting.

He could see no one following him. He arrived at the lay by under the bridge about forty minutes later and switched off his lights as instructed. He waited there in the dark for nearly half an hour. It was beginning to get spooky, and Tim had picked up the sense he was being watched. He grew increasingly uneasy and decided he could wait no longer. As he started the engine and began to pull away, Colin ran out from the shadows still wearing his crash helmet.

"Where the fuck have you been?" said Tim, he was quite irritated and uneasy by now.

"Sorry," said Colin. "I needed to make sure you hadn't been followed."

They chatted for a moment and had a quick laugh about how Colin had nearly got caught earlier as he fumbled the getaway bike keys. "Where's the bike?" asked Tim, handing Colin's passport to him through the window.

"Hidden over there," Colin indicated to where he had hidden the bike in some hedges.

"This is too spooky. I'm out of here," said Tim. "All the best mate," he began to pull away from the kerb.

"See ya," Colin whispered and started walking towards his bike. Tim had driven about two hundred yards, his lights were still off, when he heard the screaming engines. Horrified he slammed on his brakes and looked through the back window. There were few street lights and none near his car. Tim watched through his back window, transfixed. The bike and car from earlier had somehow sped up, surprised and cornered Colin as he tried to extract his bike from the hedge. To Tim's utter horror he saw one of the men draw a gun. Now Tim did not know what to do. Should he go back and help Colin? But Tim had no weapons. In any case was this not Colin's argument? Why should Tim step in? Maybe Colin did owe those guys money. What did Tim know?

But as Tim watched the scene grew even more horrifying. One man held a gun pointed at Colin's head still in his white open faced crash helmet. As Colin raised his arms, another man kicked the back of Colin's legs forcing him onto his knees in front of the gunman. "Oh my god," thought Tim. "It's an execution."

Yet still it got more terrifying. The third man now returned from the car holding in his hand, brandishing what looked to Tim like a samurai sword. Tim almost soiled himself as he continued to watch, unable to turn away from the horror.

As the man with the sword approached the kneeling helmeted Colin, Colin began to turn round. The man with the gun shouted and Colin turned back to face him. The man from behind approached, the curved blade glinted and flashed as its owner took a huge swing, as though he was playing golf.

Before Tim's eyes Colin's head, still in the crash helmet lifted up from his neck severed clean. The crash helmet span upwards maybe six or twelve inches above the neck. The headless corpse still momentarily on its knees spasmed as jugular blood fountained from the neck, then pitched forward. The crash helmet containing Colin's decapitated head landed with a crack on the concrete, like a hardboiled egg, and rolled slowly over once or twice. Finally it came to a rest. To Tim's horror he could see Colin's still wide open eyes even from where he was. They seemed to be staring right at him for a moment, then they turned cloudy.

This was too much, Tim was shaking uncontrollably with adrenal energy. Without turning his lights on he pulled the car away from where it was standing. He drove forwards slowly in the dark, expecting the men to rush up behind him any second but not daring to check in his mirror. He saw a turning on the left and took it. Then warming to his cause, he accelerated until he saw another turning. Now he looked in his mirror. There was no one behind. He stopped the car. Opening the door he leaned out and vomited two or three times, as though purging the ghastly image from his consciousness. He pulled away as soon as he was able and turned again, then another turning. Then he parked his car away from any streetlights, in a line of other parked cars. Switching his engine off he lay down on across the seats so he couldn't be seen through the windows and waited, shivering with fear and upset and eventually also, the cold. He had to leave a window open slightly to stop the windows steaming up and giving him away, and it was a freezing cold moonlit night: several degrees below freezing.

Tim stayed put without even moving a muscle, except for his involuntary spasmodic shivering, for several hours. It was about three am, when he finally got the courage to poke his head above the seat. The coast looked clear. Still shaking so much he could barely turn the key in the ignition, Tim managed to pull the car out and turn the heater on to slowly thaw him out as he drove home. It did occur to him to go and check if the corpse was still there, and see if the money was still in the backpack. He decided against it in the end, because probably the gangsters would have taken the money anyway, and because he didn't want his DNA inadvertently left at the scene. Making believe it never happened, he wiped it from his memory, and didn't ever think about it for more many years, until the distance of time had separated him sufficiently. I was the first person he ever told the story to.

"You didn't think to report it to the police then?" I asked.

"No of course not," he snorted.

"Do you think that John tipped off Kenny about Colin's meeting in his club?"

"No," he scoffed. I noticed for the first time his bulb-like eyes.

The corpse was spotted lying in the verge a couple of days later by a passing driver who notified the police.

The police investigated the scene and discovered the motorbike also hidden so it had not been noticed in the hedges. There were certain anomalies at the scene. Most notably perhaps, the fact that the head was missing. As also was the crash helmet. Neither were ever recovered. Also the wound on the neck was noted to be remarkably 'clean cut', in keeping with a blade wound, Tim explained. The cause of death was deemed suicide by the coroners and in the police reports. Somehow it was believed that after discarding his crash helmet, Colin had committed suicide by driving at such high speed towards the bridge while he lent over at a horizontal angle that he had managed to knock his own head clean off his shoulders, and atomise it in the process. All this despite the fact that there was no visible damage to the motorcycle, or the bridge, and there was no trace of blood on the bridge. The tragedy was finally documented officially, as "an inexplicable accident."

As for the remaining three, Greg, Danny and Jack, they were never caught. They would have found out about the bust a few days later through the internet and seem to have evacuated the chalet in Grenoble. Only one of the trailers was ever found. It was beaten and battered and appeared to have been rolled down the mountain side. Both the wheels were missing. Neither those wheels nor the other Land Rover, nor the two trailers were ever recovered.

It seems the three left France and crossed the border into Spain. There they sold the cocaine for £10 000 per kilo. They would have made about £800 000 each. They used this to buy new identities, and set up small business enterprises in Spain or elsewhere in Europe. Whether they have every returned to the UK to visit their parents, Jack in particular was said to be very close to his mother, is unclear.

Chapter 36

"Now that would be an interesting story," said Tim.

"What would?" I said.

"The story of Greg Jack and Danny."

"How so?"

"Well, how they got into Spain, how they bought fake ID, how they set up businesses, how they made visits to the UK. Maybe that's the story you should have written."

I had come to retrieve the manuscript I had sent to Tim as requested a couple of weeks before. He had insisted on a veto reading, before he would reveal what happened to Colin. I had posted him a manuscript, but heard nothing for a couple of weeks. Finally I received an email saying simply. "Throwing out old junk, collect script before Friday. Alt. can bin it."

I rushed round the following afternoon. Not so much to get the script back, I could always print another if I needed to. But I really wanted to find out what his impressions were, and obtain his blessing to go ahead with publication. Melanie was out for the afternoon visiting friends. I followed him into the living room. A half empty bottle or red wine stood on the coffee table next to his glass. He fetched a glass from the side cabinet and set it on the coffee table in front of me. Then he poured me a glass and topped up his own. "Thank you," I said.

"That is where I think the interesting story is:" Tim explained, as he handed me back the script, "specifically what became of John and those other three in the long run. I mean, I think there's a lot of drama there, a lot of pathos. Something that might even be of some interest to people."

"Thank you," I said again as I reached forward for my glass. He looked at me sharply.

"I don't really know what to think about your title," he started on another course. "I mean, Colin wasn't particularly nice. But nor was he very nasty; not really. No, I don't think so. He wasn't either of those things."

"Oh no," I said. "It doesn't stand for Colin." I scribbled hastily in my notepad.

"Oh," he said, surprised. "Well surely not John."

"No, no! Of course not," I said hurriedly.

"It doesn't refer to me does it?" has asked, alarmed.

"No, no," I said. "No, I don't think it stands for any of them."

"Well, who then?"

I showed him what I'd written in my notepad. It was easier to explain by writing it down. "Nice Mr 'Charlie' Nasty".

He looked at it. There was a pause while he thought for a moment. Then slowly, almost imperceptibly, and with a faint hint of chagrin, he started to nod. At length he said, "They can only make it into a film if Clint Eastwood directs it."

I laughed out loud. "You haven't even fucking read it. You bastard. Have you!"

He looked at me slightly shocked. "Well! ... I've read bits of it," he said.

Printed in Great Britain
by Amazon